THE
STRUCTURE
OF
MODERN POETRY

THE
STRUCTURE
OF
MODERN POETRY

From the Mid-Nineteenth to the Mid-Twentieth Century

WITHDRAWN

by Hugo Friedrich

Translated by Joachim Neugroschel

NORTHWESTERN UNIVERSITY PRESS

EVANSTON   1974

Originally published in German under the title *Die Struktur der modernen Lyrik*, © Rowohlt Taschenbuch Verlag GmbH, Hamburg, 1956. This translation is based on the revised German edition of 1967. Quoted material has been translated into English by Joachim Neugroschel.

Abel

For Ernesto Grassi
on his sixty-fifth birthday
May 2, 1967

CONTENTS

ABOUT THE AUTHOR

Hugo Friedrich was born in Karlsruhe, in 1904. He completed his secondary schooling (*Abitur*) there in 1923, and he then studied German and Romance languages and literature, as well as history, philosophy, and the history of art. In 1928 he received his doctoral degree at Heidelberg in the field of comparative literature. (His dissertation, on Abbé Prévost in Germany, was published in 1929.) He continued his studies in Munich, concentrating on Romance languages. After passing his *Staatsexamen* (an examination allowing the candidate to teach in secondary schools), he taught for a while. After several trips that brought him into contact with the Romance cultures, he began preparing for a university teaching career and received his *Habilitation* degree (the requisite degree in Germany) in 1934; his dissertation, published in 1935, was on antiromantic thought in modern France. In 1937 he became Professor of Romance Philology at the University of Freiburg, where he remained, despite invitations from other universities. Of all his teachers, he owes the most to Karl Vossler, Ernst Robert Curtius, C. Neumann, Karl Jaspers, and Friedrich Gundolf. In 1957 Hugo Friedrich became a regular member and, in 1961, an extraordinary member of the German Academy of Language and Literature; in 1958 he became a regular member of the Heidelberg Academy of Sciences and Scholarship and, in 1960, an honorary member of the Modern Language Association of America. He is Commendatore dell'Ordine al Merito della Repubblica Italiana (1958) and Officier des Palmes Académiques (1962), and in 1964 he won the prize for scholarly prose awarded by the German Academy of Language and Literature. Since 1969 he has been a member of the Ordre pour le Mérite (*Friedensklasse*). Among the subjects and personalities with which his books deal are Descartes, Stendhal, Balzac, Flaubert, Dante, Montaigne, Calderón, Italian poetry, and the art of translation.

PREFACE
TO THE
AMERICAN EDITION

It may strike the American reader as strange that this analysis of modern poetry hardly mentions the great American poets of the nineteenth and twentieth centuries. There are two reasons for this. One is my intent to explore modern European poetry by means of common denominators. I therefore limited myself in American literature to the pioneers Edgar Allan Poe and Ezra Pound, who have become meaningful to Europe, even though Walt Whitman with his (at the time) completely innovative poetic language would also belong here. The second reason is that I have refrained from judging such subtle images as those in lyrical verse when written in a language which I do not master completely. Yet it might have been extremely fruitful to demonstrate what the European poets have in common with American poets of the twentieth century, particularly Robert Frost, Wallace Stevens, and William Carlos Williams. Perhaps the American reader will give me credit for at least acknowledging this fact.

HUGO FRIEDRICH

CHRONOLOGY
OF MODERN POETRY

1759	Denis Diderot: *Les Salons*
1760(?)–72	Diderot: *Le Neveu de Rameau*
1776–77	Jean Jacques Rousseau: *Les Rêveries du promeneur solitaire*
1798	Novalis: *Fragmente*
1801	Novalis: *Heinrich von Ofterdingen*
1802	Victor Hugo born in Besançon
1821	Charles Baudelaire born in Paris
1827	Hugo: Preface to *Cromwell*
1840–45	Edgar Allan Poe: *Tales of the Grotesque and Arabesque*
1842	Stéphane Mallarmé born in Paris
1845–55	Baudelaire: *Curiosités esthétiques* (complete edition, 1865)
1846	Lautréamont born in Montevideo
	Poe: *A Philosophy of Composition*
1846–62	Baudelaire: *L'Art romantique* (complete edition, 1868)
1848	Poe: *The Poetic Principle*
1854	Gérard de Nerval: *Chimères*
	Arthur Rimbaud born in Charleville
	Baudelaire begins translating Poe's short stories; continues until 1865
1857	Baudelaire: *Les Fleurs du mal* (final version, 1868)
1862	Mallarmé's first poems
1863–70	Mallarmé teaches English at *lycées* in Tournon, Besançon, Avignon
1864	Baudelaire: *Petits Poèmes en prose*
1865	William Butler Yeats born in Dublin
1867	Lautréamont comes to Paris
	Baudelaire dies in Paris
1867–1916	Rubén Darío (1892, 1898, 1908–14 in Spain)
1868–69	Lautréamont: *Chants de maldoror*
1868–1933	Stefan George
1869–73	Rimbaud's poetry
1870	Lautréamont dies in Paris

1870–94	Mallarmé teaches in a *lycée* in Paris
1871	Rimbaud: *Voyant* letters
	Rimbaud moves to Paris
	Paul Valéry born in Sète
	Marcel Proust born in Auteuil
1874	Rimbaud stops writing and begins a life of wandering
	Mallarmé: *La Dernière Mode*
1874–1929	Hugo von Hofmannsthal
1875	Rainer Maria Rilke born in Prague
1876	Édouard Manet's portrait of Mallarmé
	Else Lasker-Schüler born in Elberfeld
1880	Rimbaud in Africa
	Apollinaire born in Rome
1881	Ramón Jiménez born in Moguer, Andalusia
1883	José Ortega y Gasset born in Madrid
1884	Paul Verlaine: *Les Poètes maudits* (containing material on Rimbaud and Mallarmé)
1885	Hugo dies in Paris
	Ezra Pound born in Hailey, Idaho
1886	Gottfried Benn born in Mansfeld
✓ 1887	Mallarmé: *Poésies* (containing poems written since 1862)
	St.-John Perse born in Saint Léger les Feuilles, off Guadeloupe
	Georg Trakl born in Salzburg
1888	Guiseppe Ungaretti born in Alexandria, Egypt
	T. S. Eliot born in St. Louis, Missouri
1889	Mallarmé's translations of Poe's verse
	Henri Bergson: *Essai sur les données immédiates de la conscience*
1889–97	Valéry's early poetry; he stops writing until 1917
1891	Rimbaud dies in Marseilles
	Pedro Salinas born in Madrid
	Valéry visits Mallarmé
1892–93	High point of the *mardis* (Tuesday evenings) in Mallarmé's Paris apartment
1893	Jorge Guillén born in Valladolid
1894	Claude Debussy: *L'Après-midi d'un faune*
	Mallarmé retires, lectures in England, settles in Valvins (Seine)
1895	Paul Eluard born in Saint-Denis
1896	Gerardo Diego born in Santander

	Eugenio Montale born in Genoa
	Verlaine dies in Paris
✓1897	Mallarmé: *Divagations* (prose poems and essays on poetry, written since 1864)
1898	Mallarmé: *Poésies* (definitive edition)
	Mallarmé dies in Valvins
	Apollinaire moves to Paris
	St.-John Perse moves to Paris
	Vicente Aleixandre born in Seville
1899	Federico García Lorca born in Fuente Vaqueros, Granada
1901	Salvatore Quasimodo born in Syracuse, Italy
1902	Rafael Alberti born in Puerto de Santa Maria, Cadiz
1905	Start of friendship between Pablo Picasso and Apollinaire
1908	Apollinaire: *L'Enchanteur pourrissant* (containing *Onirocritique*)
1909	F. T. Marinetti's *Futurist Manifesto* appears in Milan
1910–20	German expressionism
1911	St.-John Perse: *Eloges*
1912	Ungaretti leaves Egypt for Paris; friendship with Apollinaire and others
	Benn: *Morgue*
1913	Apollinaire: *Alcools* (containing *Zone*),
	Eluard's first poems
1913–22	Proust: *A la recherche du temps perdu*
1914	Ungaretti settles in Italy
	Trakl: *Gedichte*
	Trakl dies in Krakow
1916	Dadaism founded in Zurich
1917	Valéry: *La Jeune Parque*
1918	Apollinaire: *L'Esprit nouveau et les poètes*
	Apollinaire: *Calligrammes*
	Apollinaire dies
1919	Guillén starts writing poetry
	Ungaretti: *L'allegría*
1920	*Menschheitsdämmerung*, edited by Kurt Pinthus
	Valéry: *Album des vers anciens*
1921	García Lorca: *Libro de poemas*
	Valéry: *Charmes*
1922	García Lorca: *Poema de cante jondo*
	Proust dies in Paris

1922	T. S. Eliot: *The Waste Land* García Lorca becomes friendly with the composer Manuel de Falla
1924	First surrealist manifesto (André Breton) Eluard: *Mourir de ne pas mourir* Alberti: *Marinero en tierra* García Lorca: *Canciones*
1924-44	Valéry: *Variété*, I–V
1925	Pound: *Cantos* Ortega y Gasset: *La deshumanización del arte* García Lorca becomes friendly with Guillén and the painter Salvador Dali Diego: *Versos humanos*
1926	Rilke dies in Val-Mont, Switzerland Eluard: *Capitale de la douleur*
1927	T. S. Eliot becomes a British subject Benn: *Gesammelte Gedichte*, I
1928	Montale: *Ossi di seppia* Alberti: *Sobre los ángeles* Guillén: *Cántico* (first version) García Lorca: *La imagen poética en Don Luis de Góngora* (lecture, published 1932)
1929	García Lorca in New York; writes poems of the collection *Poeta en Nueva York* (published posthumously, in 1940)
1932	Eluard: *La Vie immédiate*
1934	'Second surrealist manifesto (Breton)
1935	García Lorca: *Llanto por Ignacio Sánchez Mejías* Ungaretti: *Sentimento del tempo*
1936	García Lorca shot in Spanish Civil War Benn: *Ausgewählte Gedichte*
1938	Valéry: *Introduction à la poétique*
1939	Yeats dies near Menton Montale: *Le occasioni*
1940	St.-John Perse moves to the United States
1941	Diego: *Alondra de verdad* (containing earlier poetry)
1942	Louis Aragon: *Les Yeux d'Elsa* St.-John Perse: *Exile* Quasimodo: *Ed è subito sera* Igor Stravinsky: *Poetics of Music*
1944	T. S. Eliot: *Four Quartets* Alberti: *Poesía* (1924–44)

1945	Valéry dies in Paris
	Lasker-Schüler dies in Jerusalem
1948	Benn: *Statische Gedichte*
1950	Breton: *Anthologie de l'humour noir*
	Guillén: *Cántico* (definitive version)
1951	Salinas dies in Boston
1952	Benn: *Probleme der Lyrik*
	Eluard: *Choix de poèmes* (expanded version)
	Eluard dies in Charenton-le-Pont
1956	Montale: *La bufera e altro*
	Benn dies in Berlin
1957	St.-John Perse: *Amers*
1958	Jiménez dies in San Juan, Puerto Rico
1959	Ungaretti: *Il taccuino del vecchio*
1960	Aleixandre: *Poesías completas* (1924–57)
	Benn: *Sämtliche Gedichte* (1912–56)
1961	St.-John Perse: *Poésie* (speech at receiving the Nobel Prize)
1965	T. S. Eliot dies in London
	Diego: *Poesía amorosa* (1918–61)
	Karl Krolow: *Gesammelte Gedichte* (1944–64)

THE
STRUCTURE
OF
MODERN POETRY

I

THEN AND NOW

A PREVIEW OF PRESENT-DAY POETRY:
DISSONANCE AND ABNORMALITY

There is no easy approach to European poetry in the twentieth century. It speaks in enigmas and obscurity. Yet is is remarkably abundant. We can no longer deny the stature of the German poets, from Rilke and Trakl to Gottfried Benn; the French, from Apollinaire to St.-John Perse; the Spanish, from García Lorca to Guillén; the Italians, from Palazzeschi to Ungaretti; or the English and Americans, from Yeats to T. S. Eliot. Their works show that poetry has no less relevance for the intellectual situation of our time than does philosophy, fiction, theater, painting, or music.

These lyricists offer the reader an experience which, before he even realizes it, brings him very close to an intrinsic feature of modern poetry: the obscurity is as fascinating as it is confusing. The verbal magic and mystery are gripping but disorienting. "Poetry can communicate before it is understood," T. S. Eliot remarked. We may call this combination of incomprehensibility and fascination a dissonance, because the result is a tension that creates agitation rather than calm. Dissonant tension is an aim of the modern arts in general. Stravinsky writes:

> Nothing forces us to be constantly looking for satisfaction that resides only in repose. And for over a century music has provided repeated examples of a style in which dissonance has emancipated itself. It is no longer tied down to its former function. Having become an entity in itself, dissonance frequently neither prepares nor anticipates anything. Dissonance is thus no more an agent of disorder than consonance is a guarantee of security.[1]

1. Igor Stravinsky, *Poetics of Music* (New York, 1942), pp. 34 f.

3

The same holds true for poetry.

Its obscurity is intentional. Baudelaire wrote, "There is a certain glory in not being understood." For Gottfried Benn, writing poetry meant "elevating crucial things into the language of incomprehensibility, devoting ourselves to things which do not merit our convincing anyone of them." St.-John Perse apostrophizes the poet ecstatically: "O two-tongued one, amidst all two-pointed things, and yourself a struggle between all things that struggle . . . man speaking in the ambiguous! . . . like a man entangled in a confusion of wings and thorns. . . ." Montale is more restrained: "No one would bother to write verse if the poet's goal were to make himself understood."

The best advice one can offer the serious but uninitiated reader is to try to adjust his eyesight to the darkness enshrouding modern poetry, whose tendency to avoid as much as possible the communication of clear contents is everywhere apparent. A poem is now a self-sufficient entity of multiple meanings — a taut network of absolute forces that act suggestively upon prerational levels of the mind and make the secret areas of concepts vibrate.

The dissonant tension of the modern poem is revealed in other ways as well: elements of archaic, mystic, occult origin clash with keen intellectualism, straightforward modes of expression with complicated ideas, balanced language with unresolved content, precision with absurdity, insignificant themes with turbulent styles. These tensions are in part formal and often are meant to be just that. But at other times they appear in the subject matter.

Whenever a modern poem touches on realities — of objects or people — its treatment is nondescriptive, omitting the warmth of familiar seeing and feeling. It makes those realities seem unfamiliar, estranges and deforms them. The poem is not to be measured against what is ordinarily accepted as reality, not even when it assimilates vestiges of this so-called reality as a springboard for its freedom. Reality departs from the spatial, temporal, material, and psychological order of things, transcending those distinctions which are necessary to a normal orientation in the world but which are now rejected as detrimental: the distinctions between beauty and ugliness, nearness and remoteness, light and shadow, pain and pleasure, earth and heaven. Of the three possible modes in lyric poetry — feeling, observing, and transmuting — the last predominates in the modern age, with regard to both the world and language. Definitions based on German romanticism (and employing improper generalizations) claim that poetry is the language of the heart, the emotions, the individual soul. This concept of *Gemüt* points to an easing of tension through self-communion in a psychical habitat which even the loneliest of men can share with anyone capable of sentiment. Such communicative coziness is exactly what the modern poem eschews.

4

It prefers, instead, to disregard humanitarianism in the conventional sense of the word, "experience," feeling, and often even the personal "I" of the poet. The modern poet participates in the poem not as a private individual but as a verse-writing intelligence, a manipulator of language, an artist testing the transformational acts of his imperious imagination or of his unreal visual power, trying them out on an arbitrary and insignificant theme. This does not rule out the possibility that such a poem originates in, or arouses, the enchantment of the soul. But this is neither "heart" nor "sentiment." It is the multivoiced and absolute quality of pure subjectivity, which cannot be broken down into individual emotional values. "Sentiment? I have no sentiment," Gottfried Benn avowed. Any hint of emotive tenderness is instantly mangled by harsh, disharmonious words.

We may speak of *aggressive dramatics* in modern poetry. They prevail in the relationship between the themes and the subjects, which are pitted against, rather than coordinated with, one another. These dramatics are also present in the relationship between the themes or subjects and an uneasy style that forces the sign and its designatum as far apart as possible. Yet these dramatics also determine the relationship between the poem and the reader, precipitating a shock effect in the victim, the reader, who feels alarmed rather than secure. Admittedly, poetic diction has always been distinct from the normal communicative function of language. But, apart from rare exceptions (e.g., Dante, Góngora), the difference between the two was always moderate and one of degree. Then suddenly, in the latter half of the nineteenth century, this distinction turned into a radical split between ordinary parlance and poetic language, a hypertension that, allied with obscure contents, produced bewilderment. Poetic diction took on the character of an experiment, bringing forth combinations which created, rather than grew from, the meaning. Familiar linguistic material appeared in unusual senses. Words from areas of remote specialization were given a poetic charge. Syntax either splintered apart or shrank down to deliberately primitive nominal statements. The oldest elements of poetry — simile and metaphor — were handled in a new fashion: the poet avoided the natural term of comparison, forcing an unreal union of logically and objectively incompatible elements. In modern painting, an autonomous structure of colors and forms now dislocates or totally eliminates the object; in verse, the autonomous dynamics of language, the need for nonmeaningful sequences of sound and curves of intensity, can go so far that the poem is no longer intelligible from its statements. Its actual content is the dramatics of external and internal formal forces. Since the poem still consists of language — although without communicable subject matter — it has the dissonant effect of simultaneously beguiling and bewildering the reader.

Confronted with such phenomena, the reader is left with a definite

5

impression of abnormality. And this is in keeping with a basic concept of modern poetics: surprise, amazement. The poet who wants to surprise and amaze must resort to abnormal means. True, abnormality is a perilous concept, implying the existence of a timeless norm; yet one era's "abnormality" is often the next era's norm, thereby proving itself capable of being assimilated. However, this does not apply to the poetry with which we are dealing, nor to the Frenchmen who founded it. Rimbaud and Mallarmé have not been assimilated by the public at large, not even today, although so much is being written about them. Nonassimilability is typical of even the most recent poets.

Let us instead use *abnormality* and *normality* as heuristic terms. Disregarding historical factors, we shall posit as normal the psychology and consciousness capable of grasping a text by Goethe or Hofmannsthal. This allows us to recognize all the more clearly those examples of contemporary poetry that deviate enough from the kind practiced by the above-mentioned writers to be labeled "abnormal." This term is not a value judgment, nor does it signify "degenerate" (which we cannot emphasize too strongly). The uncritical admirer of modern poetry tends to defend it against bourgeois inhibitedness and the taste created by school and home. This is a childish reaction, having little to do with the aims of such poetry and evidencing a naïve ignorance toward three thousand years of European literature. Modern poetry (and art) is not to be admired or rejected per se. An inherent phenomenon of our times, it has the right to be examined and appreciated. And the reader has the right to derive his standards from older literature and to set them as high as possible. We shall refrain from judging by such standards, but we shall take the liberty of referring to them when describing and trying to understand.

Cognition is possible even with poetry that is not primarily meant to be understood, poetry which, as T. S. Eliot writes, contains no meaning "satisfying a habit of the reader." Eliot goes on to say: "Some poets are restive towards such meaning, because it seems superfluous, and they see possibilities of poetic intensity that come from ridding oneself of the meaning." Such poetry is cognizable and describable, even though it may contain a freedom so great that the best that understanding can do is to determine the existence of that freedom without grasping the contents — especially since (according to Eliot) these contents have such incalculable meaning that the poet himself, while writing, has only a limited knowledge of the sense of what he is creating. The cognition of such poetry registers, as a primary feature of stylistic intention, great or total unintelligibility. And other characteristics can be determined. Cognition can still be hopeful, because it directs itself at historical circumstances, poetic technique, and an undeniable consistency of language that links the most diverse authors. Finally, cognition yields to the plethora of meanings in these texts by incorporating itself into the process that such poetry tries to initiate in the audience: the reader's attempts at interpretation continue the creative act of poetry, endlessly and boundlessly.

NEGATIVE CATEGORIES

In attempting to understand modern poetry, we are faced with the task of finding descriptive categories. We cannot sidestep the fact (on which all critics concur) that negative categories predominate. *However — and this makes all the difference — these negative categories are definitional, not pejorative.* They are, in fact, applied as a result of the historical process by which modern poetry has departed from older literature.

The change occurring in the poetry of the nineteenth century led to a parallel change in the concepts employed by criticism and aesthetics. Until the start of the nineteenth century, and to some extent even beyond, poetry stood in the resonance chamber of society, which expected it to idealize well-known themes or situations, to offer therapeutic solace even when presenting the demonic; poetry itself, while set apart from the other literary genres, was not placed above them. But when poetry began to oppose a society intent on economic security and to lament both the scientific deciphering of the universe and the prosaism of the general public, a sharp break with tradition resulted. The poet's originality was justified by his abnormality; poetry became the language of self-centered suffering, which, rather than struggle for relief, sought nuances in words; poetry, now viewed as the purest and loftiest form of literature, opposed all other forms, arrogating the freedom of recklessly and boundlessly voicing anything inspired by an imperious imagination, by a subjectivity extending into the unconscious, and by a play with empty transcendence. This change was accurately mirrored in the categories used by poets and critics when discussing poetry.

Writers of the previous period, when judging poems, focused on thematic qualities, describing them with the aid of positive categories. Goethe's critiques of poetry include such terms as *pleasure, joy, lovingly harmonious richness*: "Everything boldly ventured submits to the law of moderation"; catastrophes turn into blessings; base things are elevated; poetry is beneficent in that "it teaches us to regard the human condition as something desirable"; poetry has "inner serenity," a "happy view of reality," and raises individual things to a universal rank. Formal qualities are the meaningfulness of words, "restrained diction" that "proceeds with quiet prudence and precision," and an accurate and unambiguous choice of words. Schiller uses similar terminology: the poem ennobles; it lends dignity to the emo-

7

tions, idealizes its subject, or else it would not deserve to be called a poem; it avoids "peculiarities" incompatible with the "ideally universal"; its perfection depends on a serene soul, its beautiful form on the "consistency of a coherent whole." Since such requirements and value judgments are defined by their opposites, the older period had to employ negative categories as well, but only for the purpose of condemning: fragmentary, "confused," "a mere hodgepodge of images," night (instead of light), "witty sketchiness," "wavering dreams," "frivolous texture" (Grillparzer).

But with the new type of poetry, different and almost constantly negative categories emerged, and they were increasingly applied to the form rather than the content. Novalis was one of the first to use these categories, not to censure, but to describe and even to laud. Poetry, he said, is allegedly based on "deliberately aleatory production"; it presents its themes "in a free and random catenation"; "the more personal, more local, more temporal a poem is, the closer it comes to the central pole of poetry." (Note that in German aesthetics of the day, terms like *temporell* generally referred to inadmissible limitation.)

Subsequently, the densest accumulation of negative categories can be found in Lautréamont. His clairvoyant blueprint of future literature (1870) was apparently meant to be a warning (as far as it is possible to interpret the changing masks of this cryptic *chaotique*). Yet, amazingly enough, this poet, who helped pave the way for later poetry, was able to characterize its features in such a manner that it makes no difference whether he (perhaps) wanted to halt the development that he foresaw. His prognostication: anxiety, confusion, degradation, distortion, the reign of anomaly and peculiarity, obscureness, burrowing imagination, somberness, a sundering into extreme antitheses, a predilection for the Void. And then, abruptly, in the flood of Lautréamont's prophecies, a "sawing." This "sawing" crops up elsewhere. (The French word *scie* also denotes "nuisance"; in the following quotation it is used primarily in this sense and then concretely as well.) Eluard's poem *Le Mal* (1932), an accumulation of images of destruction, begins: "There was the door just like a saw." Various paintings by Picasso depict a saw, or merely its jagged teeth veering through geometric planes, with no apparent bearing on the subject matter; in one canvas, the strings of a mandolin appear as a sawlike structure. We need not assume any direct influence, but the recurrence of this symbol may be viewed as one of the most significant indices of the structuralism governing modern art and literature since the second half of the nineteenth century.

Here are some more key terms from German, French, Spanish, and English writings on modern poetry. We must, however, emphasize again that these terms are descriptive and not derogatory. Thus: *disorientation, disintegration of the familiar, loss of order, incoherence, fragmentism, reversibility, additive style, depoeticized poetry, bolts of annihilation, strident imagery, brutal abruptness, dislocation, astigmatism, alienation.* And finally there is the statement by a Spaniard, Dámaso Alonso: "At the moment we have no choice but to apply negative terminology to our art." Written in 1932, this line could have been repeated in 1955 without misrepresenting the current state of poetry.

The use of such terms was honest. And, of course, different ones were used. Verlaine called Rimbaud's verse "Vergilian." Yet the same has been said of Racine's verse. Such a positive adjective can only approach the mark without hitting it exactly, as long as it glosses over the dissonances in Rimbaud's subject matter and vocabulary. One French critic speaks of the "peculiar beauty" of Eluard's poetry. But this positive description is lost amid an array of totally negative ones, and they alone characterize that "peculiar beauty." We come across similar problems with the interpreters of painting. They label a neck painted by Picasso "elegant"; but this adjective, even though applicable, does not quite convey the particular elegance of this neck, the elegance of a totally unreal construction that looks less like a human figure and more like a wooden contraption. Why are the critics not courageous enough to include this in their definition of the specific elegance?

We now come to the question of why negative categories describe modern poetry more accurately than positive ones do. It is a question pertaining to the historical function and the future of modern verse. Are all these poets so far ahead of us that no suitable terminology can catch up with them? Must our cognition therefore make do with the expedient of negative concepts? Or would a possibility hinted at above be closer to the truth: namely, that we are dealing with ultimate nonassimilability as an intrinsic feature of modern poetry? Either alternative might be correct, but we cannot tell for sure. All we can ascertain is the existence of abnormality. Consequently, if we want to know the precise elements of such abnormality, we must use the terms that it has forced upon even the most reluctant observers.

THEORETICAL PRELUDES IN THE EIGHTEENTH CENTURY: ROUSSEAU AND DIDEROT

In Europe, during the second half of the eighteenth century, writings appeared which may be interpreted, in the light of later poetry, as its preludes. It will suffice to point this out in the works of Rousseau and Diderot.

In Rousseau's case, we are thinking not so much of the author of political and social blueprints or of the ethical enthusiast intoxicated with nature. That is, we can consider these aspects only as poles of an unresolved tension omnipresent in his works: the antithesis between intellectual acumen and emotional excitement, between a gift of logical thought development and a submission to the utopias of the feelings — a very specific case of modern dissonance. However, others of his characteristics are of greater importance for us.

Rousseau may have been an heir to many traditions, but for his purposes they were no longer binding. He seemed to prefer standing alone, pitted solely against himself and nature. And this desire made all the difference. Rousseau stationed himself at a zero hour of history. He repealed history with his plans for government, society, and life, plans that can only be distorted by any inquiry into their historical determinants. His egocentric stance embodied the first radical form of modern antitraditionalism and, at the same time, rejected all mankind. Rousseau is frequently labeled a psychopath, a classical paranoiac. But this diagnosis fails to explain why in both his own age and the subsequent one he was admired for his self-imposed isolation and the eccentricities that it justified. The absolute self, joined in his case to the lofty suffering of misunderstood genius, forced a rift between him and society. The pathological element in Rousseau may have contributed to this rift, but his sense of alienation obviously corresponded to a growing general feeling among his contemporaries. Viewing one's own abnormality as a warrant for one's vocation, being so convinced of an inevitable irreconcilability between the self and the world as to establish the maxim, Better to be hated than to want to be normal — all these things formed a pattern of self-interpretation easily recognized among the poets of the following century. Verlaine coined an apt expression for them: *poètes maudits*, "outcast poets." The suffering of the misunderstood self because of a self-inflicted banishment from society and the retreat into a self-involved inwardness became acts of pride; exile was a claim to superiority.

In his last work, *Les Rêveries du promeneur solitaire*, Rousseau succeeded in proclaiming a prerational certitude of existence. The substance of this certitude is a dream twilight submerging from mechanical time into inner time and no longer differentiating between past and present, chaos and comfort, fancy and reality. The discovery of internal time was nothing new; Seneca, Augustine, Locke, and Sterne had thought about it. But the lyrical intensity of Rousseau's commitment to it, and the idea of inner time as belonging particularly to an antisocial psyche, helped pave the way for later poetry, an influence that could never have proceeded from earlier philosophical analyses of time. Mechanical time, the clock, became the hated symbol of technological civilization (for Baudelaire and many later poets, such as Antonio Machado); internal time became the refuge of a poetry fleeing the confines of reality.

The distinction between imagination and reality was further abolished by Rousseau throughout his writings. In *La Nouvelle Héloïse*, he claimed that only the imagination can bring real happiness, whereas the materialization of a fantasy destroys happiness: "The land of illusion is the only land worth inhabiting in this world; the human creature is so trivial that only that which is not is beautiful." Along with this goes the idea of creative imagination, which has the right to use the authority of the self to create something nonexistent and to set it above existing reality. The significance of such ideas for later poetry cannot be overemphasized. Rousseau may have been speaking from the perspective of a personal sentimentality of happiness. But, if we discount this feeling, we see that he boldly raised the imagination to a power that is well aware of, and yet desires, its own illusion, for it is convinced that the Void — which Rousseau conceived of as moral vacuity — allows no intellectual productiveness other than that of the imagination, and that this is the only kind of productiveness that fulfills the needs of creative inwardness. Thus we are no longer obliged to measure the products of the imagination by the standard of the objectively and logically permissible; we no longer have to separate those products from pure fancy. Imagination has become absolute. And in the nineteenth century it will again be absolute, heightened to a dictatorial force and definitively free of Rousseau's sentimental coloring.

Diderot, too, granted the imagination an independent status and the right to judge itself by its own standards. His trains of thought are different from Rousseau's. They are connected with a discussion of genius, which he elucidated dialectically in *Le Neveu de Rameau* and linearly in his *Encyclopédie* article on *génie*. In the former work, the discussion leads to the thesis that the frequent and perhaps inevitable conjunction of immorality and brilliance, social incapacity and great intellectual stature, is a fact that we must admit even though we cannot explain it. Diderot's boldness is extraordinary; he abolished a concept current since antiquity, the equation of the aesthetic faculties with cognition and ethics. He ascribed an independent rank to artistic genius. For the sake of comparison, one may examine Lessing's and Kant's attempts to link the extraordinary character of the genius to the standards of truth and goodness. Diderot's *Encyclopédie* article is no less daring. He did accept the older theory of genius as a visionary force of nature, at liberty to flout all rules. But no predecessor of his ever wrote that a genius also has the right to err. It is, he wrote, precisely the astonishing and surprising errors of genius that inflame; a genius sows brilliant errors. Enraptured by the soaring flight of his own ideas, a genius builds houses that reason would never tenant; his creations are free combina-

11

tions which he loves as much as poetry; his ability is to create rather than to discover. Thus, "True and false are no longer the distinguishing features of a genius." In the passages summed up here, the concept of imagination crops up frequently. It is the pilot force of genius; and it is granted the same privilege of being a spontaneous action of intellectual powers. Its quality is measured by the scope of the images produced, the efficacy of its ideas — a pure dynamics no longer bound to any contents and beyond all distinction of good and evil, truth and error. This, too, is not very far from the dictatorial imagination of later poetry.

There is more to be found in Diderot, primarily in *Les Salons*, a critical appreciation of contemporary painting. Here he is highly sensitive to the atmospheric values of a painting and presents entirely new insights into color and light as they exist independent of the subject matter. But, even more important, he interweaves analyses of painting and of poetry. This has little to do with the old doctrine supported by Horace's (misunderstood) phrase, "ut pictura poesis."[2] It is actually the specifically modern rap-prochement of art and literary criticism, reappearing with Baudelaire and still current today. Nothing in Diderot's time compares to his insight into poetic processes in his *Salons* (with the possible exception of G. B. Vico's works, which were, however, unknown to Diderot). Diderot saw that tone is to verse as color is to painting, and he called this correspondence "rhythmic magic." It strikes the eye, the ear, and the imagination more deeply than objective precision could. "Clarity is detrimental." Therefore, "Poets, be obscure," which means that poetry should turn to nocturnal, out-of-the-way themes that terrify and create mystery. However, for Diderot, poetry is no longer primarily a concrete statement. It is emotional movement by means of free creation of metaphors, at liberty to "hurtle to extremes," and by means of equally extreme levels of tone. A decided superiority of linguistic magic over linguistic contents, of the dynamics of the image over its meaning, is here proclaimed. The extent to which Diderot could sometimes go in his dissociation from thematic objectiveness is shown in his groping and yet astounding words: "The pure and abstract dimensions of [subject] matter are not devoid of a certain expressiveness." Baudelaire will repeat this point, but much more emphatically, thereby establishing that modernity of verse-making which we may call abstract poetry.

In addition, Diderot developed a theory of comprehension which may be summed up as follows: Comprehension is ideally self-comprehension;

---

2. For the correct interpretation of this formula, see Horace, *Epistolae*. [The phrase means "as with the painter's work, so with the poet's." "Horace had only intended to say that like certain paintings, some poems please only once, while others can bear repeated readings and close critical scrutiny" (Mario Praz, *Mnemosyne* [Princeton, 1970], p. 4). — *Trans.*]

whereas, because of the inability of language to render meanings exactly, the contact between poetry and the reader is not one of comprehension but one of magical suggestion. And, finally, Diderot initiated an expansion of the concept of beauty. He made a bold, if extremely cautious, attempt to conceive of disorder and chaos as aesthetically depictible and to view shock as a permissible artistic effect.

These notions, all of them astoundingly modern, are the brilliant products of an intellect whose wealth of ideas, intuitions, and stimulations led to Diderot's being likened to the elements of fire and water, to a volcano, to Prometheus, to a salamander. To be sure, Diderot's ideas came into their own only after they were taken up by others, long after Diderot's time.

NOVALIS ON FUTURE POETRY

The new functions of imagination and poetry set down by Rousseau and Diderot acquired greater importance in German, French, and English romanticism. Their subsequent development through the middle and late nineteenth century can be traced precisely and has often been described. Rather than repeat it here, we can limit ourselves to assembling those major features of romantic theories that also characterize modern poetry.

We must begin with Novalis. His lyrics can be disregarded; his reflections, written down in *Fragmente* and on several pages of his unfinished novel *Heinrich von Ofterdingen*, are far ahead of them. With the aim of interpreting romantic verse, they outline a conception of future poetry; when this theory is measured against versecraft from Baudelaire to the present, its full significance becomes clear.

Everything Novalis says about poetry refers almost wholly to lyric verse, which now appears as "the poetic per se." He lists as essential features its indefinability and its endless remoteness from all other literature. Although occasionally referring to it is a "depiction of the emotions," he also interprets the lyrical "I" as a neutral state of mood, as a totality of inwardness which never consolidates into a precise feeling. In the act of verse-making, "cool thoughtfulness" is uppermost. "The poet is pure steel, hard as flint." In both concrete and spiritual subject matter, poetry produces a blend of heterogeneous elements, a phosphorescence of transitions. It is a "bulwark against ordinary life." Its imagination enjoys the privilege of "jumbling all images." Poetry is a singing opposition to a world of habits, a world in which poetic men cannot live, for they are "visionary, magic men." Thus, once again we have a likening of poetry to magic — an idea coming from ancient traditions but appearing in a new

context, linked to ''construction'' and ''algebra,'' as Novalis calls the intellectual property of poetry, a feature he would often underscore. Poetic
magic is severe, a ''union of imagination and intellectual power,'' a
''manipulation''; its effect is a far cry from mere enjoyment, which can
no longer accompany poetry. From magic, Novalis derives the concept
of evocation. ''Every word is evocation,'' a summoning up, a conjuring
of the thing it names: hence, ''sorcery of the imagination'' and ''the wizard
as poet,'' as well as vice versa. The poet has the power of compelling
the enchanted to ''see a thing, believe it, feel it as I want them to'': dictatorial (''productive'') imagination. That is the ''greatest boon of the mind,''
and it is independent of ''external stimuli.'' The language of imagination
is therefore ''self-discourse,'' not meant to communicate. Poetic diction
''is like mathematics; it constitutes a world unto itself, plays only with
itself.'' Its language is obscure; at times even the verse-maker ''does not
himself understand it.'' He is concerned only with ''the musical states
of the soul,'' sequences of tones and tensions no longer contingent on
the meaning of the words. An attempt at understanding is still made, but
only by very few initiates. These initiates no longer look to poetry for
the qualities of ''lower genres,'' i.e., ''correctness, lucidity, purity, com-
pleteness, order.'' There are higher qualities: harmony, euphony. And then,
emphatically, comes the modern separation of language and content in favor
of the former: ''Poems, purely harmonious, but also devoid of any sense
or coherence, at most only a few stanzas comprehensible, like mere fragments of the most disparate objects.'' Thus, linguistic magic, in the service
of enchantment, is allowed to smash the world into fragments. Obscurity
and incoherence are prerequisite to lyrical suggestiveness. ''The poet uses
words like piano keys,'' stirring up powers in them that are unknown to
everyday speech; later on, Mallarmé will talk about a ''keyboard of words.''
Novalis, protesting against older poetry, which ''placed its supplies in an
easy-to-grasp order,'' writes: ''I would almost say that chaos must glimmer
through any poem.'' Modern poetry causes universal ''alienation'' so as
to lead the way to a ''higher homeland.'' Its ''manipulation,'' ákin to
''mathematical analysis,'' consists in deriving the unknown from the
known. The themes in verse-making are random; the methods are based
on the abstractions of algebra, and these are like ''the abstractions of fairy
tales'' in their independence of the ordinary world, which suffers from
''hyperclarity.''

An impassive inwardness in lieu of feelings, imagination instead of
reality, universal ruin rather than unity, an amalgam of heterogeneous
things, chaos, the fascination of obscurity and verbal magic, as well as
an impersonal manipulating, conceived of as analogous to mathematics
and making the familiar alien — this is precisely the structure for

14

Baudelaire's aesthetics as well as for the poetry of Rimbaud, Mallarmé, and the twentieth century. And the structure is the same, even though individual parts may have been dislodged or developed.

All this could be supplemented by Friedrich Schlegel's comments on the separation of beauty from truth and ethics, the poetic necessity of chaos, and "the Eccentric and the Monstrous" as requirements for poetic originality. Novalis and Schlegel were read in France, thereby inducing some of the cardinal ideas of French romanticism. This movement must be discussed briefly, for it conveyed the German ideas to Baudelaire, the first great poet of modernity and the first European theorist of modern poetry and art.

FRENCH ROMANTICISM

As a literary fashion, French romanticism became obsolete in the mid-nineteenth century. But it has remained the intellectual fate of ensuing generations, even of those who wanted to wipe it out and introduce other fashions. It may have shed its extravagance, its attitudinizing, its ostentatiousness, its short-lived triviality; yet it provided the means of expression for the increasingly deromanticized sensibilities of the latter half of the century. Its harmonies concealed the dissonances of the future.

In 1859 Baudelaire wrote, "Romanticism is either a divine or a diabolical blessing to which we owe eternal stigmata." This remark accurately describes the way in which romanticism, even while dying out, stigmatized its followers; they revolted against it because they were under its spell. Modern poetry is deromanticized romanticism.

Bitterness, a taste of ashes, somberness, are compulsive and yet cultivated experiences fundamental to the romantic. From antiquity up to the eighteenth century, joy was the supreme psychic value indicating the perfection of the sage or the believer, the knight, the courtier, the educated man of the social elite. Sorrow, if not transitory, was considered a negative value by most people, and a sin by theologians. But following the preromantic moods of suffering of the eighteenth century, this situation was reversed. Joy and serenity in literature subsided, to be replaced by melancholy and *Weltschmerz*. These new values required no *raison d'être*; they were self-sustaining and became signs of spiritual nobility. The romantic author Chateaubriand discovered unmotivated melancholy, made the "science of sorrow and anxiety" the goal of art, and interpreted spiritual disunity as a blessing of Christianity. The romanticists regarded themselves as belonging to a late cultural phase. They indulged in the spreading awareness of decadence as a source of unusual fascination, and considered destructiveness, morbidity, and crime intriguing. In Vigny's poem *La Maison du berger*, poetry becomes a lament on technology's threats to the soul. The concept of the Void begins to play its part. Musset was its first spokesman, within a field of experience in which illusionist youth, inflamed by Napoleon, collided with a passionless world of profit-making and saw both illusion and profit-making collapse into absurdity, desolation, silence, nothingness. "I believe in the Void, as I do in myself," he wrote. Melancholy and lament eventually turned into a fear of the uncanny. In Gérard de Nerval's *Vers dorés* (1845), a poem which contains a dissonance between the title and the contents, and which puts the human and the nonhuman on the same level, we find the following line: "Fear, in the blind wall, eyes that watch you." We shall see how all these moods recur — and change — in Baudelaire.

Emulating German works, which featured watered-down versions of Platonic traditions, the French romanticists viewed the poet as a misunderstood seer, a priest in the sanctuary of art. The poets formed a party against the bourgeois public and, eventually, broke up into opposing factions. Madame de Staël's utterance (1801) that literature is an expression of society lost its meaning. Writers, repeating the Revolution's protest against the social establishment, turned out a literature of opposition or one of the "future" and, finally, a literature of seclusion with increasing pride in its isolation. Rousseau's schema of uniqueness rooted in abnormality became the systematic pattern of these generations — and of those that followed.

The self-consecration of the poet, as well as the genuine or bogus experiences of suffering, melancholy, and the vanity of the world, indubitably released forces beneficial to poetry. During the romantic period, French poetry, for the first time since its period of glory three centuries earlier, flourished richly. Much of it had stature, if not European scope. One factor instrumental in this blossoming was the ubiquitous idea (formulated in France, too) that poetry is the primal speech of mankind, the total language of the total subject, allowing no boundaries between different themes or even between religious and poetic inspiration. French romantic poetry treated internal experience comprehensively and subtly; it contained a creative sensitivity to southern, Oriental, exotic atmospheres; it produced enchanting verse on love and nature, and evinced a virtuoso artistry. Victor Hugo's poetry is coruscating, gesticulatory, overly abundant, oratorical; and yet it manages to create moods of quiet intimacy as well as images of visionary forcefulness. Musset's verse becomes a mixture of cynicism and pain; Lamartine's achieves — occasionally — a pure tone which, the author himself aptly said, is as soft as velvet.

Romanticism marked the beginning of poetic practice rooted in lan-

16

guage, a reaching for the impulse inherent in the word itself. This process was a momentous one for the modern age. Victor Hugo did not merely use it; he established it, with the assistance of numerous and ancient predecessors. In a well-known passage in the *Contemplations* one reads: "The word is a living creature, more powerful than he who employs it; issuing from the darkness, it creates any meaning it wishes; it is all the things — and even more — that thought, vision, and feeling await outside: it is color, night, joy, dream, bitterness, ocean, infinity; it is the *logos* of God." We will have to recall this passage, as well as Diderot's tentative words and Novalis' more decisive statements, if we want to understand Mallarmé's ideas on the initiatory power of language — although his rigor is a far cry from Victor Hugo's chaotic ecstasy.

THEORY OF THE GROTESQUE AND THE FRAGMENT

Equally momentous was the theory of the grotesque. Diderot had circled in on it in *Le Neveu de Rameau*. Victor Hugo developed it in the preface to his *Cromwell* (1827) as part of a theory of drama. It was probably the most important French contribution to the ideology of romanticism. Its roots presumably go back to Friedrich Schlegel's comments on humor and irony, which he linked with such concepts as chaos, eternal agility, and fragmentary, transcendental buffoonery. Several details in Hugo seem, however, to be original; they are brilliant flashes of insight on the part of the twenty-five-year-old poet, and we should not demand too much careful thought of them. They are symptoms anticipating modernity.

Originally, *grotesque* was a term used by painters to describe ornamental tendril-shaped designs, usually representing legendary motifs. In the seventeenth century it came to include the bizarre, the droll, the burlesque, the distorted, and the peculiar in any respect. That was how Victor Hugo, partly under the influence of Friedrich Schlegel, used the term. However, the French poet added the notion of ugliness. His theory of the grotesque was a further step, and the most energetic one, toward equalizing beauty and ugliness. The latter, previously disqualified, allowed at best in the lowest literary genres and on the periphery of the fine arts, was raised to a metaphysical expressive value. Victor Hugo based his ideas on the conception of a world intrinsically split into antitheses and able to exist as a higher unity only by virtue of that split. This thought, frequently formulated before Hugo, goes back to antiquity. But Hugo emphasized the role of ugliness in a new way. No longer the opposite of beauty, it is in itself an absolute value. In a work of art it appears as the grotesque, a formation of incompleteness and disharmony; however, for Hugo, incompleteness is "the appropriate way to be harmonious." We can see how the concept of disharmony invades the semantically shifting term *harmony* to become a disharmony of fragments. The grotesque is meant to relieve us of beauty and, with a "shrill voice," to do away with beauty's monotony. It mirrors the dissonance between man's animal nature and his higher levels. Smashing appearance into fragments, it says that the "whole" is perceptible only as a fragment, because the "whole" is not concordant with man. But what "whole"? Characteristically, the answer is either lacking or confused. Even though Hugo believed it to be a Christian "whole," his idea of it is simply one of empty transcendence. All that exists for him are the ruins of the "whole" in the grimaces of the grotesque, and these grimaces have nothing to do with laughter. The mirth of the grotesque, as he interpreted it, gives way to grinning or horror, becoming a grimace, a provocative excitement, and a stimulus to a disquiet which the modern soul longs for more strongly than peace.

These are romantic theories. They recur only a few years later in Théophile Gautier. They belong to the "stigmata" of which Baudelaire spoke. They point out the road to Verlaine's Harlequin poems, as well as to the "grimacing" verse of Rimbaud and Tristan Corbière, the black humor of the surrealists and their forerunner, Lautréamont, and the absurdities of the most modern writers. The ultimate obscure purpose is to indicate in dissonances and fragments a transcendence whose harmony and wholeness can never be perceived again.

II

BAUDELAIRE

THE POET OF MODERNITY

With Baudelaire, French poetry became a matter of concern for all Europe, as can be seen by the effect it had in Germany, England, Italy, and Spain. In France, as well, it soon became obvious that the influence exerted by Baudelaire, reaching Rimbaud, Verlaine, and Mallarmé, was different from, and more exciting than, anything from the romantics. Mallarmé admitted that he had begun where Baudelaire had had to leave off. Valéry, nearing the end of his life, traced a direct line of communication from Baudelaire to himself. T. S. Eliot called Baudelaire's work "the greatest example of modern poetry in any language." In 1945, Jean Cocteau wrote: "From behind his grimaces, his gaze slowly wanders over to us, like light from the stars."

Many such statements speak of the poet of "modernity." This is a perfectly justifiable designation, since Baudelaire was one of the first to use this word. Employing it in 1859, he apologized for the neologism, explaining that he needed it to express the modern artist's special ability to look at the desert of a metropolis and not merely see the decline of mankind but also sense a mysterious beauty hitherto undiscovered (pp. 891 ff.).[1] This was Baudelaire's own problem: how is poetry possible in our commercialized and technologized civilization? His verse points out the way, and his prose makes an exhaustive study of it. The road leads as far as possible from the banality of real life to a zone of mystery, but in such a way that the subject matter found in civilized reality is brought

---

1. [All references in this chapter are to *Œuvres complètes*, ed. J. G. Le Dantec (Paris, 1954). — *Trans.*]

19

into this zone and thus becomes poetically viable. This new outlook touched off modern poetry, creating its corrosive but magical substance.

Basic characteristics of Baudelaire are his intellectual discipline and the lucidity of his artistic consciousness. He united poetic genius and critical intelligence. His insights into verse-making are, as with Novalis, even superior to his own poetry. Indeed, Baudelaire's critical insights had a stronger effect on later times than did his verse. His ideas are set down in his essay collections *Curiosités esthétiques* (1865) and *L'Art romantique* (1868), which contain interpretations and programs developed from an observation of contemporary painting and music as well as literature. As in Diderot, but on a higher level and with new goals, his ideas on poetry draw upon the other arts. The essays constantly expand into analyses of contemporary sensibilities, of modernity in general, because Baudelaire conceived of poetry and art as converting the fate of an era into form. He thus anticipated Mallarmé's contribution: ontological poetry and an ontological theory of poetry.

DEPERSONALIZATION

Scholars have made great headway in revealing Baudelaire's connections with the romantics. But here we want to discuss his uniqueness and what it was that enabled him to transmute the romantic legacy into verse and thought, which in turn evoked later poetry.

Les Fleurs du mal (1857) is neither confessional poetry nor a diary of private states and circumstances, no matter how much it may contain of the suffering of a sick, lonely, unhappy man. Unlike Victor Hugo, Baudelaire never dated any of his poems. None of them can be thematically elucidated by biographical data. Baudelaire sparked off the depersonalization of modern poetry, at least in the sense that the lyrical word no longer derives from a fusion of the poetic persona and the empirical person, which fusion had been a goal of the romantics, as opposed to many of the poets of earlier centuries. We cannot overestimate the importance of Baudelaire's comments on this subject. Nor are they weakened by their indebtedness to similar statements by Edgar Allan Poe. On the contrary, this fact merely puts them in the proper context.

Outside of France, it was Poe who most decisively separated poetry and the heart. He wanted the subject of poetry to be an enthusiastic excitement that had no connection with personal passion or the "intoxication of the heart." What he meant was a comprehensive mood which, for want of a better name, he called "soul," but always added, "not heart."

Baudelaire repeats such statements faithfully, varying them in his own words. "The sensitivity of the heart" — as opposed to "the sensitivity of the imagination" — "is not beneficial to the poetic process" (pp. 1031 ff.). Here we must take into account that Baudelaire considers the imagination an intellectually guided operation (as remains to be shown). This conception sheds the necessary light on the above-quoted words, which demand a rejection of any personal sentimentality in favor of a lucid imagination far more capable of solving difficult problems. Baudelaire provides the poet with a motto: "My task is extrahuman" (p. 1044). In a letter, he talks about the "deliberate impersonality of my poetry," by which he means that his poetry can express any human sensibility, preferably the most extreme. Tears? By all means, but only those which "do not come from the heart." Baudelaire justifies poetry for being able to neutralize the personal heart. He gropes along; his ideas are often clouded by older ones. And yet we can recognize the historical necessity of the future development, from the neutralization of the person to the dehumanization of the lyrical persona (the "I"). Baudelaire introduced the depersonalization which T. S. Eliot and other poets later viewed as a requirement for the precision and validity of versecraft.

In almost all the poems in *Les Fleurs du mal*, it is the "I," the poetic voice, that is speaking. Baudelaire is totally wrapped up in himself. But, egocentric as he may be, the poet pays scant heed to his empirical ego when he writes his verses. He writes out of himself only insofar as he considers himself a sufferer of modernity, which is cast over him like a spell. He explained often enough that his own suffering was not peculiar. Characteristically, any vestiges of his personal life to appear in his poems are expressed hazily. He would never have written anything like Victor Hugo's poem on the death of a child. With a dogged, methodical thoroughness, he subjectively goes through all the phases growing out of modernism: anxiety, inescapableness, the collapse of ardently desired, but Void-bound, ideality. Baudelaire talks of his obsessive wish to make that destiny his own. *Obsession* and *destiny* are two of his key words. Others are *concentration* and *centralization of the ego*. He adopts Emerson's dictum: "He who is immovably centered is a hero." Its antithetical concepts are "dissolution" and "prostitution." The latter term, derived from the French illuminati of the eighteenth century, means abandonment, an illegitimate remission from one's intellectual fate, flight to others, betrayal through dissipation. These are the symptoms of modern civilization, as Baudelaire points out, dangers even he must beware of — he, "the master by virtue of the fate of his faculties" (p. 676), by virtue of the concentration on a self that has canceled out the aleatoriness of the individual person.

CONCENTRATION AND AWARENESS OF FORM:
POETRY AND MATHEMATICS

Les Fleurs du mal, permeated with a network of themes, is a concentrated organism. One might even speak of a system, especially since Baudelaire's essays, journals, and even some of his letters provide for this carefully thought-out network. There are not many themes. And they crop up astonishingly early — in the 1840s. From the publication of *Les Fleurs du mal* up to his death, Baudelaire scarcely went beyond them. He preferred revising an early draft to writing a new poem. Although some critics have viewed him as unproductive, his was the productivity of intensity, which, having attained a breach, increases in depth and strength. His was a productivity activating artistic perfectionism, because the suprapersonal validity of the contents is assured only in the maturity of the form. Baudelaire's themes, few in number, are to be seen as a set of conveyers, variations, metamorphoses, of a basic tension which we can characterize as a struggle between satanism and ideality. The tension is never resolved. But, as a whole, it has the same order and logic as every individual poem.

Two possibilities of future poetry are united here. In Rimbaud, the unresolved tension will increase into an absolute dissonance, destroying all order and coherence. Mallarmé, too, will intensify the conflict, but will shift it to other themes, creating a Baudelaire-like order only to mask it in a new obscure language.

With the concentration of themes in his verse, Baudelaire was abiding by the decree of not surrendering to "intoxication of the heart." This state may occur in poetry but is not poetry per se; it is only material. The act leading to pure poetry is labor, systematic construction of an architecture, manipulation of the impulses of language. Baudelaire often pointed out that *Les Fleurs du mal* was not meant to be an album, but a whole, with a beginning, an articulate development, and an end. His indication is valid. The poems embrace despair, paralysis, feverish soaring into the unreal, a death wish, a morbid playing with sensation. But all these negative themes can be encompassed by a methodical composition. Next to Petrarch's *Canzoniere*, Goethe's *Westöstlicher Divan*, and Guillén's *Cántico*, *Les Fleurs du mal* exhibits the most rigorous architecture of any book of European poetry. Everything Baudelaire added to the initial publication was planned in such a way (according to his letters) as to fit into the framework he had laid out in 1845 and completed in the first edition. Here, even the old custom of numerical composition played a part. The original edition contained one hundred poems divided into five groups — a further sign of the poet's formal intention, definitely corresponding to a general romantic striving for form. Moreover, the obvious

22

vestiges of Christian ideas suggest that the conspicuously precise formal structure is an echo of high medieval symbolism, which reflected cosmic order in compositional forms.

In subsequent editions, Baudelaire gave up the numerical system but strengthened the internal order. This can easily be discerned. After the introductory poem, which anticipates the entirety, the first group (*Spleen et idéal*) offers a contrast between elevation and downfall. The next group (*Tableaux parisiens*) shows an abortive escape into the external world of a metropolis; the third set (*Le Vin*), the attempt to flee into an artificial paradise. This flight, too, fails to bring peace. Hence, there is a surrender to the fascination of the destructive: this makes up the contents of the fourth group, which bears the same name as the whole book (*Fleurs du mal*). The result is the scornful rebellion against God in the fifth group (*Révolte*). The final endeavor, in the sixth and last group (*La Mort*), is the search for peace in death, in the absolute unknown. The architectural plan is also evident within the individual groups as a kind of dialectical reasoning in the poems. A demonstration is unnecessary, since the essential form can be seen in the book as a whole. It is an agitated order whose lines change in themselves, an order that forms an over-all downward curve. The lowest point is the end, the "abyss," because only the abyss offers a hope of seeing the "new." What "new"? The hope in the abyss has no word for it.

Baudelaire's architectural construction of *Les Fleurs du mal* proves his renunciation of romanticism, whose books of poems are mere collections, their haphazard arrangement a formal echo of the chance inspiration. His methodical architecture also bears witness to the role of formal energy in his verse. These forces mean more than simple decoration or proper form. They are means of salvation, sought after to the utmost in an extremely unsettling intellectual situation. Poets have always known that grief dissolves in song, that suffering is purged and purified by being transmuted into sublimely formed words. But it was only in the nineteenth century, when purposeful suffering turned into purposeless suffering, desolation, and ultimately nihilism, that forms became so crucial to salvation, although their rigidity and calmness were a dissonant contrast to restless contents. Once again we encounter a basic dissonance of modern poetry. Just as the poem has separated from the heart, so the form has separated from the content. Language is rescued by the salvation of form, while the content is left unresolved.

Baudelaire often spoke of salvation through form. An example is the following, whose meaning is more provocative than the conventional wording would make it seem: "It is a wonderful privilege of art that if something terrible is expressed artistically it becomes beautiful, and that pain, rhythmically arranged and articulate, fills the mind with a calm joy'' (p. 1040). This sentence veils something that has already occurred in Baudelaire's work: the ascendancy of the desire for form over the desire for mere expression. Yet these words reveal the extent to which he longed for security through form — the "life preserver of form,'' as Guillén put it. Elsewhere Baudelaire writes: "Obviously, metrical laws are not arbitrarily invented tyrannies. They are rules demanded by the organism of the mind itself. They have never prevented originality from manifesting itself. The very opposite is infinitely closer to the truth: they have always helped originality to mature'' (p. 779). Stravinsky will refer to this passage in his *Poetics of Music*. The idea will be reiterated by Mallarmé and Valéry — not only because it confirms the old romantic sense of form but also because it supports a practice favored by many of the moderns: i.e., handling the conventions of rhyme, metrics, and stanza like instruments that cut into the language and provoke reactions which would never have emanated from the thematic plan of the poem.

Baudelaire extols Daumier's ability to depict with precision and clarity the base, the trivial, the degenerate. He could have similarly praised his own poems. They unite deadliness and precision and are thus a prelude to future verse. Novalis and Poe introduced the concept of calculation into poetics, and Baudelaire followed suit. "Beauty is the product of reason and reckoning,'' he writes in a highly characteristic discussion of the superiority of the artificial (that is, the artistic) over mere nature (p. 911). He even considers inspiration to be mere nature, impure subjectivity. As the poet's only impulse, it leads to lack of precision, as does intoxication of the heart. But it is welcome as a reward for the artistic labor which precedes it and which has the status of an exercise; in this case inspiration assumes grace, akin to a dancer who "has broken his bones a thousand times in private before exhibiting himself to an audience'' (p. 1133). The high quota of intellectual and voluntative factors that Baudelaire assigns to the poetic act is not to be overlooked. Like Novalis, he draws the concept of mathematics into such reflections. Thus, in characterizing the accuracy of style, Baudelaire compares it to the "wonders of mathematics.'' The metaphor is given the value of "mathematical precision.'' All these ideas go back to Poe, who spoke of the relationship between poetic tasks and "the strict logic of a mathematical problem.'' The effects are apparent in Mallarmé as well as in the poetics of our time.

A TERMINAL ERA AND MODERNITY

Even in Baudelaire's themes we can discern his withdrawal from romanticism. Everything he inherited from that period — and the legacy is

Baudelaire

great — he turned into such a difficult experience that, by comparison, the romantics look like dilettantes. They had taken the eschatological interpretation of history — which, Greco-Roman and Christian in origin, had been gaining ground since the late Enlightenment — and had developed it further, defining their own era as a terminal one. Yet this was primarily a mood, rendered harmless by the lovely hues that they managed to capture from the cultural sunset. Baudelaire, too, placed himself and his time in this terminal era; but he did so with different images and emotions. The eschatological consciousness permeating Europe since the eighteenth century and reaching into our own time went through a phase of terrified and terrifying sagacity with Baudelaire. In 1862 he wrote the poem *Le Coucher du soleil romantique* [Romantic sunset], which contains a series of lessening degrees of light and joy, descending to cold night and a horror of swamps and repulsive beasts. The symbolism leaves no doubt as to its meaning. It alludes to ultimate darkening, to a loss of the soul's self-intimacy, which can survive even in decline. Baudelaire knew that a poetry suitable to his time could be achieved only by seizing the nocturnal and the abnormal: they constitute the only place where the self-estranged soul can produce poetry and escape the triviality of "progress," the disguise of the terminal era. Accordingly, he called his *Fleurs du mal* a "dissonant product of the muses of the terminal era."

Baudelaire's exhaustive pondering of the concept of modernity was very different from that of the romantics. It is a highly complex notion. Negatively, it signifies the world of big cities, devoid of vegetation, with their ugliness, their asphalt, their artificial lighting, their stone canyons, their sins, their lonely crowds. Furthermore, it refers to the technological era of steampower, electricity, and progress. Baudelaire defined progress as "the progressive decay of the soul and the progressive domination of matter" (p. 766), and then again as "atrophy of the mind" (p. 1203). We hear of his "utter disgust" at advertising posters, newspapers, and the "rising tide of all-leveling democracy." The same was said by Stendhal and Tocqueville and, a bit later, by Flaubert. However, Baudelaire's concept of modernity goes further. It is dissonant and turns the negative into something fascinating. Poverty, decay, evil, the nocturnal, and the artificial exert an attraction that has to be perceived poetically. They contain secrets that guide poetry on to new paths. In the refuse of urban centers, Baudelaire smells a mystery, which his poetry depicts as a phosphorescent shimmer. In addition, he approves of anything that banishes nature in order to establish the absolute realm of the artificial. Since the cubic stone masses of cities are unnatural, and since, although constituting the place of evil, they belong to the freedom of the mind, they are inorganic landscapes of the pure intellect. Only vestiges of this rationale will appear among later poets.

25

But even twentieth-century poetry will bathe the metropolis in the mysterious phosphorescence that Baudelaire discovered.

In his lyrics, the dissonant images of the big city are extremely intense. They join gaslight and evening sky, the fragrance of flowers and the reek of tar; they are filled with desire and lament, and they contrast with the sweeping oscillation of the verses. Extracted from banality, like drugs from toxic plants, the images are poetically transmuted into antidotes for "the vice of banality." The repulsive is joined to the nobility of sound, acquiring the "galvanic shudder" (*frisson galvanique*) that Baudelaire praises in Poe. Dusty windows with traces of rain; gray, washed-out façades; the venomous green of metals; dawn as a dirty splotch; the animal sleep of prostitutes; the roar of busses; faces without lips; old hags; brass bands; eyeballs soaked in gall; stale perfumes: these are some of the contents of the "galvanized" modernity in Baudelaire's poetry. And they survive in Eliot.

THE AESTHETICS OF UGLINESS

Baudelaire frequently speaks of beauty; yet, in his lyrics, beauty is confined to the metrics and vibration of language. The subject matter no longer fits in with older ideas of beauty. He uses complements that are paradoxical and reinterprets the "splice of amazement" in order to lend beauty an aggressive attraction. To shield itself against the banal and to provoke banal taste, beauty must be bizarre. "Pure and bizarre" is one of his definitions of the beautiful. But he frankly desires ugliness as the equivalent of the secret that must be fathomed anew, as the possible beginning for an ascent to ideality. "From ugliness, the poet evokes new enchantment" (p. 1114). The deformed creates surprise, which in turn causes the "unexpected assault." More violently than ever before, abnormality becomes a goal of modern verse-making, as does one of the reasons for abnormality —⁌ irritation at the banal and conventional, which, in Baudelaire's eyes, exist even in the beauty of older style. The new "beauty," which can coincide with ugliness, acquires its restlessness by both assimilating the banal and being deformed into something bizarre, and through the "union of the terrifying with the foolish."

These are intensifications of ideas that were current since Friedrich Schlegel's "transcendental buffoonery" and Victor Hugo's theory of the grotesque. Baudelaire expressed his approval of Poe's title *Tales of the Grotesque and Arabesque* (1840) "because the Grotesque and the Arabesque are offensive to human sight." For Baudelaire, the grotesque has nothing to do with the comical. Intolerant of "simple comedy," he welcomes the "gory fool's-play" in Daumier's caricatures, develops a

26

"metaphysics of the absolute comical," views the grotesque as a clash
of ideality with the devil, and adds to it a concept that is to make a mark
for itself: the absurd (pp. 710 ff.). His own experiences, as well as those
of man, who is torn between ecstasy and collapse, are derived from "the
law of the absurd" (p. 438). It is the law that compels man to "express
suffering through laughter." Baudelaire speaks of the "justification of the
absurd," and lauds dreams because things impossible in reality are endowed
by them "with the terrible logic of the absurd." The absurd becomes a
view of unreality, which Baudelaire and later poets want to penetrate in
order to flee the constriction of reality.

"THE ARISTOCRATIC PLEASURE OF DISPLEASING"

A poetry requiring concepts like the above for its justification will either
annoy the reader or elude him. Rousseau's chasm between the author and
the audience had led to the notion of the lonely poet, a favorite theme
of the romantics, who treated it with some degree of melodiousness.
Baudelaire took up the theme, but his tone was sharper. He added the
aggressive dramatics that henceforth were to characterize European art and
literature — even when the intention to shock, though not proclaimed as
a principle, was sufficiently obvious in the work itself. Baudelaire still
had such principles. He spoke of "the aristocratic pleasure of displeasing,"
called *Les Fleurs du mal* "the passionate joy of resistance" and "a product
of hate"; he was glad that poetry caused a "nervous shock" and prided
himself on irritating the reader and no longer being understood by him.
"Poetic consciousness, once an endless source of delight, has now turned
into an inexhaustible arsenal of instruments of torture" (p. 519). All this
is more than an imitation of romantic ways. The internal dissonances of
poetry have logically become dissonances between the work and the reader.

RUINOUS CHRISTIANITY

These inner dissonances do not have to be treated in detail here. Only
the previously mentioned over-all dissonance between satanism and ideality
will be gone into further. This is necessary because it contains a thematic
feature of later poetry, one that we shall call "empty ideality."

"To fathom a poet's soul, one must look for those words which occur
most often in his works. The word reveals his obsession" (p. 1111). These
lines of Baudelaire's contain an excellent principle of interpretation, one
that can be applied to Baudelaire himself. The rigor of his intellectual

world, the persistence of its few but intense themes, allows us to find its focal points in the words occurring most frequently. They are key words and can easily be arranged in two polar groups: on the one side, *darkness, abyss, fear, desolation, desert, prison, cold, black, rotting*; on the other, *elevation, azure, heaven, ideal, light, purity*. The elaborate antithesis runs through almost every poem. Often compressed in a minimal space, the antithesis becomes a lexical dissonance, as in "dirty greatness," "decaying and enchanting," "beguiling horror," "dark and light." Such a union of normally incompatible things is known as an oxymoron — an old artistic figure of poetic diction, designed to articulate complicated psychological situations. In Baudelaire, the oxymoron is used to a conspicuous degree. It is the key figure of his fundamental dissonance. And it was a good idea on the part of Baudelaire's friend H. Babou to employ an oxymoron in the title *Les Fleurs du mal*.

These word groups conceal traces of Christianity. Baudelaire's work is inconceivable without the Christian religion. But he is no longer a Christian. This fact is not refuted by his frequently discussed "satanism." The man who knows himself to be possessed by Satan may bear Christian stigmata; but this is quite different from Christian belief in salvation. As far as it may be stated succinctly, Baudelaire's satanism is the victory of the evil devised by the intelligence over the merely animal evil (and thereby, the banal), with the goal of gaining in an acme of evil some entry into ideality: hence, the cruelties and perversities in *Les Fleurs du mal*. Out of "thirst for infinity," they degrade nature, laughter, and love into the satanic in order to find the point at which to escape into the "new." According to another key word, man is "hyperbolic," always straining upward in his intellectual fever. Yet, essentially torn asunder, he is a *homo duplex* who must satisfy his satanic pole in order to understand his heavenly one. Manichaean and Gnostic forms of early Christianity return in this schema via the illuminati of the eighteenth century and Joseph de Maistre. However, the recurrence cannot be attributed solely to outside influences. This schema voices a need of Baudelaire's. Symptomatically, and not just for him, the modern intellect falls back upon ancient ways of thinking that correspond to its inner dissension.

Nor do the many quotations culled from Baudelaire as proof of his Christianity alter the picture. Baudelaire manifested a will to pray, spoke in all earnestness about sin, and was deeply permeated with a sense of human sinfulness — so much so that he would have smiled at the clever psychologists of our day who diagnose his illness as a "repressed mother-fixation." He himself could not find a road. His praying languished into impotence and finally ceased to exist. He wrote of suffering, viewed it as the insignia of man, and knew damnations that hint at the existence of an isolated Jansenism within him. Yet there was no other determination than to exacerbate his dissension, which grew more and more excessive. One can see it in his attitude toward women. His malediction misses the more human intermediary position. His "hyperbolic" tension would be Christian only within the context of faith in the mystery of salvation. But this very belief is lacking. Christ occurs in Baudelaire's poems only as a fleeting metaphor or as he whom God abandoned. Behind the awareness of being damned, there is a desire "to enjoy damnation intensely." Naturally, all this is inconceivable without a Christian legacy. But what remains is a ruinous Christianity. In the Thomistic conception of creation, evil has only accidental significance. But, like the ancient Manichaeans, Baudelaire isolates it as an essential force. In the depth and the paradoxical complexities of this force, his poetry develops the courage of abnormality. Later poets, except for Rimbaud, forget that abnormality grew out of the purulence of moribund Christianity. But abnormality itself has remained. Even poets who are more rigorously Christian cannot or will not escape it. T. S. Eliot is a prime example.

EMPTY IDEALITY

This ruinous Christianity explains another peculiarity of Baudelaire's poetry, and one of great consequence for later times, a peculiarity attached to concepts like "ardent spirituality," "ideal," "elevation." But elevation to where? Occasionally God is named as an end, but more often the names are indefinite. What is it? The answer is supplied in the poem *Elévation*. Its content and tone are lofty. Three stanzas appeal to the *esprit* ("spirit," "mind") to soar above the ponds, valleys, mountains, forests, clouds, seas, sun, ether, and stars into the fiery sphere beyond, which purges of the miasmas of earthliness. The apostrophe ends. A more general statement follows: Happy is the man who can ascend to these heights and learn to grasp the language of "flowers and mute things."

The poem moves within a familiar schema of Platonic and Christian-mystical origin. According to this schema, the spirit rises to a transcendence which so alters it that, upon looking back, it can see through the outer covering of the earthly and perceive the true essence. It is the schema known in Christian terms as *ascensio* or *elevatio*. The latter designation gave the poem its title. Further congruities can be observed. In both ancient and Christian doctrines, the highest heaven is true transcendence, the heaven of fire, the empyrean. Baudelaire calls it "clear fire." And the imperative, "Purge thyself," recalls the well-known mystical act of *purificatio*. Finally, mysticism tended to divide elevation into nine levels; the substance of each level was not always consistent, the sacred number nine being the important thing. And the same number occurs in our poem. There are exactly nine realms that the spirit is to transcend. A striking feature! Was this compelled by the mystical tradition? Perhaps. It would be akin to the compulsion that the Christian heritage exercised on Baudelaire. No decisive answer can be given, especially since possible influences of Swedenborg and other modern mystics must be taken into account. But we are concerned with something more important. For the very reason that the poem corresponds to so great an extent to the mystical schema, it becomes apparent that something is lacking to make them *fully* congruent: the arrival at the elevation, the very will to arrive. The Spanish mystic St. John of the Cross once wrote: "I flew so high, so high, that my hunt reached its goal." In *Elévation*, the possibility of arrival is known, and yet it is not granted to Baudelaire, as the closing stanzas explain. They speak vaguely of "divine beverage," of "profound immensity," "limpid space." There is no mention of God. Nor do we learn what the newly understood language of flowers and mute objects is. Not only is the goal of transcendence far; it is empty as well, an ideality devoid of content, a mere pole of tension, hyperbolically striven for but never reached.

This process is ubiquitous in Baudelaire's works. Empty ideality has a romantic source. But Baudelaire dynamically transforms it into a force of attraction that arouses an excessive upward tension and simultaneously repulses a downward tension. Like evil, it is a compulsion that must be obeyed, although obedience will bring no relief of tension: hence the equation of "ideal" and "abyss"; hence expressions like "gnawing ideal," "I am shackled to the pit of the ideal," "inaccessible azure." Such phrases are familiar to us from the classical mystics, for whom they connoted the painfully pleasurable compulsion of divine grace, the first step toward bliss. In Baudelaire, the two poles of satanic evil and empty ideality are meant to sustain the excitement made possible by escape from the banal world. Yet such flight is directionless, never exceeding dissonant excitement.

Le Voyage, the final poem in *Les Fleurs du mal*, scrutinizing all attempts at escape, ends with a decision to die. The poem does not know what death will bring; yet death is enticing, for it constitutes an opportunity leading into the "new." And what is the "new"? The indefinable, the empty antithesis to the desolation of reality. At the peak of Baudelaire's ideality we find the completely negative and new meaningless concept of death.

The chaos of such modernity resides in its being both tormented to the point of neurosis by an intense craving for escape from reality, and powerless to believe in or create a substantially precise, meaningfully structured transcendence. This chaos brings the poets of modernity to a dynamic of tension devoid of release and to secrecy and mysteriousness for their own sake. Baudelaire often speaks of the supernatural and of mystery. What he means can be comprehended only by refusing, as he does, to fill these words with any meaning other than absolute mysteriousness itself. The empty ideality, the vague "otherness"— even vaguer in Rimbaud, and turning into nothingness in Mallarmé — and the involuted mysteriousness of modern poetry correspond to one another.

LANGUAGE MAGIC

Les Fleurs du mal is not obscure poetry. It frames its abnormal consciousness, its mysteries and dissonances, in comprehensible verse. And Baudelaire's theory of poetry, too, is entirely lucid. Yet he developed judgments and programs which, although not carried out in his own poems (or, at best, to a rudimentary degree), paved the way for the obscure poetry that followed. The two main points were the theories of language magic and imagination.

Poetry, especially in Latin and the Romance languages, had always known moments in which the verse achieved an absolute sonority more compelling than the semantic content. Acoustic figures of harmonious vowels and consonants or of rhythmic parallels enchanted the ear. Yet older poetry never abandoned the content at such moments; instead, it strove to intensify the meaning through the sound. Examples can be easily culled from Vergil, Dante, Calderón, Racine. Ever since European romanticism, different circumstances have prevailed. There are verses that sound rather than say. The acoustic material acquires suggestive force. In conjunction with words full of associative overtones, it discloses a dreamy infinity. A case in point is Brentano's poem that begins, "Wenn der lahme Weber träumt, er webe [When the lame weaver dreams, he's weaving]." [2] Such lines are not meant to be understood but are to be taken as sonorous suggestiveness. Language experiences a stronger division than ever between its function to communicate and its function as an independent organism of musical fields of energy. But language also determines the poetic process itself, which surrenders to the impulses residing in language. Poets realize the possibility of creating a poem with the aid of mathematical combinations that handle the acoustic and rhythmic elements of language like magic formulas. It is those elements, rather than the thematic planning, that produce the meaning — a vague, gliding meaning whose enigmatic quality

2. [Or Poe's "silken, sad, uncertain rustle of each purple curtain." — *Trans.*]

is embodied not so much in the essential denotation of the words as in their sonorous forces and semantic peripheries. This possibility became the dominant practice in modern verse. The poet became a wizard of sound.

The knowledge that poetry and magic are related is as old as time but had to be reacquired after being discarded by humanism and trans-Alpine classicism. This reacquisition began at the end of the eighteenth century and led to the theories of Edgar Allan Poe. His ideas met the growing, specifically modern need to join poetry to archaic practices and to intellectualize it. Novalis' juxtaposition of concepts like mathematics and magic in his discussions of poetry is characteristic of such modernity. Both (or similar) concepts may be found, from Baudelaire right down to the present, whenever poets think about their art.

Baudelaire translated Poe, thereby precipitating his influence in France, even in the twentieth century — to the great astonishment of Anglo-Saxon writers (most recently, T. S. Eliot). The works of Poe to be taken into account are his essays *A Philosophy of Composition* (1846) and *The Poetic Principle* (1848). Monuments to an artistic intelligence, they arrive at their conclusions by an observation of Poe's own verse. They embody that marriage of poetry and equally great (in this case even greater) reflections on poetry which constitutes another essential feature of modernity. Baudelaire translated the first essay and part of the second, and explicitly adopted their theories. They can therefore be regarded as his own.

It was Poe's idea to reverse the order of poetic acts as stated in earlier poetics. What seems to be the result, the "form," is actually the origin of the poem; what seems to be the origin, the "meaning," is actually the result. The beginning of the poetic process is the "tone," an insistent tone that precedes meaningful language, a shapeless mood. To give it shape, the author seeks in language the acoustic material that comes closest to such a tone. The sounds are attached to words, which are then grouped into themes, which are ultimately joined into a cohesive context of meaning. Novalis' adumbration has thus become a consistent theory: poetry is born of the impulse of language which, obeying the prelinguistic "tone," points the way for the content. The content is no longer the true substance of the poem; content conveys the tonal powers and overtones of the poem, which are superior to the meaning. Poe shows, for example, that the word *Pallas* in a poem of his owes its existence to a free association in the preceding lines and to its sonorous attraction as well. A bit further on, he describes the (incidental) train of thought as a mere suggestivity of vagueness, since in this way the tonal dominant is kept and does not lose its effect because of the semantic dominant. Such versification is understood as a surrender to the magic forces of language. The poet, in attributing a subsequent meaning to the primary tone, must be "mathematically precise." The poem per se is complete in itself. It does not communicate

32

truth, "intoxication of the heart," or anything else, it *is*: the poem per se. These ideas of Poe's establish the modern theory of poetry that will gravitate around the concept of *poésie pure*.

Novalis and Poe probably were familiar with the teachings of the French illuminati; and Baudelaire certainly was. These teachings (which contain many roots of symbolism) include a speculative theory of language: A word is not a chance human product; it proceeds from the cosmic Primal One; to speak it is to establish a magic contact between the speaker and the source; the poetic word reimmerses trivial things in the mystery of their metaphysical origin and illuminates hidden analogies between parts of being. Since Baudelaire was conversant with these ideas, it was natural that he borrow Poe's thoughts on poetry, which probably were inspired by the same source. The French poet, too, spoke of the necessity of the word, in a sentence that Mallarmé was to quote later. "There resides in the Word, the *logos*, something sacred that prohibits our turning it into a game of chance. Handling a language skillfully is tantamount to practicing a kind of evocative sorcery" (p. 1035). The formula *sorcellerie évocatoire* recurs often, even being applied to the fine arts. It expresses a thinking that belongs to the realm of magic and secondary (occult) mysticism. Phrases such as "magic formulas" or "magic operation" are no less frequent. And, finally, we have another key word, *suggestion*, which we shall presently discuss.

It makes no difference that such pure linguistic magic obtains at only a few points in *Les Fleurs du mal* — in the form of unusual rhyme clusters, distant assonances, tonal curves, vowel series guiding, rather than guided by, the senses. Baudelaire's theoretical discussions go a good deal further. They anticipate a poetry which, for the sake of magical sound forces, will more and more do away with thematic, logical, emotional, and even grammatical order, and will acquire its content from verbal impulses, a content which would never have been found by methodical reflection. The meaning is abnormal; it exists on the periphery, or beyond the pale, of understanding. Here the circle closes; here we see a further logical consistency in the structure of modern poetry. A poetry whose ideality is empty escapes reality by creating an incomprehensible mysteriousness. Thus it can be supported all the more by language magic. For, by operating in the acoustic and associative possibilities of the word, the poet releases further obscure contents, as well as mysterious magical powers of pure sound.

CREATIVE IMAGINATION

Baudelaire frequently speaks of his "disgust with reality." This applies to any part of reality that is banal or merely natural — both of which

33

are, for him, synonymous with the unspiritual and the material. Characteristically, the thing that most upset him in the legal judgment against *Les Fleurs du mal* was the charge of realism. Who can blame him, especially since, in those days, the term referred to a literature that depicted the morally and aesthetically repugnant dregs of reality simply for the sake of depicting them? Baudelaire's poetry does not aspire to copy, but to transform. It dynamically changes instinctive evil into the satanic, ignites images of misery into "galvanic shudders," treats more neutral phenomena in such a way that they symbolize inner states of being or that vague world of mystery which (for him) fills empty ideality. Labeling Baudelaire a realist or a naturalist is nonsense. His harshest and most shocking themes are violently ablaze with his "ardent spirituality," which tends to recede from all reality. Furthermore, this tendency can be observed in many details of his poetic technique. The precision of the objective statement grasps mainly a reality that is driven to a downward extreme, i.e., one that is already transformed, while otherwise there is a conspicuous lack of fixed location in the imagery; there is a tendency to use emotional adjectives instead of objectively accurate ones; there is a synesthesia that removes the borders between different sensory areas; and so forth.

Baudelaire applies various names to this ability to transform reality and make it unreal, and two of these names recur persistently: *dream* and *imagination*. He is more decisive than Rousseau or Diderot about raising the same thing that they meant to a level of superior "creative" power. The Romance word *creative* is more precise in this case than the German *schöpferisch*. The latter has certain associations that could divert attention from the intellectual and voluntative forces so crucial in Baudelaire: these forces are found in his concepts of dream and imagination, which include references to mathematics and abstraction.

This is not to say that Baudelaire does not use the concept of dream in its older sense — for example, when he applies it to the various forms of subjectivity, inner time, yearning for faraway places. But here, too, the superiority over concrete proximity, the qualitative contrast between the distance of dreams and the confinement of the world, is apparent. The term must be taken in its highest and hardest sense: there where the dream is expressly distinguished from "mellow melancholy," from mere "outpouring," from the "heart." In the preface to his *Nouvelles Histoires*, a translation of Poe's tales, he calls the dream "sparkling, mysterious, perfect as crystal." It is a productive rather than a perceptive power, one that works in an exact and systematic rather than a chaotic and haphazard fashion. No matter what this power may focus on, the crucial factor is the production of unreal contents. The dream may be a natural poetic talent, but it can also be fueled by narcotics or result from a psychopathic state.

All such impulses are suitable to the "magic operation" with which the dream puts created unreality above reality.

In calling the dream "perfect as crystal," Baudelaire was not making use of a random simile. This expression guarantees the position of the dream by assimilating it to inorganic material. It was Novalis who wrote: "Stones and matter are supreme; man is the true chaos." This reversal of the hierarchy (going back to alchemistic sources) recurs regularly in Baudelaire, whenever he touches on the dream. He adds to it by degrading nature to chaos and impurity. This attitude may come as no surprise in a romantic author, yet it cannot be explained in terms of romantic thinking alone. For Baudelaire, "nature" means not only the vegetative, but also the banal lowness of man. Together with inorganic formations, the symbol of the absolute intellect is placed so high that once again a dissonant tension issues forth. This still occurs among painters of the twentieth century. In line with their cubic pictures and their unreal colors, they (Marc, Beckmann, et al.) speak of nature as something impure and chaotic: structural compulsion and not influence. In Baudelaire's eyes, the inorganic achieves its supreme significance when it is used as artistic material: a statue is worth more than a living body; the sylvan backdrop on a stage, more than a natural forest. This is certainly romantic thinking; but the extreme application is modern. Such a strong equation of art and the inorganic, such a categorical banishment of reality from literature, can, at best, be found in the literature of earlier ages from which secret trails lead to modern poetry: baroque literature in Spain and Italy.

But even that era could never have produced a poem like Baudelaire's *Rêve parisien*, the chief text of his spiritualization of the artificial and the inorganic. Not a real metropolis, but a dream city, deliberately artificial; cubic forms from which all vegetation has been banished; gigantic arcades surrounding water, the one element that — although dead — moves; diamond abysses, tunnels of precious stones; no sun, no stars, a blackness that shines out of itself; a whole city devoid of human beings, devoid of place, time, and sound. We can see what the title word *rêve* ("dream") signifies: a constructive intellectuality has become an image, an intellectuality that pronounces its victory over nature and man in symbols of mineral and metal, one that projects its constructed images into empty ideality, from which they shine back, glittering to the eye and uncanny to the soul.

ANALYSIS AND DEFORMATION

Baudelaire's discussions of imagination are probably his most significant contribution to the genesis of modern poetry and art. For him,

THE STRUCTURE OF MODERN POETRY

imagination — which he equated with dreaming — meant the creative faculty itself, "the queen of human faculties." How does it operate? In 1859 he wrote: "Imagination decomposes all creation; according to laws that emerge from the depths of the soul, it gathers and coordinates the parts and creates a whole new world" (p. 773). Prefigured in theories since the sixteenth century, this idea has become a tenet of modern aesthetics. Its modernity consists in its placing at the beginning of the artistic act an analysis, a decomposition, a destructive process; Baudelaire emphasizes this in a similar passage in which he supplements "decompose" with "separate." Analyzing, decomposing, separating reality (i.e., what can be perceived by the senses) into its parts means deforming it. The concept of deformation is frequent in Baudelaire and is always meant positively. The act of deforming evinces the power of the intellect, whose product has a higher rank than the thing deformed. The "new world" resulting from such destruction can no longer be a world structured by reality. It is an unreal formation that cannot be measured by normal standards of reality.

For Baudelaire, these ideas remain theoretical sketches. His poems rarely correspond to them. One example might be the passage in which "clouds jostle the moon" (p. 341). But viewed retrospectively — and it suffices to think of Rimbaud — the boldness of those lines concerning the imagination and their meaning for the future become clear. We should not, however, lose sight of the main direction: a striving away from confining reality. The true subtlety of the concept of imagination becomes comprehensible when imagination is contrasted with a process of mere copying: hence Baudelaire's protest against the recent invention of photography — a protest that can be found near the above-quoted sentence (p. 773). The working of the imagination is called "forced idealization" (p. 891). Idealization no longer means what it did in older aesthetics: embellishment. It now refers to the process of depriving something of its reality; it signifies a dictatorial act. It seems that at the very point at which the modern world applied its technological skill and knowledge to a mirroring of reality (in the form of photography), this positive, limited reality wore out all the more quickly, and artistic energy turned all the more vigorously to the nonobjective world of the imagination. This situation is analogous to the reaction sparked by scientific positivism. Baudelaire's condemnation of photography is on the same level as his condemnation of the natural sciences. Such artistic sensibilities experience the scientific fathoming of the world as a narrowing of the world and a loss of mystery, and therefore respond with an extreme increase in the power of the imagination. Two decades after Baudelaire's death, the same answer to the loss of mystery will be labeled "symbolism."

36

The process that took place in Baudelaire has had an incalculable significance right up to the present. Baudelaire once said, "I would like fields dyed red, flowers dyed blue." Rimbaud was to write of such fields, and artists of the twentieth century were to paint them. Baudelaire's term for an art arising from the creative imagination was *surnaturalisme*. He meant an art which deobjectifies objects into lines, colors, movements, autonomous accidentals, and which bathes them in the "magic light" that annihilates their reality in mystery. In 1917, Apollinaire was to transform the word *surnaturalisme* into *surréalisme* — and rightfully so, for this new term signified a continuation of Baudelaire's aims.

ABSTRACTION AND ARABESQUE

Another statement of Baudelaire's unites imagination and intelligence: in 1856 he wrote, "The poet is the highest intelligence, and the imagination is the most scientific of all faculties." The paradox in this line sounds no less paradoxical today: poetry which escapes from a scientifically deciphered and technologized world and flees into unreality claims, in its creation of the unreal, the very same precision and intelligence that have made the world confining and banal. Later on, we shall go into this in greater detail; for the moment, it suffices to note Baudelaire's train of thought. It leads logically to a new concept of this kind: abstraction. Friedrich Schlegel and Novalis had already used abstraction as an essential characteristic of the imagination. This is understandable, since imagination is construed as the faculty of creating the unreal. Baudelaire employs abstract mainly in the sense of "intellectual, spiritual," i.e., "not natural." Further beginnings of abstract poetry and art become visible here, acquired from the concept of an unlimited imagination whose equivalents are nonobjective lines and motion. Baudelaire calls them "arabesques"— and this concept, too, will have a future. "The arabesque is the most spiritual of all designs" (p. 1192). The rapprochement of the grotesque and the arabesque goes back to Novalis, Gautier, and Poe. And Baudelaire brought the two concepts even closer together. In his aesthetic system, the grotesque, the arabesque, and the imagination all belong together: the imagination is the power of the free spirit to perform abstract (i.e., nonobjective) motion; the grotesque and the arabesque are products of this power.

The prose poems contain a short piece on the Bacchic thyrsus. The creative imagination transmutes it into a formation of dancing lines and colors, for which, as the poem puts it, the staff is merely a pretext — a pretext, as well, for the "curving motion of words." This phrase indicates a connection with linguistic magic. The concept of the arabesque, the mean ingless linear pattern, fits in with the concept of the "poetic sentence." The latter, as Baudelaire writes in a draft of the foreword to *Les Fleurs du mal*, is a sequence of pure sound and motion; it can form a horizontal, a rising, or a falling line, a spiral, a zigzag of superposed angles. And for this very reason, poetry borders on music and mathematics.

Dissonant beauty, the removal of the heart from the "I" of poetry, abnormal consciousness, empty ideality, deobjectification, mysteriousness, all of which were produced from the magic powers inherent in language and from the absolute imagination, and were brought close to the abstractions of mathematics and the curving motion of music, were used by Baudelaire to prepare possibilities that were to be realized in future poetry.

The way was paved by a poet who bore the stigmata of romanticism. He turned romantic play into unromantic seriousness, and, with peripheral ideas of his mentors, he erected an intellectual system that had its back toward them. We can therefore call the poetry of his heirs deromanticized romanticism.

III

RIMBAUD

INTRODUCTORY DESCRIPTION

A life that lasted thirty-seven years; a poetry begun in his early adolescence but terminating after four years; then, complete literary silence, restless traveling (he wanted to go as far as Asia but had to be content with the Near East and Central Africa), a checkered career in colonial armies, stone quarries, export companies; finally, gun-running for the Negus of Abyssinia and reporting about unexplored parts of Africa for geographical societies; within that brief period of poetry a furious pace of development, which led him, within two years, to burst the shackles of his own beginnings as well as those of the literary tradition behind them and to create a seminal language of modern poetry: these are some of the facts about Rimbaud.

The turbulence of Rimbaud's life was matched by his work. His *œuvre* is small; but a key word of his may be applied to it: *explosion*. He began with regular rhyme and meter, moved into disarticulated free verse, and ended with the asymmetrical rhythm of the prose poems in *Les Illuminations* (1872–73) and *Une Saison en enfer* [A season in hell] (1873).[1] This leveling of forms, prepared for by earlier poets, produced a dynamic verse employing both subject matter and form as arbitrary means for its freedom. There is no need to divide Rimbaud's work into poetry and prose. A more sensible division would be as follows: the first period (until the middle of 1871), including all the "easier" verse; and the second, comprising the obscure, esoteric verse.

1. These dates have been challenged by Bouillane de Locaste; his arguments are prepossessing but not totally convincing. He claims that *Les Illuminations* was Rimbaud's final work.

Rimbaud's poetry can be understood as the realization of Baudelaire's theoretical designs. Yet the over-all result is totally different. The unresolved but ordered and rigorously formal tensions of *Les Fleurs du mal* are turned into absolute dissonances. Rimbaud's themes are connected only at times and, then, in an instinctive fashion; they are fractured at a great many points and jumbled together. The quintessence of this poetry is no longer the theme but an ebullient excitement. As of 1871, rather than comprehensible structures of meaning, Rimbaud offers fragments, broken lines, sensually precise but unreal images — yet with chaos vibrating in the unity for whose formulation chaos is required: the unity of a sonorousness superior to meaning and traversing all cacophony and harmony. The poetic act shifts more and more from a thematic predication to a dictatorial mode of seeing and, thereby, to an unusual technique of statement. This technique need not even depend on destroying syntactical order. In fact, such destruction is quite infrequent with the eruptive poet Rimbaud and, strangely enough, much more typical of the calm lyricist Mallarmé. Rimbaud is content to articulate his chaotic themes in sentences that are simplified to the point of being primitive.

DISORIENTATION

The effect of such poetry is confusion. In 1920 Jacques Rivière wrote of Rimbaud: "His mission is to disorient us." This comment is also correct in recognizing that Rimbaud had a mission. This was borne out by a letter from Claudel to Rivière in which the playwright, speaking of the first time he read *Les Illuminations*, says, "At last I came out of the loathsome world of a Taine or a Renan, out of that revolting mechanicalism ruled by inflexible and, what's worse, knowable and teachable laws. *Les Illuminations* was a revelation of the supernatural." Claudel is referring to scientific positivism, which is based on the conviction that both man and the universe are totally explicable, and which stifles artistic and spiritual powers in need of arcana. Consequently, obscure poetry, which flees from the explicable world of scientific thought into the extremely enigmatic world of the imagination, can seem like a mission that will help the receptive reader to make the same escape. This is probably a major reason behind Rimbaud's attraction for Claudel and for many other readers as well. Rimbaud's chaos of unreality spelled salvation from the confines of reality. It was the impulse leading to Claudel's conversion, although this act itself was entirely Claudel's responsibility. Rimbaud, even more than Baudelaire, should not be interpreted as a Christian, although his poetry contains powers akin to those of religious ecstasy. These powers, however, vanish into the nothingness of an empty supernaturalism.

The impression conveyed by Rimbaud's poems is all the more disorienting because of the language, which can wound with brutal blows and yet produce spellbinding melodies. At times it seems as if Rimbaud were floating along in ethereal beatification, as if he came from another world, radiant and enraptured. Gide called him a "burning bush." Others called him an angel; Mallarmé speaks of an "angel in exile." Rimbaud's dissonant *œuvre* has evoked extremely contradictory criticism: he is exalted as the greatest poet or dismissed as a disturbed adolescent with an aura of legends recklessly overrating him. A dispassionate examination will easily dismiss the excessive praise, which can be interpreted as a result of the power that Rimbaud exerts. However critics may differ, they all agree that we cannot escape the phenomenon of Rimbaud, who soared like a meteor and vanished, leaving a fiery trail in the firmament of poetry. Experienced writers who become familiar with him state that their work issues from the same expressive compulsion as his, the compulsion of "inner states of being" that recur during a period of civilization. Gottfried Benn has recently said this.[2]

THE *VOYANT* LETTERS: EMPTY TRANSCENDENCE, STRIVING FOR ABNORMALITY, DISSONANT "MUSIC"

In 1871 Rimbaud wrote two letters in which he drafted a program for future poetry, a program that coincides with the second phase of his own work. Since the letters focused on the concept of the prophet (*voyant*), critics have called them the *voyant* letters (pp. 251 ff.).[3] They reveal that for Rimbaud, too, the modern poet's verse and his reflections on poetry are of equal value.

There is certainly nothing new about regarding the poet as prophet. One of the sources of this idea is Greek. Renaissance Platonism reintroduced it. Rimbaud got the idea from Montaigne, who, in one of his essays, combined two Platonic quotations on poetic madness. While still a *lycée* pupil, Rimbaud memorized that passage. Victor Hugo may also have stimulated him. The important thing, however, is the use that Rimbaud made of this ancient thought. What does the poet see, and how does he become a prophet? The answers are quite un-Greek and very modern.

---

2. Benn, *Lyrik des expressionistischen Jahrzehnts* (Wiesbaden, 1955), p. 8.
3. [All references in this chapter are to *Œuvres complètes*, ed. A. Rolland de Renéville and J. Mouquet (Paris, 1954). — *Trans.*]

The goal of writing poetry is "to attain the unknown," or "to view the invisible, to hear the unheard." These concepts are familiar. They come from Baudelaire, for whom, as for Rimbaud, they are key words of empty transcendence. And Rimbaud, too, fails to define them more precisely. He stops with the negative designation of the goal to be seen. This goal is discerned as the unfamiliar and the unreal, as simply something else, but nothing more. Rimbaud's poems confirm this. Their eruptive thrust beyond reality is primarily the release of this very pressure, followed by the deformation of reality into images that, although unreal, are not signs of a true transcendence. The "unknown" remains, for Rimbaud, too, a tension pole devoid of content. The poetic vision sees through a deliberately demolished reality into empty mystery.

Who is the subject of this viewing? Rimbaud's answer has become famous. "For 'I' is someone else. When brass awakes as a trumpet, it cannot be blamed. I am present at the flowering of my thoughts; I witness, I listen. I execute a stroke of my bow — and a symphony stirs in the depths. It is wrong to say, 'I think.' One should say, 'I am thought.' " Thus, the proper subject is not the empirical "I," the self. Other powers supplant it, powers from below and of a prepersonal nature, but whose authority is compelling. They alone constitute the suitable organ for viewing the "unknown." In such lines, one can sense the mystic schema: the sacrifice of the self, the ego overpowered by divine inspiration. But now this overpowering comes from below. The ego sinks downward, deprived of its powers by collective strata in the subconscious (*l'âme universelle*). This is the threshold of modern poetry, which no longer takes experiences from a worn-out world matter, but from the chaos of the unconscious. It is understandable that the twentieth-century surrealists claimed Rimbaud as one of their ancestors.

The following idea is also significant: the ego's self-deprival of power must be accomplished by an operative act directed by the will and the intelligence. "I want to be a poet and I am *working* toward becoming one" is Rimbaud's tenet of volition. Its application consists in "a long, unlimited, rational confusion of the senses." Even more incisive: "One must create a deformed soul, like the man who plants warts on his face and cultivates them." The poetic impulse is set in motion by self-mutilation, by an operative maiming of the soul, all for the purpose of "reaching the unknown." The seer of the unknown, the poet, is "the great invalid, the great criminal, the great outlaw — and the supreme scholar." Thus, abnormality is no longer a destiny merely to be endured (as it was for Rousseau); it is a state of intentionally remaining outside. Poetry is based on the premise that the will distorts the structure of the soul, because such a distortion makes possible a blind thrust into both prepersonal depth and empty transcendence. We are far from the smitten prophet of the Greeks, to whom the Muses brought tidings of the gods.

The poetry resulting from such an operation is called "new language," or "universal language," for which it makes no difference whether or not verse has form. Poetry is an interlocking of "the astonishing, the unfathomable, the repulsive, and the delightful." All values are identical, including beauty and ugliness. Their validity resides in their excitement and their "music." Rimbaud is always talking about music. He calls it "the unknown music," hearing it in "castles built of bones," in the "iron song of telegraph poles." It is "the sonorous singing of new disaster," "the most intense music," from which all "purely melodious suffering" of a romantic nature has been removed. His poetry does offer sounds of objects or creatures, but the song and the singing are always smashed by shouts and roars: dissonant music.

The *voyant* letters contain a lovely passage: "The poet defines the degree of the unknown that stirs in the collective soul of his era." This is immediately followed by the programmatic announcement of abnormality: "[The poet] is abnormality turned into the norm." These proclamations reach an acme: "The poet reaches the unknown, and even if ultimately he no longer understands his own visions, still he has seen them. Although he may perish from his giant leap through unheard and unnamable things, other terrible laborers will come and begin at those horizons where he collapsed."

The poet: laboring toward the world explosion by virtue of his outrageous imagination, which smashes into the unknown and crumbles. Did Rimbaud sense that the enemy forces in the modern age — the technological proletariat and the poetic "laborer"— would secretly meet, both being dictators: one, the tyrant of the earth; the other, the tyrant of the soul?

BREAK WITH TRADITION

The revolt in this program, and in the poetry itself, also points backward, to demolish tradition. We know that during his childhood and adolescence, Rimbaud had a mania for reading. His verses are full of echoes from both contemporary and earlier authors of the nineteenth century. But even these echoes have the sharpness of tone that is distinctly Rimbaud's and not of the writers who influenced him. He either overheated or undercooled all that he used, transforming it into a totally different substance. These echoes are of secondary importance for any criticism of Rimbaud. They merely confirm here what they confirm elsewhere: that no writer can start in a vacuum. Thus they yield nothing specific about Rimbaud. One can

more easily grasp the distinctive quality of his nature in his violent permuta-
tion of the works he read and in his desire to break with tradition, an
attitude that grew into hatred of the past. "To curse one's ancestors" is
a phrase from the second *voyant* letter. It is said that he called the Louvre
ridiculous and demanded that the Bibliothèque nationale be burned to the
ground. Such remarks may sound childish, but they correspond to the
attitude permeating his final work, *Une Saison en enfer*, which, though
written by a teen-ager, is anything but adolescent. Rimbaud's aggressive
self-exile from his era and the general public is, consistently, a rejection
of the past as well. The reasons are historical rather than personal. The
fact that the past was becoming burdensome with the decay of a genuine
sense of continuity, and that this sense was being replaced by historicism
and museum collections, created in several minds of the nineteenth century
a counterpressure leading to a distaste for anything historical. And this
antipathy has remained a constant in modern art and letters.

Rimbaud's schooling was thoroughly humanist. But in his poems
antiquity is lampooned. Myth is vilified by vulgarity: "slum bacchants";
Venus bringing booze to workers; in a metropolis, deer sucking Diana's
teats. The grotesque, which Victor Hugo saw in medieval farces, spreads
(as it did for Daumier) to Mount Olympus. One example is the radical
disfigurement in the sonnet *Venus Anadyomène*. The title refers to one
of the loveliest of myths, the birth of Aphrodite (Venus) from oceanic foam.
The text offers a bizarre contrast: from a green zinc bathtub emerges a
fat female body with a gray neck, a reddish spine; the loins are engraved
"Clara Venus"; at a precise anatomical place, a sore. Critics have interpreted this sonnet as a parody of certain conventional trends and schools
of the times (especially the Parnasse, a group of French poets who treated
Greco-Roman myths with ceremonial accuracy). But Rimbaud's sonnet
is parody without humor, attacking myth itself, tradition per se, beauty.
It is an attack sublimating a deformational drive that, stranger still, contains
enough artistry to leave the mark of consistent and logical style on the
ugliness depicted.

There is an even more violent assault on beauty and tradition in *Ce
qu'on dit au poète à propos de fleurs*. Rimbaud mocks the poetry of flowers
— roses, violets, lilies, lilacs. Modern poetry requires a different flora.
Sing not of vines, sing of tobacco, cotton shrubs, and potato fungus; the
tear on a candle is worth more than a flower; the dripping woolly texture
of exotic plants is worth more than French vegetation. Beneath a black
azure, in the age of iron, black poems shall be written, their rhymes welling
up "Like a ray of sodium / Like liquid rubber," their lyre — telegraph
poles; and someone will come and speak the great love, that "thief of
dark indulgences."

MODERNITY AND CITY POETRY

A text like the above reveals Rimbaud's attitude toward modernity, an ambivalent attitude, like Baudelaire's — aversion when modernity means material progress and scientific enlightenment, acceptance when modernity brings new experiences whose harshness and night require a harsh, "dark" poem. The result: Rimbaud's "city poetry." It can be found in *Les Illuminations*; its power is grandiose, changing Baudelaire's dream city into a superdimensional one. The best sections are those entitled *Ville* or *Villes* (pp. 180 ff.). Incoherent clusters of imagery conjure up imaginary or future cities, spanning all ages, reversing all spatial order; massive things move, sound, roar; the concrete and the abstract crisscross one another; between crystal chalets and copper palm trees, above craters and chasms, there occurs the "collapse of apotheoses"; there are artificial gardens, an artificial sea, a church dome, fifteen thousand feet wide, made of steel, giant candelabras; the upper parts of the city are so high that the lower parts are out of sight. These cities have rejected all familiar things, there is no monument of superstition, none of the millions of inhabitants knows the others, and yet one life is as compulsively monotonous as the next. These people are ghosts; their forest shade and summer night are coal smoke. Death is without tears, love without hope, and "a pretty crime whines in the filth of the street."

Who could unravel these intermeshed images; who could find a calm sense in them? Their meaning resides in the chaos itself. Produced by an excited imagination, the superdimensional chaos becomes the cerebrally inexplicable yet sensorily perceptible token of the material and psychical conflicts in urban modernity — the token of its terrors, which are its fascinations.

REBELLION AGAINST CHRISTIAN TRADITION: *UNE SAISON EN ENFER*

Rimbaud's Christianity is not the ruinous Christianity of Baudelaire. Rimbaud's works show that he begins with rebellion and ends with martyrdom, unable to escape his Christian heritage. His mentality is certainly much more a Christian one than one of indifference or enlightened irony. Rimbaud's opposition is of the kind that remains under the control of the very power against which it rebels — as he himself was well aware. In *Une Saison en enfer* this awareness becomes poetry. But the protest against Christianity does not calm down. It merely grows more tormented and more intelligent — to break off into silence. It is part of a rebellion against

45

all heritage per se, and part of a passion for the "unknown," for that empty transcendence which Rimbaud can proclaim only by demolishing. The poems of his initial phase contain the most outspoken attacks, developing into a psychologizing decomposition of the Christian soul. For example, in *Les Premières Communions* an adolescent girl succumbs to her rebellious drives, which sin against Christianity because it repressed them by making them sinful. Rimbaud goes even further. He wrote a prose piece (probably in 1872) that begins with the words: "Beth-Saïda, la piscine des cinq galéries [Bethesda, the pool of the five galleries]." This passage is based on Christ's miraculous healing of a sick man at the lake of Bethesda (John 5:1–15). But the biblical tale is completely transformed. Cripples descend into the yellow water, but no angel comes, no one heals them. Christ leans against a pillar, staring motionlessly at the bathers, and from their faces Satan grins at him. One of them stands up and, with a steady gait, walks toward the town. Who cured him? Christ said nothing; he did not even glance at the paralytic. Could the healer have been Satan? The text remains silent on this point; it merely places Christ near the invalid. This allows us to sense that neither Christ nor even Satan effected the cure; it may have been a force whose whereabouts and identity are unknown. Empty transcendence.

It is time for a brief discussion of *Une Saison en enfer*, which contains Rimbaud's final word on Christianity. The text consists of seven long pieces in prose. There are a great number of different movements placed side by side without transition: jolting thrusts of statements begun but not ended, harassing and delirious accumulations of words, unanswered questions, and the enchanting and sinister melody of madness swooping along the huge, periodical curves. In the content of this work, Rimbaud has revised all of his earlier phases, but in such a way that by attempting to surmount them, he gets involved in them anew before finally disposing of them. The result is a chaotic oscillation: everything he loves he hates, then loves again, and then hates. A thing is described as positive in one sentence, transcended in the next, and then repeated in still another. The revolt revolts against itself. Only the conclusion carries everything to an end, to a departure from all mental existence.

Homelessness in the conventional world of objects, psyche, and reason: this sums up the over-all meaning of these zigzag lines, as well as the meaning of the passages on Christianity. Rimbaud uses Christian words — *hell, devil, angel* — but they waver between literal and metaphorical meanings. They are consistent only as emblems of blind excitement. "Ugly leaves from my journal of damnation," presented to the devil — this is what Rimbaud called the work. "Pagan blood is returning, the Gospel is past, I am leaving Europe, I will swim, tear out grass, hunt, smoke,

46

drink liquors as strong as boiling metal, . . . be saved." And yet he says, "I wait for God greedily." Then, a few pages later, "I was never a Christian; I belong to the race of those who sang while under torture." He calls for the "joys of damnation," but they fail to come. Both Christ and Satan fail to come, but he feels their shackles. "I know I am in hell; therefore I am in hell." Hell is bondage to the catechism; pagans have no hell — which is why paganism also rejects him.

Such utterances seem to mean that the speaker suffers from Christianity as from a trauma. Agitation becomes a grimace — an attack and at the same time a bondage. This, for him, is hell. Calling it hell is Christian. A tacit but perceptible question haunts the text: Is the chaos of the modern world and of one's own inwardness a perverted Christian fate? But the question is never resolved. The second main theme of *Une Saison en enfer* crops up: to leave the Continent, leave the "swamps of the West," the folly of Europe, "prove what is obvious," and not notice that Christ's birth coincided with the birth of the Philistine. Gradually this theme frees itself from the zigzag lines, follows a definite course leading to autumn, winter, night, deliberately to misery —"worms in my hair and in my armpits and in my heart." Totally spent and consumed, he decides "to embrace wrinkled reality," flee Europe, and commence a life of hard deeds.

Rimbaud abided by his resolution. He capitulated to the invincible tensions and conflicts of spiritual existence. The poet who pierced farther into the unknown than anyone else could never elucidate what the unknown is. He did an about-face and took inner death upon himself, growing silent before the world that he had blown apart. The heritage of Christianity offered him the strongest resistance. But it never sated his immense craving for what was beyond reality, and it seemed as confining as all earthly things. Rimbaud's explosion of all reality and tradition ripped Christianity to shreds. Baudelaire had managed to turn his damnation into a system. But, for Rimbaud, damnation became chaos and ultimately silence. Accordingly, his sister's claim that he died in the faith has proved to be a pious fabrication.

THE ARTIFICIAL "I": DEHUMANIZATION

The "I'" that speaks in Rimbaud's poetry can no more be explained biographically that can the "I" in *Les Fleurs du mal*. One may, if one cares to, present a psychological analysis of Rimbaud's poems, citing his boyhood and adolescent experiences. But such material is of little use to an understanding of the poetic persona. The process of dehumanization is accelerated. Rimbaud's "I" is, in its multivoiced dissonance, the product of operative self-transformation (mentioned above) and therefore a result of the same style from which his imagery emerges. This "I" can wear any mask, extend to any mode of existence, any era, any nation. Rimbaud's lines about his Gallic ancestors (at the beginning of *Une Saison en enfer*) can be taken literally. But a few sentences later we read: "I have lived everywhere; there is no family that I do not know. My head contains roads in the Swabian plains, views of Byzantium, the ramparts of Solyme [Jerusalem]." This is motional imagination, not autobiography. The artificial "I" feeds on "idiotic pictures" with enticing material from the Orient and primitive society, becomes planetary, turns into an angel and a magician. Rimbaud institutes the abnormal divorce of the poetic "I" from the empirical self, a division to be found in such poets as Ezra Pound and St.-John Perse and sufficing to forbid any interpretation of modern poetry as biographical statement.

Rimbaud, too, traces his spiritual destiny back to the over-all conditions of modernity. "A spiritual struggle is as brutal as a battle of men" (p. 230). In the same passage, addressing Verlaine, he defends his own lot of having fallen deeper and thereby viewing greater distances, but remaining comprehensible to no one and deadly even in gentleness. His is the pride of knowing that this "strange suffering possesses disquieting authority" (p. 161). Rimbaud is said to have claimed that "my superiority consists in my not having a heart." He is repulsed by the "sensitive hearts" of romantic poetry. A line from *L'Eternité* reads: "You break loose from human approval, common striving, and fly" (p. 132).

Such utterances are not mere programs. The poetry itself is dehumanized. The verses speak to no one, soliloquize, make no attempt to curry favor with the audience, seem to speak in a voice belonging to no palpable owner, especially when the imagined "I" gives way to an "I"-less statement. Discernible feelings are replaced by a neutral vibration even stronger than in Edgar Allan Poe. A good example is the prose poem *Angoisse* [Anxiety] (p. 188). The title seems to indicate a precise psychic condition. Yet there is none. Even anxiety has lost its familiar countenance. Is this really anxiety? We perceive mercurial intensity compounded of many things: hope, collapse, jubilation, grimace, inquiry — all spoken swiftly and passed over swiftly, until the text swerves into wounds, torments, tortures, whose origins and purposes remain unknown. There is a frenzy of vagueness in image and emotion, as hazy as the two female beings mentioned fleetingly. Emotion may mean anxiety, but it is so far removed from the normal shapes of emotion as to bear no longer the human label "anxiety."

When Rimbaud introduces human beings into his poetry, they appear as rootless aliens or as caricatures. The various parts of the body, dispropor-

48

tionate to the whole, are overexposed, labeled with anatomic terms that assure a stern objectivity. Even a seemingly calm poem like *Le Dormeur du val* can be mentioned as an instance of dehumanization. The sonnet begins in a small valley meadow "foaming with rays," and it ends in death. The language runs parallel, from the quietly rapturous opening lines to the sober conclusion, which reveals that the still sleeper is a dead soldier. The descent into death is gradual; the revelation is delayed and erupts only at the very end, quickly and unexpectedly. The artistic substance of the poem is the progression from light to dark. Yet the poem advances without sympathy, in cool peacefulness that makes no mention of death but simply uses the same noun that was applied to the meadow: "a verdant *hole*," and then, in the plural, "two red *holes* in his right side." The dead soldier is pure imagery in the eyes of the onlooker. Any possible reaction of the heart is left out, to be supplanted by an artistic style of motion which uses human death as an oblique thrust, bringing the movement to an abrupt halt.

BURSTING THE LIMITS

Rimbaud's poetic "I" acquires more and more of an agitation that presses into imaginary distances. A compulsive drive toward the "unknown" makes him speak (as Baudelaire did) of the "abyss of the azure." This altitude, inhabited by angels, is simultaneously an abyss of defeat, "a well of fire in which seas and fables meet." The angels are points of light and intensity, tokens that gleam and immediately vanish again, signs of loftiness and distance and inconceivable superabundance, yet angels without God and without tidings. The very earliest poems demonstrate an urge of the finite toward the infinite — for example, *Ophélie*. The Ophelia has nothing to do with Shakespeare's. She floats down the river, but a faraway space opens up around her, with golden stars that release a mysterious singing, with enormous mountains, with the death rattle of oceans, with the terror of the infinite. She is transmuted into an eternal figure: for more than a thousand years she has been drifting down the river; for more than a thousand years her song has been singing the madness of those "great visions" that strangle speech.

This conversion of nearness into distance is a dynamic schema throughout Rimbaud's works. It recurs with increasing rapidity, often within a single sentence. The agitation becomes dithyrambic. "I hung ropes from steeple to steeple, garlands from window to window, golden chains from star to star, and I dance" (p. 178). It is the chaotic dance of an aimless dancer, as at the end of Baudelaire's *Les Sept Vieillards* [The seven old men]. Eventually, distance no longer transforms; it destroys. The prose poem *Nocturne vulgaire* (p. 187) begins: "A blast [of air] pierces gaps in the partitions, . . . blows away the limits of homes." These words may be viewed as programmatic for Rimbaud's writings. The poem itself carries them out, with exploding images from all kinds of space; the conclusion is a burdenlike repetition of the opening words. The chaotic removal of limits is not contained by the relative brevity of this prose poem. The end of such a text could just as easily come earlier or later.

A subsequent, rather obscure poem, *Larme* (p. 125), poses enigmas which cannot be solved by the totally unrelated title or by anything in the contents. (Unrelated titles will remain a basic feature of modern poetry; see below, p. 124.) As always in modern verse, it is better to interpret this poem not so much in terms of the dynamic imagery as on the basis of the progression of dynamics. A man sits drinking near a river. His beverage disgusts him. This is prelude. A sudden vehemence occurs at an asymmetrical point: a storm transforms the sky; black lands, lakes, poles, columns beneath a blue night, and railroad stations emerge above; masses of water pour down upon the forests; ice floes drop into the stagnant ponds. What has happened? A finite landscape on earth has been abruptly changed into a diluvial landscape in the sky, a landscape in which the earth participates. The text closes with the drinker's reeling words — a conclusion that does not conclude, that renews the riddles. Only one thing is perceptible: the act that wipes out limits by the invasion of raging distances.

Hunger and *thirst* are frequent in Rimbaud's diction. These are the same words that the mystics and Dante used, in keeping with biblical language, to denote sacred yearning. In Rimbaud, however, such passages point toward the unquenchable. The conclusion of *Comédie de la soif* runs: all creatures, the pigeons, the game, the fishes, the last butterflies, are thirsty — but who could melt where the unguided cloud melts! (p. 128). That same year, 1872, Rimbaud wrote *Fêtes de la faim*. These hunger feasts are of stones, coal, iron, pebbles, under shreds of black air and sonorous azure. Hunger — insatiable because the path to the azure is blocked — craves hard things, becomes a poetry of resistance, a "feast" of dark frenzy that knows how to be evil. "Sick thirst darkens my veins" (p. 131).

LE BATEAU IVRE

We can now discuss Rimbaud's most famous poem, *Le Bateau ivre* [The drunken boat] (1871). He wrote it without knowing the exotic seas and lands that flash up in it. Some critics have assumed that illustrated magazines provided the imagery. This may be so, but it merely supports what can be gained directly from the text. The poem has nothing to do with realities of any sort. A powerful and violent imagination creates a febrile vision of exaggerated, whirling, totally unreal spaces. Scholars usually point out certain borrowings from other poets. Yet even these borrowings, which are actually recastings, cannot hide the fact that this poem has its own center of gravity. It has been compared to Victor Hugo's *Plein Ciel* (in *La Légende des siècles*): both have a ship plunging into the sky. But Hugo's imagery serves a trivial grandiloquence of progress and happiness. *Le Bateau ivre*, on the other hand, leads to the destructive freedom of a lonely failure. The motional structure of this poem has no predecessor other than Rimbaud himself. The design is an extreme but consistent heightening of the process in *Ophélie*, of surmounting the finite with the infinite.

The boat is bearer of the events. Tacitly, but unmistakably, the events simultaneously denote a process taking place in the poetic "I." The images possess such vehement power that the symbolic equation of ship and man is recognizable only in the course of the over-all movement. The dynamic contents are visible, specified details. The more unreal and exotic the images, the more sensuous their description. This is helped by the poetic technique which makes the text an absolute metaphor throughout, speaking only of the boat and never of the symbolized "I." Banville's adverse criticism reveals the boldness of this technique. When Rimbaud read the poem to him, Banville complained that it should have begun, "I am a ship that. . . ." He failed to realize that the metaphor, no longer a mere figure of comparison, now creates an identity. The absolute metaphor will remain a dominant characteristic of later poetry. For Rimbaud, it corresponds to a basic feature of his writings (to be treated below, under the heading "Sensory unreality").

Le Bateau ivre is one great act of expansion. There is an occasional retardation, after which, however, the expansion resumes with new vehemence, exploding into chaos at several points. The action begins with a certain calm — the boat drifting down the river. But even this calm was preceded by a violent break: the boat is unconcerned about the murder of the crew on shore. Next, everything solid dissolves. The drifting turns into a dance of the boat, shattering in storms and seas, passing all lands, a dance in green nights, putrefaction, danger, under signs of death and "singing phosphorus"; the boat is hurled into the birdless ether, smashing holes into a "reddening sky like a wall"— until the change: nostalgia for Europe. But homesickness leads back to no homeland. The ship muses about a brief idyl, a child playing at a pond on a balmy evening. This vision remains a helpless dream. For, after breathing the spaciousness of oceans and starry archipelagoes, the ship knows it is too spoiled for confinement to Europe. Just as the opening calm absorbed the violent rejection, so, at the end, the weary calm of the ship absorbs the destructive expansion of the preceding stanzas. It is the calm of total exhaustion and impotence, of shipwreck in boundlessness, of incapacity for the finite.

The poem demonstrates a high degree of technical correctness. The syntax is simple, giving the statements a formal clarity. The explosions are in the ideas rather than in the sentence structure. And the effect is all the more vehement for the formal disharmony in regard to the syntax. The ideas are protuberances of the imagination; to the wildness and distance they add even more wildness and distance, not merely in successive stanzas, but from line to line, and sometimes even within a single line. There is no coherence linking the images. No image develops inevitably from a preceding one; the random order would permit a rearrangement of whole stanzas. Furthermore, individual image complexes mix extreme opposites, uniting things that are incompatible in practice — beauty and repulsiveness, slovenliness and rapture — making bizarre use of technical terms, especially nautical jargon. The chaos rages in an unshaken syntactical framework.

And yet the chaos is articulate. Once again, the direction of the movement is more important than the dynamic content. The dynamics of the poem allow for the random and incoherent occurrence of the images because those images are simply bearers of the autonomous motion. The motion clearly proceeds through three acts: vehement rejection and revolt, escape into the superdimensional, decline into the calm of annihilation. These acts make up the motional structure not just of *Le Bateau ivre* but also of Rimbaud's entire work. Many details of his thematic chaos are no longer explicable. But such poetry can be understood if we proceed to the structure of its dynamics. Hence it is consistent of such poetry to become more and more abstract. Within this context, the term *abstract* is not limited to the nonperceptual and nonobjective. It refers to those lines, verse groups, and sentences which are autonomous and which constitute purely linguistic motive forces by means of which they destroy to the point of incomprehensibility, or even prevent, any possible connection between the subject matter and reality. This "abstraction" exists in a large number of modern poems, especially those akin to Rimbaud's kind of writing.

In his verse, the tripartite structure of the dynamics represents his relation to both reality and transcendence: a raging deformation of reality, a craving for space and the faraway, an ultimate failure because reality is too confining and transcendence too empty. A prose series of concepts sums this up: "Religious or natural mysteries, death, birth, future, past, creation of the world, nothingness" (p. 213). The end is the Void.

52

Rimbaud

DESTROYED REALITY

No one would think of evaluating any poetry, especially lyrical verse, according to how accurate and complete the imagery is with regard to external reality. Poetry has always had the license to shift, transpose, and suggestively abbreviate reality, to stretch and demonize it, to make it the medium of subjectivity, the symbol of a comprehensive position of life. Yet one can check the extent to which the transformation relies on practical conditions, is connected — despite any fabrication — to the real world, remains within the framework of the metaphorical powers inherent in all languages, and therefore is comprehensible. Since Rimbaud, poetry has become less and less reliant on these factors. It cares less and less about the interrelations of the parts of speech and their hierarchical values. Hence, more than ever before, the observer must heuristically draw upon reality for comparison. Only then will the scope of the destruction of reality and the vehemence of release from earlier traditions of metaphor be evident.

In his final poem, Rimbaud has his lover, Verlaine, say: "How many nights have I lain awake next to his sleeping body, trying to fathom why he [Rimbaud] was so intent on escaping from reality" (p. 216). Rimbaud is speaking in Verlaine's fictive words: he is unable to explain the reasons for his flight. His *œuvre*, however, does show an explicable parallel between his attitude toward reality and his passion for the "unknown." The latter, which can no longer be sated by faith, philosophy, or mysticism, is — to a greater degree than for Baudelaire — a pole of tension; and the tension boomerangs to reality because the pole is dead. Since reality is experienced as insufficient for empty transcendence, the passion for transcendence becomes an aimless destruction of reality. This destroyed reality constitutes the chaotic emblem for the insufficiency of any reality and for the unattainability of the "unknown." We may call this relationship the dialectic of modernity. It is crucial to European art and literature far beyond Rimbaud. Picasso was to say, later on: "For me, a painting is a sum of destructions."

We are reminded of Baudelaire's statement that the initial act of imagination is a "dissection." This dissection, which for Baudelaire was connected with "deformation," became an actual poetic practice for Rimbaud. If reality is still present at all (or if we can heuristically compare the poem with reality), it undergoes expansion, dismemberment, defacing; it experiences tensions of contrast — and all this to such a degree that reality becomes a transition to the unreal. Two of the most important elements in Rimbaud's objective world are water and wind. Under restraint in the early works, they subsequently evolve into stormy raging and roaring, diluvial powers smashing spatial and temporal orders: ". . . deserts, prairies, horizons are wearing the red dress of tempests" (p. 124). An over-all

53

THE STRUCTURE OF MODERN POETRY

look at the objects and creatures in Rimbaud's poetry reveals his restless stretching toward the width and height and depth of the entire universe, his ceaseless wandering, his alienation of familiar things and beings (usually by omission of a spatial or temporal connection): highways, vagabonds, prostitutes, drunkards, and taverns; forests, stars, angels, and children; volcano craters, steel skeletons, glaciers, mosques, and the circus and sideshow world, which he calls "the paradise of the mad grimace" (p. 172).

INTENSITY OF UGLINESS

Such realities are no longer coordinated according to any standard set up for the others by *one* thing, *one* country, or *one* being. These realities are heatmarks left by a feverish intensity. Their depiction has nothing in common with any realism. The ugliness that Rimbaud stamps on the vestiges of reality in his works is to be understood as intensity. And so is the beauty. Certain passages in his writings *are* "beautiful" — in the imagery or in the melody of the language. The point is, however, that they are not absolute; they occur in proximity to other passages, "ugly" ones. Beautiful and ugly are no longer opposing values; their contrast is meant to fascinate. Any objective difference between them is done away with, as is the difference between true and false. The rapprochement of beauty and ugliness produces the all-important dynamic of contrast, which is also within ugliness alone.

In earlier poetry, ugliness was usually a burlesque or a polemical sign of moral inferiority: in the *Iliad* (Thersites), Dante's *Inferno*, the high medieval poetry of knighthood in Germany (which depicted noncourtly people as ugly). The devil was ugly. But as early as the second half of the eighteenth century, then in Novalis, and subsequently in Baudelaire, ugliness was considered "interesting"; it complied with an artistic sensibility that needed intensity and expressiveness. Rimbaud made ugliness serve a sensuous energy that craved the most violent deformation of sensory reality. A poetry whose objects signify not so much the contents as the metaobjective tension relations needs ugliness, which, challenging one's natural sense of beauty, creates a dramatics of shock between the text and the reader.

In 1871 Rimbaud wrote the poem *Les Assis* — the title can be translated as "The Sitters" in light of the bold language. Verlaine claims that the poem alludes to a municipal librarian in Charleville who had hurt Rimbaud's feelings. Although this claim may be true, it does not help us understand the poem. Permeated with anatomical terms, linguistic innovations, and slang, the poem creates a myth of monstrous ugliness. There is no mention

54

of librarians or books. The lines tell of a hoard of brutish, squatting, malicious old men. First come macabre details: black wens; pockmarks; eyes with green rings; coiled fingers clenching thighbones; "vague cankers" on their foreheads, like leprous blossoms on old walls. Then come the figures: whimsical frames grafted in epileptic passion on the great black skeletons of their chairs, their feet intertwining in the rachitic bars of the chairs from dawn to dusk forever. Hot suns "percolate" their skin; their eyes stare at the windows "where snows droop." The bound-up souls of old suns blaze in the straw plaiting in which grain used to ferment. The old men crouch with their teeth on their knees; they are "green pianists," their ten fingers drumming on the bottom of their seats, their heads nodding in the love motions of their senile imaginations. If anyone calls them, they snarl like slapped cats. They slowly open their shoulder blades, drag their crooked feet along, banging their bald pates against dark walls; and their suit buttons catch your eye from the ends of corridors. Their eyes filter the black venom of cowed bitches. When they sit down again, they sink their fists into grimy cuffs; beneath their scrawny chins, tonsils throb to the bursting point. They dream about finer seats. Ink blossoms spitting comma pollen cradle them.

Such ugliness is not mimesis; it is creation. Multiple creatures that are ubiquitous and everlasting; carcasses rather than human beings, fused with objects that are the companions of those who crouch upon them; impotent malice and the twilight of senile sexuality: all this is stated with infernal scorn concealed in the near-melody of the lines. The whole poem is a dissonance between song and image. Even the incorporated vestiges of "beauty" serve the dissonance or are themselves dissonant; they join lyrical potency and banality: "ink blossoms," "comma pollen." And the banality is embellished by the simile of a dragonfly's soaring over gladioli. The part played by ugliness is clear. Were we to measure its role against that of normal ugliness, we would see that Rimbaud's poetic ugliness deforms normal ugliness, just as it deforms all reality, in order to show, in this destruction, the escape into the realm beyond reality — an escape into emptiness.

Twelve years earlier, Baudelaire had written *Les Sept Vieillards*. Here, too, there is an ugliness of people and objects, but in a multiple orientation. The scene and the action are developed precisely and gradually: first the teeming city, next the suburban street, then the indication of time (early morning). An old man appears; his portrayal is precise and thorough. Another just like him comes along. There are seven in all. The lyrical "I" responds with precise reactions: dismay, horror, and a concluding verdict. Ugliness is present in sensory exactitude, but restrained in itself and, above all, coordinated in space, time, and emotion. One old man is likened to Judas. This, too, is an orientation. By referring to a familiar personage, the poem makes possible a return to a familiar atmosphere, just as the agitation of the "I" brings something like warmth into the dreadful spectacle because, for all its torment, the agitation is human. Such orientations are nowhere to be found in Rimbaud. His old men are visible only as a collective group, and the group consists of anatomical and pathological details rather than of individuals. As for space, there is only a vestige. Time is "forever." Characteristically, Rimbaud does not even hint at what Verlaine mentions as the source of inspiration, the library in Charleville; this would have meant too much orientation toward reality. The overabundance of ugliness is not brought back into any familiar sphere, which would have been possible, even in horror. The deforming will of the modern poet has made ugliness completely abstract.

SENSORY UNREALITY

Any comparison of Rimbaud's images with reality can have only heuristic value. Deeper inquiry will reveal that such concepts as "real" and "unreal" do not suffice. There is a more useful concept: "sensory unreality." The deformed subject matter taken from reality often speaks in word clusters of which each component part has a sensory quality; yet such groups combine incompatible things, and in such an abnormal way that the sensory qualities form an unreal structure.[4] The latter always consists of clear, palpable images, but only such as the physical eye would never encounter. They go far beyond the license that has always been permitted poetry by the metaphorical forces inherent in language. "The zwieback of the street," "the king, standing on his stomach," "azure snot": such images may occasionally make characteristics of reality more effective, yet they are not aimed at reality; they are moved by a dynamics of destruction which, as a surrogate for the invisible "unknown," shifts the form boundaries of reality and forces its extremes together, thereby turning reality into the sensorily agitated and agitating unknown. Changing the order of reality and yet staying within the same meaning is a practice of earlier poetry. There are discreet instances of it in Rimbaud. A red flag is called "a flag of bleeding flesh." The real stimulus of this image, the color red, is not mentioned; the language instantly joins the (characteristically gruesome) metaphor to the object. But

4. See Hugo von Hofmannsthal's comment about Novalis: "The most wonderful poetic sentences are those that describe with great physical precision and clarity something that is physically impossible; such sentences are true verbal creations" (*Aufzeichnungen* [1959], p. 183).

such examples merely show the germ of what is fully developed in most cases and which makes Rimbaud's sensory reality the true setting for his shock dramatics.

"Flesh blossoms that flower in starry woods," "pastorals wearing wooden shoes [snarling] in the garden," "city dirt, red and black as a mirror when a lamp revolves in the next room": all these images are elements of sensory reality but are elevated beyond reality by contraction, omission, dislocation, recombination. This is why the resulting creation no longer refers to reality; instead, it rivets one's attention on the act that produced it, the act of a dictatorial imagination. This concept, which describes the impetus in Rimbaud's poetry, makes any measuring of his verse according to reality unnecessary. (Such measuring is done only for heuristic reasons.) We are now in a world whose reality exists in language alone.

DICTATORIAL IMAGINATION

Dictatorial imagination does not perceive and describe; it functions in unlimited creative freedom. The real world shatters before the peremptory decree of an "I" that would rather create contents than receive them. A statement that Rimbaud made while living in Paris has come down to us: "We must root out painting's old habit of copying, and we must make painting sovereign. Instead of reproducing objects, painting must compel agitation by means of lines, colors, and shapes that are drawn from the outer world but simplified and restrained: genuine magic." People have referred to this statement when explaining twentieth-century painting (as in the catalogue of the Picasso exhibition at Paris, 1955). These words, like Rimbaud's poetry, actually anticipate modern painting, which cannot be interpreted in terms of objects. The absolute freedom of the "I" wants to be seen as painting itself. We can easily discern the great extent to which Baudelaire's theoretical reflections on the imagination paved the way for poetic and artistic practice far into the twentieth century.

Rousseau, Poe, and Baudelaire spoke of "creative imagination," with emphasis on the creative faculty. Characteristically, Rimbaud dynamically charges this formula in its main word. He speaks of the "creative *impulse*" in a sentence that sums up his aesthetics: "Your memory and your senses should be merely food for your creative impulse. But when you leave the world one day, what will have become of it? One thing is certain: it will not in any way look the way it looks now" (p. 200). The artistic impulse leaves the face of the world distorted and unfamiliar. This impulse is an act of violence. A key word of Rimbaud's is *atrocious* (*atroce*).

Dictatorial imagination scrambles spatial order: coaches drive across the sky, a parlor lies at the bottom of a lake, the ocean hovers above the highest mountain peaks, railroad tracks run through and over a hotel. The imagination also reverses the normal relationship between man and objects: "The notary hangs from his numbered watch-charm" (p. 59). The imagination forces extremes together, the sensory and the imaginary: "Deeply moved to the point of death by the murmur of the milk of morning and of the night of the last century" (p. 163). The imagination assigns unreal colors, colors that do not ordinarily fit the objects, making them all the more alien, in fulfillment of Baudelaire's wishes: "blue cress," "blue mare," "green pianists," "green laughter," "black moons". Reaching toward endlessness, the imagination pluralizes things that exist only in the singular: Etnas, Floridas, Maelstroms. The result is a sensuous intensification and an escape from reality. This pluralizing matches Rimbaud's tendency to preclude details of locality or any other delimitation by using the word *all*: "all murders and all battles," "all snows." Plurals and summations are the powerful instruments of an imagination that ransacks reality, throws it away, and masses it into something new beyond reality.

As in Baudelaire, dreamlike visions reach for the nonorganic in order to become hard and alien. "In hours of bitterness, I picture balls of sapphire, of metal" (p. 170). One of the most nearly perfect prose poems is *Fleurs* (p. 186). Its periods heave upward, creating a tension which the conclusion resolves but leaves unintelligible. The motion of the imagery forms curves of absolute imagination and absolute language which benefit from the nonorganic as a token of the unreal and, in this poem, as a token of a magic beauty: a golden stairway, green velvet, crystal discs that blacken like bronze in sunshine; foxglove blossoms upon a carpet of silver filigree, eyes, and hair; yellow pieces of gold strewn on agate, mahogany pillars supporting an emerald dome, slender ruby stems. In this environment the roses are assailed by a hard nonreality and have a mysterious relationship to the poison of the foxglove. For in the depth of this imagination, magical beauty is identical with destructiveness.

Poisonous plants and roses; elsewhere, filth and gold: an image formula for the dissonances that such an imagination adds to its products. The dissonances are frequently verbal; word clusters condense heterogeneous objects or values in the smallest possible space: a tar-drunk sun, a July morning with the wintery taste of ashes, copper palm trees, dreams "like pigeon droppings." Anything sounding cozy or comfortable is smashed, usually at the end of a text and with a brutal or vulgar word. Such poetry wants to rip open rather than close. The dissonance between a statement and its form is to be noted. Rimbaud uses a folksonglike tone in one of his most obscure poems, *Chanson de la plus haute tour*. In another poem, *Les Chercheuses de poux*, he transposes garbage, dense sexuality,

Rimbaud

and the rite of lice-picking into the linguistic vibration of pure lyricism. Chaos and absurdity appear in sober terseness, opposites imperturbably linked without a *but, however,* or a *nevertheless.*

LES ILLUMINATIONS

Les Illuminations can be described similarly. The title, characteristically ambiguous, can mean "colored drawings in a manuscript," "lighting," or "inspiration." An analytical division of the contents is impossible. Enigmatic imagery and action glide past. The language alternates between intoxication and harshness, monotonously insistent repetitions and free-floating strings of words. Rarely does a title of one of the prose poems help us to understand it. The atomized themes ricochet between hindsight and foresight, hatred and transfiguration, prophecy and renunciation. Agitation is scattered about in space that reaches from the stars down to graves, a space that is peopled by anonymous figures — murderers and angels. Epirus, Japan, Arabia, Carthage, and Brooklyn meet in a single setting. Conversely, things that normally belong together are separated to the point of total divorce (e.g., *Promontoire* [p. 191]. The dramatics in the poems involve the destruction of the world, with disorder as the epiphany of invisible arcana. A text starts so far away from the motive idea or object that it seems like a fragment, chancing upon us from another world. Here and there we find narrative, as in *Conte* (p. 170). A prince — what prince? — kills women; they come back. He kills his men; they follow him. "How can one be enraptured by destruction, rejuvenated by cruelty!" A genie of ineffable beauty comes to him, and the two of them die. "But the prince passed away in his palace and at a normal age." Ecstatic killing and dying are not successful. The victims live; the man who has died with the genie subsequently dies an ordinary death. This may mean that even destruction fails and merely leads into the trivial. Yet the most salient feature of this "fairy tale" is the fact that it expresses absurdity with narrative accuracy, knowing all the while that not even absurdity suffices. "Our desire lacks knowledgeable music" is the hatchetlike conclusion.

Les Illuminations ignores the reader. It does not wish to be understood. It is a tempest of hallucinatory discharges, and it hopes at best to arouse the fear of danger that stems from love of danger. It is also a text without an "I." The "I" that appears in a few of the pieces is the alien, artificial voice adumbrated in the *voyant* letters. Nevertheless, *Les Illuminations* bears witness that its author, as one line puts it, is an "inventor more meritorious than all [his] predecessors" (p. 174). *Les Illuminations* is the first great monument of the modern imagination become absolute.

59

CROSSFADE TECHNIQUE

Recently editors have included *Marine* in *Les Illuminations* (p. 188), and the poem may belong in that work. It was written in 1872 and is the first example of free verse in French: ten lines of varying length, unrhymed, and without the usual regular alternation of masculine and feminine rhymes. In French, the abandonment of strict meter was (and still is) more conspicuous than in other languages and was felt to be a more violent symptom of abnormal poetry. Rimbaud adjusted form to his dismembered imagination; he put form awry, producing asymmetrical verse similar to his lyrical prose. This was an energetic step beyond Baudelaire. Since *Marine*, free verse has more and more come to dominate French poetry. Gustave Kahn, Apollinaire, Max Jacob, Henri Régnier, and Paul Eluard were to be twentieth-century virtuosos of *vers libres*, which became a formal characteristic of the type of poet who — knowingly or not — followed in Rimbaud's footsteps.

MARINE	SEASCAPE

Les chars d'argent et de
    cuivre —
	The wagons of silver and
	    copper —

Les proues d'acier et d'argent —	The prows of steel and silver — Churn the foam —
Battent l'écume —	Lift the rootstocks of bramble.

Soulèvent les souches des
    ronces.
	The currents of the sandy
	    moor,

Les courants de la lande,	And the immense ruts of the
Et les ornières immenses du reflux,	ebbing tide,
Filent circulairement vers l'est,	Circle smoothly eastward,
Vers les piliers de la forêt,	Toward the pillars of the forest,
Vers les fûts de la jetée,	Toward the posts of the jetty,

Dont l'angle est heurté par des
    tourbillons de lumière.
	Its corner colliding with whirls
	    of light.

The poem contains two contrasts: one between the metrical dearticulation and the carefully articulate, quiet tone; the other between the tone and the extraordinary boldness of the content. With great restraint, the poem arrays statement after statement. They are joined together at only two points (ll. 6, 10) by almost insignificant connective particles. This avoidance of syntactical links is what raises the diction beyond mere prose, making the subdued ''I''-less tone mysterious: magical restraint. The lines are not merely a typographical isolation of clauses, which would require breaks in prose, too. The isolation actually lends a greater intensity to the word clusters and an almost biblical parallelism to the tone. Furthermore, most of the words are nouns. The few verbs are overshadowed by the subjects and objects, whose image value is more important than their movement. And yet something revolutionary occurs due to the authority of unreal imagination. The poem commences with a line that does not fit in with the title: "wagons of silver and copper." The second line is more in keeping: "prows of steel and silver." Both the wagons and the prows "churn the foam," "lift the rootstocks of bramble." There are "currents of the sandy moor," "ruts of the ebbing tide," which glide "toward the pillars of the forest" and "the posts of the jetty," all of which are flooded with colliding "whirls of light."

We can see what the text creates: two areas, one maritime (ship, sea), one territorial (wagon, moor). But the two are crisscrossed to such an extent that they cinematically fade into one another, transcending all normal separation. The seascape is also a landscape and vice versa. This identification may have been inspired by a metaphor common in Latin and current in French: the metaphor of a ship "plowing" the ocean. But the poem goes beyond this possible stimulus in that its verbs, as well as its word clusters, merge both areas ("the currents of the sandy moor," etc.). Thus we are not dealing with metaphors. They are superseded by the equation of empirically discrete things. In addition, we note that the text does not name the sea; it speaks of foam and the ebb tide. It does not name the ship; it simply mentions the prow. Putting the part for the whole (synedoche) has always been a technique available to the poet. But, in Rimbaud, the effect is keener than ever. By including only parts of objects, he initiates a destruction, which then assails the order of reality per se.

This calm, laconic poem is not only the first clear appearance of free verse in French; it is also the first example of the modern crossfade technique, which is itself a special case of reality destruction and sensory unreality. What new thing is created? In terms of objectivity, we can offer only a negative definition: nonreality, the removal of objective distinctions. The resulting enigma is insoluble. The objects joined by this technique are haphazard and interchangeable, as is the text itself: of the ten lines, at least three or four could be rearranged without disturbing the organism. The imagination that produces all this may be called "freedom," a positive term. But if we want to define the freedom more precisely, we will be faced with a mass of negative concepts. For such freedom is an escape from the systems of reality; it is an unreal merging of dissimilar things. Such freedom of the imagination is generally powerful and artistically convincing, yet its individual steps are not inevitable. And this factor will become a basic characteristic of modern poetry: its contents are interchangeable, whereas the style obeys a law that has its own evidence. The cinematic crossfade is still one of the many features common to both poetry and painting. Interestingly enough, Proust discusses it in great detail. In *Seascape with Frieze of Girls* (found in *Within a Budding Grove*) he describes a visit to the fictitious painter Elstir. The passage includes reflections that coincide amazingly with the aesthetics of modern painting. We may also view them as an affirmation of Rimbaud's methods and, consequently, of the fact that poetry cleared the way for modern painting. The determining power of the artist (to sum up Proust's words) is the "dream," imagination superior to reality. Poetry uses metaphors, and painting uses "metamorphoses," to translate objects into creations that do not exist in the real world. As applied to the painter Elstir, some of his most frequent metamorphoses consisted in removing the boundary between ocean and land in his seascapes. The town is depicted in "marine terms"; the sea, on the other hand, in "urban terms." The result is a painting of the "unreal and the mystical," in which the unities of objects and areas are taken apart and transformed, in their parts, into an unreal "equation" of dissimilarities: the very same process that we observed in Rimbaud's *Marine*. The fact that Proust developed this aesthetic by using seascapes as examples is a coincidence, but an amazing one.

ABSTRACT POETRY

The dictatorial imagination of *Les Illuminations* can reach the point of absurdity. Thus, in *Après le déluge* (p. 167) a hare stopping in clover and speaking through a cobweb prays to the rainbow; madame sets up a piano in the Alps. The imagination can create a frenzy of image shreds, as in *Matinée d'ivresse*. But it has other possibilities as well: the ones that Baudelaire meant when he used the word *abstraction*. This term may be applied to texts of Rimbaud's in which lines and motion form a nonobjective (abstract) network over the contents of the imagery.

One instance is the short piece *Les Ponts* (p. 179). For the sake of elucidation, we include both the original and a translation.

LES PONTS	THE BRIDGES
Des ciels gris de cristal. Un bizarre dessin de ponts, ceux-ci droits, ceux-là bombés, d'autres descendant en obliquant en angles sur les	Crystal gray skies. A strange design of bridges, some straight, some curved, some dropping obliquely upon the foremost ones, and these

premiers, et ces figures se renouvel-
ant dans les autres circuits éclairés
du canal, mais tous tellement longs
et légers que les rives, chargées de
dômes, s'abaissent et s'amoin-
drissent. Quelques-uns de ces ponts
sont encore chargés de masures.
D'autres soutiennent des mâts, des
signaux, de frêles parapets. Des
accords mineurs se croisent, et
filent; des cordes montent des
berges. On distingue une veste
rouge, peut-être d'autres costumes
et des instruments de musique. Sont-
ce des airs populaires, des bouts de
concerts seigneuriaux, des restants
d'hymnes publics? L'eau est grise
et bleue, large comme un bras de
mer.

Un rayon blanc, tombant du haut
du ciel, anéantit cette comédie.

figures recurring in the other
illuminated windings of the canal,
but all of them so long and light that
the dome-laden banks subside and
diminish. Some of these bridges are
still laden with hovels. Others bear
posts, signals, fragile parapets.
Minor chords intersect, and speed
along; bridge cords rise from the
steep banks. A red jacket can be
made out, perhaps other clothes and
musical instruments. Are they folk
songs, scraps of baronial concerts,
remnants of patriotic songs? The
water is gray and blue, wide as
ocean sounds.

A white ray, falling from the top
of the sky, destroys this show.

The passage is a precise description. Its subject matter, however, is imaginary: an "excerpt" of a city devoid of geographical or temporal context
and created by vision rather than mimesis. Bridges: yet their main feature
is not so much their physical volume as their linearity: straight, curved,
oblique lines, "a strange design." (We are reminded that, for Baudelaire,
"strange" (*bizarre*) was part of the world of the "abstract" and the
"arabesque.") Summarily, these lines are thus called "figures." The
figures are repeated in "the other"— which other? — windings of the
canal. The law of gravity does not obtain, for the figures (to be seen simply
as bridges, too) are so light that they weigh down the heavy river banks:
lightness weighs down heaviness. New lines consisting of striplike tones,
quick evocations of a red jacket and some musical instruments, and then
the hatchetlike conclusion: everything remains incomprehensible. Again,
an uncomplicated syntax houses something totally alien. The alien quality
is heightened by the cold accuracy of the predications. There are no human
beings here. The red jacket is isolated; like the music (devoid of origin),
it makes the absence of people all the more obvious. Objects dominate,
but in the vagueness of plurals, in the absurdity of their interrelations;
there is no normal connection between cause and effect. The objects are
distilled into pure movements and geometric abstractions. Unreal as the
content may be, it is made even more so by the annihilating conclusion.

63

Rimbaud moves about in this nowhere world without lofty rhetoric. He can give up the rebellious escapes of his earlier poetry into alien worlds. Now he *is* in an alien place. A keen sense of vision registers the bizarreness that it has created, stating this bizarreness in a language that is matter-of-fact in tone, but without passing it on.

MONOLOGUE POETRY

As of 1871, Rimbaud's poetry became more and more monologic. Preliminary drafts of certain passages in his prose works have survived. If we compare them with the final versions, we can see in what direction Rimbaud changed. His sentences are even more pithy than before, his high jumps over intermediary links or terms more daring, his bizarre word clusters more frequent. Contemporary accounts claim that Rimbaud would use up whole piles of paper before arriving at a satisfactory version, scrupulously mull over every single comma and adjective, and collect rare and unusual words for his writings. This merely goes to show that Rimbaud's work methods were no different than those of the classic authors of clarity. His soliloquizing obscurity is no uncontrollable lunging; it is planned craftsmanship and, as such, is perfectly logical in a poet whose unfulfillable passion for the "unknown" has no other choice than to turn the familiar into alienating chaos. Rimbaud later wrote: "I set down the inexpressible; I captured whirlwinds" (p. 219); but, a few pages further on: "I can't speak anymore." Rimbaud's dark poetry is suspended between these two extremes: its darkness is the obscurity of what has never been said or what can be said no more, on the brink of silence.

Why does a poet who speaks for no one write poetry? The question is probably unanswerable. We might, however, interpret such poetry as an extreme attempt at enlisting dictatorial imagination and using abnormal speech in order to save the freedom of the spirit in a historical situation — one in which scientific enlightenment and cultural, technological, and economic power structures have organized and collectivized freedom, thereby robbing it of its essence. A homeless spirit can create a place to live and work only in poetry. Perhaps that is why the poet writes poetry.

THE DYNAMICS OF MOTION AND THE MAGIC OF LANGUAGE

The network of tensions in any poem by Rimbaud is produced by energies known in music. The analogy to music resides, however, not so much in tonal figures as in the passage of degrees of intensity, the absolute motion of rising and falling, the alternation of tension and release. Here lies the source of the fascination of this arcane poetry that speaks into the Void.

The methods of such dynamics can be studied in the prose poem *Mystique* (p. 185). Something happens in an imaginary landscape, and the event is itself part and parcel of the landscape. First, angels are dancing on sloping "meadows of steel and emerald." The fields are not static; "fields of flame leap up to the peak of the mamelon." To the left, a ridge is being "trampled by all homicides and all battles, and all disastrous din curves by." The upper part of the picture "is made of the whirling, heaving din of seashells and human nights." At the end, "the flower-strewn sweetness of stars and sky . . . sinks . . . into the blue and fragrant abyss." Sight and sound are blended with one another and with abstractions; thus, another ridge is called a "line of orients [Orients, orient pearls, or sunrises?] and progress." Removing the boundaries of individual objects, the poet correspondingly wipes away the boundaries and corporeity of the whole by means of vast movements: first, a horizontal motion below; then, an ascending movement; then, once more, a horizontal one, but this time high above (a movement paradoxically consisting of objects from the deep, seashells); and, finally, a rising motion that terminates far below. These movements, more perceptible than visible in the unreal material objects, are absolute dynamisms. And so are the movements of the syntactical periods: at first, and until the middle of the poem, lively, occasionally retarding rises; thereafter, a wide descending sweep, gliding and then slackening off, until the end, with its brief, isolated "down below," abruptly hurling the curve down. It is such movements, and not the "contents," that structure the poem. The more one reads the poem, the more fascinating it becomes.

We explained language magic in the foregoing chapter. Poets from Novalis to Poe and Baudelaire mulled over this method of creating a lyric not just out of themes and subject matter but also, perhaps exclusively, out of the combinative possibilities of the sounds of language and the associative overtones of word meanings. Rimbaud practices this method more daringly than anyone before him. A poet who cares little for normal intelligibility can use a method like this all the more readily since it divorces the word as sound and suggestion from the word as conveyer of communicable sense. The word now releases nonlogical energy that guides the statements and, by means of unusual successions of sound, practices an unusual sorcery. The latter helps make the "unknown" vicariously perceptible as much as the sensory unreality and the absolute motion do.

Rimbaud speaks of the "alchemy of the Word [*logos*]" (pp. 218 ff.). Critics have construed this statement and others to mean that he was conver-

65

sant with magic and was inspired by occult literature. As a matter of fact, such writings had been gaining popularity in France ever since the middle of the nineteenth century, even among the literary elite. These works included the so-called hermetic books (dealing with Hellenistic black art and attributed to the legendary Hermes Trismegistus), which were translated by Lewis Ménard in 1863. Yet no one has offered substantial evidence that Rimbaud was acquainted with such writings. Occasional attempts to interpret Rimbaud's poetry as secret texts in code for occultists are nonsensical.[5] The rapprochement of poetry with magic and alchemy has been common since the eighteenth century and need not be taken literally. The important thing about this rapprochement is that it sees an analogy between the poetic act and magical and alchemistic operations, which, through the use of a secret material, try to convert base metals into gold. The fact that modern poets refer more and more to this analogy is part of the specifically modern tendency to make poetry bridge the gap between intellectuality and the arcana of ancient sorcery.

In the piece entitled *Alchimie du Verbe*, Rimbaud wrote: "I regulated the form and the movement of every consonant, and I felt sure that with instinctive rhythms I would invent a poetic Word [*logos*] which would eventually be accessible to all the senses." Passages like this, which can be found in Rimbaud's final work, are meant to indicate a state through which he had already passed; yet even in this last piece of writing he practices methods of language magic to various degrees. The resulting works, when read aloud, plainly show the careful reckoning of vowel nuances and consonant affinities. This becomes particularly daring when the auditory intention is so dominant that the verse or sentence which it directs achieves only an absurd meaning: "Un hydrolat lacrymal lave [A lachrymal hydrolate washes]"; "Mon triste cœur bave à la poupe [My sad heart drools at the stern]." One can compare this poetry to atonal music. The dissonance between the absurd meaning and the absolute sound is never resolved.

We can study one example more closely, a line from the prose poem *Métropolitain* (p. 189): ". . . et les atroces fleurs qu'on appellerait cœurs et sœurs, damas damnant de langueur." (A variant reads "longueur," but the difference is negligible.) If we tried to translate this phrase, the result would be: ". . . and the atrocious flowers that might be called hearts and sisters, damask damning languidly." The translation is poor, not because it sounds absurd (so does the original), but because the source of the line is missing: linguistic creation. The sentence is an abstract series of assonances and alliterations. Similarities of vowels and consonants shape

5. See J. Gengoux, *Le Symbolisme de Rimbaud* (Paris, 1947).

the sound to so great an extent that the meaning of the words produces no coherence in image or thought. Why should flowers be called "hearts and sisters"? For no other reason than that these nouns rhyme with *flowers: fleurs, cœurs, sœurs*. What should a translator do? He would have to make a hopeless attempt at finding something that would formally match the counterpoint of pure sound and bizarre meaning in the original, e.g., "the fearful ferns that we find fraternal and eternal, damask damning burningly." But this leads nowhere. Rimbaud is untranslatable. He demonstrates his own statement: "A tap of your finger on the drum releases all sounds and starts the new harmony" (p. 175). Frenchmen may hear the new harmony. But it is drawn from such deep strata of their language that no other tongue is capable of duplicating it. A translation can only be an incomplete account of the content, a factor of far less importance than in other poetry.

The growing abnormality of modern verse makes translating more and more improbable — and not just translating French. The breach between the magical language of poetry and the language of communication has become a chasm separating the national languages of Europe.

CONCLUSION AND VERDICT

Rivière, in his monograph on Rimbaud (which remains unsurpassed), writes: "The help he brings us consists in his making our stay on earth impossible. . . . The world sinks back into its primal chaos; things emerge with the terrible freedom that was theirs when they served no purpose." Rimbaud, foundering before the "unknown," evoked chaos in order to replace it. He is a great poet because he captured chaos artistically, in a language of mysterious perfection. Like Baudelaire, he courageously, and with prescience, took upon himself "the brutal spiritual struggle" of which he spoke and which became the destiny of his era.

When his poetry, which deformed both his self and the outside world, reached a point of self-destruction, the nineteen-year-old had enough character to put down his pen. His silence is an act of his poetic existence.

IV

MALLARMÉ

INTRODUCTORY DESCRIPTION

Mallarmé's poetry seems unlike anything produced by his predecessors or his contemporaries. It was written by a man whose life ran a normal, bourgeois course, and who, for all his great suffering, was kindness itself, never displayed his inner torment, and tended to treat his own person ironically. But calm as his life may have been, his mind worked slowly on thoughts and poetry whose abstractions went even further than Rimbaud's tumult. The obscurity of Mallarmé's verse is intimidating. It has to be deciphered from a language that is his alone. And yet his poetry, too, is part of a structure whose components go back to romanticism and have been growing stronger and stronger since Baudelaire.

The reader who has come with us this far will be able to orient himself if we offer a few key words of explanation. In Mallarmé, too, we find the following: an absence of emotional and inspirational poetry; imagination guided by the intellect; destruction of reality and of both logical and emotional order; the use of the inciting forces in language; suggestivity instead of comprehensibility; the sense of living in a terminal era of civilization; a dual relationship to modernity; a breach with humanistic and Christian traditions; isolation which sees itself as a badge of honor; equal status of poetry and reflections on poetry, with negative categories predominant in these thoughts.

All these features, indicating that Mallarmé is a typical representative of modern poetry, were transformed and deepened by him; but, complicated as the result may be, the consistency inherent in the process is still discernible. A new type of modern poetry emerged. And a paradox similar to

Rimbaud's prevailed: the enigmatic, abstruse Mallarmé canon exerted a considerable influence. This effect is in itself a symptom of the condition of modern poetic practice. The uncommunicative loner is disquieting; he is listened to and constantly reinterpreted; he attracts pupils and makes them masters. His very unusualness attracts minds weary of normality. His *œuvre* is not literary sloth, aestheticism, or the like, but the product of the highest demand that a poet can make upon himself. Mallarmé was heard, and his work bore fruit, as shown by other poets: Stefan George, Valéry, Swinburne, T. S. Eliot, Guillén, Ungaretti.

We can sum up Mallarmé's specific traits in advance. As in the discussion that will follow, we will concentrate on his second phase, which began around 1870. His poetry — quiet, unobtrusive, but perceptible — vibrates in a near vacuum. Each poem has multiple levels of meaning surpassing one another and leading to the limits of intelligibility. Mallarmé perfects the view, current since Baudelaire, that by imitating reality, the artistic imagination does not idealize it but deforms it. Mallarmé gives this view an ontological foundation. He does the same for the obscurity of poetry and its avoidance of a confining intelligibility. That is, he heightens the unity of craftsmanship and aesthetic reflection by adding ideas that revolve around absolute being (equated with nonbeing) and its relationship to language. Mallarmé formulates his ideas theoretically and always cautiously in the essays in *Divagations* and in several letters. The ideas take true shape in his poems, but the results are by no means didactic. For him, poetry is the only place in which language and the absolute can meet. Poetry thus reached an acme such as it had not attained since antiquity. Yet this is not a happy height; it lacks true transcendence, and it lacks gods.

An explanation will follow below. The reader may wonder: Is this still poetry? Why does Mallarmé not discuss his ontological ideas in a theoretical and unequivocal exposition? The answer is simply that any unequivocal precision would entail a loss of mystery. And mystery is crucial; the poet wants to come as close to it as possible. His poetry and his ideas do not move from the empirical world into ontological universality; they take the opposite course. His poetry uses simple objects: a vase, a console, a fan, a mirror. They may lose their objective essence and become conveyers of an invisible current of tension; but the word that names them makes them present for the imagination. And in this presence they acquire an unusual increase in meaning, because that invisible current of tension enters into them so fully that these simple objects of our world become totally instinct with mystery. This process takes place vicariously for all the objectivity surrounding us. By eschewing concepts, by deeply imprint-

70

ing absolute being — i.e., nonbeing — upon simple objects, by rendering them enigmatic before our eyes, Mallarmé creates essential mystery out of the familiar. And that is why this is poetry: a singing of mystery with words and images, at the perception of which the soul vibrates, even though it is led into alien territory.

INTERPRETATION OF THREE POEMS: *SAINTE, EVENTAIL (DE MADAME MALLARMÉ), SURGI DE LA CROUPE*

It will prove useful to discuss three poems by Mallarmé as an introduction to this difficult author. Some pedantry will be necessary.

The first text is *Sainte* (p. 53),[1] the final version of which was written in 1884. The French-speaking reader should read this, as well as the other two poems, aloud, but softly. For such verse is meant to affect the ear before anything else; the interlocking phonic sensations prepare the reader for the inner perception of the abnormal content.

A la fenêtre recélant
Le santal vieux qui se dédore
De sa viole étincelant
Jadis avec flûte ou mandore,

Est la Sainte pâle, étalant
Le livre vieux qui se déplie
Du Magnificat ruisselant
Jadis selon vêpre et complie:

A ce vitrage d'ostensoir
Que frôle une harpe par l'Ange
Formée avec son vol du soir
Pour la délicate phalange

Du doigt que, sans le vieux santal
Ni le vieux livre, elle balance
Sur le plumage instrumental,
Musicienne du silence.

At the window which conceals
The old tarnishing sandalwood
Of the viol that sparkled
Once with flute or mandola

Is the pale Saint, spreading out
The old unfolding book
Of the Magnificat that shimmered
Once according to vesper and complin:

At this monstrance glasswork
Grazed by a harp that the Angel
Formed with its evening flight
For the delicate phalanx

Of her finger which, without the old sandalwood
Or the old book, she poises
On the instrumental plumage,
She, the musician of silence.

1. [All references in this chapter are to *Œuvres complètes*, ed. H. Mondor and G. Jean-Aubry (Paris, 1951). — *Trans.*]

71

The text, metrically faultless, speaks in a single yet unconcluded sentence. The syntax, far from all oratorical pomp, is as simple as can be, even if it takes the reader a while to work the sentence out: "A la fenêtre . . . est la Sainte . . . à ce vitrage. . . ." The author uses an adverbial phrase, a short main clause with the most unemphatic of verbs (*est*), and a belated apposition. Yet this basic structure is veiled by the insertion of the first stanza, the complementary second stanza — which sounds like a relative clause — and, finally, the relative clauses of the third and fourth stanzas. The apposition ("à ce vitrage") dangles: the adjoining subordinate clauses do not complete the sentence, but leave it open. The simple and yet elliptic syntax provides space for a murmuring tone on the periphery of silence (named in the closing word).

There is a version of the poem written twenty years earlier: *Sainte Cécile, jouant sur l'aile d'un Chérubin*. The title has been reduced to *Sainte*, i.e., the most general and indefinite. The negation of reality has affected the title, depriving it of delimitation to anything unequivocal.

The poem lists a few objects: a window, an old instrument made of sandalwood, a monstrance window, a harp, a Magnificat book. But their relationship to one another is enigmatic; physically they are not even present. Syntactically, the monstrance seems to be an elucidating appositive of the window. Does this mean that the two are identical? This would be inconceivable according to the normal order of things. The harp in the third stanza was formed by the evening flight of an angel. Is the harp a metaphor for the angel's wing? Yet it seems to be a harp, a plumage used as a musical instrument. It is *both* a harp *and* a wing — not just a metaphor, but an identity, a process already known to us in Rimbaud. The poem exists in a realm in which real differences are transcended and an interpenetration takes place on many levels of meaning. Yet something else happens. The viol, *concealed* by the window, exists linguistically but not objectively. The flute and the mandola (a kind of lute) are present only as memories of "once." The book of the Magnificat, although at hand, is characterized in such a way that it no longer is part of the present: it shimmered "once," in the past. And, beginning in the third stanza, the removal of the objects becomes more comprehensive. The transition is in the harp, which is simultaneously an angel's wing — an unreal identity. Everything that follows is total absence. The Saint plays *without* the old sandalwood, *without* the old book. Is she playing at all? She is actually silent, a musician of silence.

We can see that there are few objects present, that they are either indefinite or unreal identities of disparate things, and that they are ultimately annihilated and relegated to absence and silence. This process is not the result of any act of the Saint; the language alone is responsible. By removing and thereby annihilating the objects, the diction gives them an existence in language. These rejected objects have no existence other than in language. Their presence is spiritual and becomes more absolute the more their empirical existence is transcended.

The poem *is* a process, taking place not in the objects but in the language, and in a special tense which likewise banishes the objects. The very beginning reveals this process. The dying gold of the sandalwood creates an impression of declining light, eventide. "Vesper" and "complin," referring to the past, also emphasize this impression. But this is no precise evening hour in which we could imagine the presence of the Saint. It is, if we may word it thus, evening time per se, absolute lateness, the proper time category for decline and destruction. This impression is heightened by the precise naming of the "evening flight" in the third stanza. The flight beyond empirical time, the frequent mention of "old," and the antique mandola add up to a plethora of signs indicating the absolute lateness. All concreteness is annihilated; the temporal characteristics, seemingly attached to the concreteness, detach themselves and become absolute. In an unreal harmony with absence and nothingness, they create the existence of lateness and pastness — an existence which becomes totally free unto itself only on the premise of a nonconcrete space devoid of objects.

The viol is hidden by the window; the flute and the mandola are evoked only by the language. Why are they here at all, even if "only" in the language? They are musical instruments, like the unreal harp. Even these hidden or absent or unreal objects are conveyers of an existence — the acoustic existence of music. But what sort of music is it? The Saint does not play. The music is silent — and for this very reason it is an entity that, together with the lateness and the absence of objects, has a spiritual existence in — and only in — language.

This poem, one of Mallarmé's finest and purest, calls upon our visual and perhaps our aural perception, and transforms the perceptible into something unfamiliar, even sinister. In the immaculateness of the meter, in the innocence of dreamy murmuring, the poem achieves the abnormal. It destroys objects in order to raise them to absolute entitities which, because they no longer have anything to do with the empirical world, exist all the more definitively in the language. The language draws them into an interrelationship beyond any system of reality.

It takes time to realize all this. We really need those "brain glasses," to which Maurice Barrès refers sarcastically in his criticism of Mallarmé. For such poetry has little to do with lyrics of emotion, personal experience, or the phenomenal. Exotic, yet quietly fascinating, Mallarmé's poetry speaks from an incorporeal, lonely inwardness in which the mind, no longer blotted by reality, observes itself and feels, in the interaction of its abstract tensions, the same satisfaction of sovereignty as in the formula systems of mathematics.

Our second text is the sonnet *Eventail (de Madame Mallarmé)* [Fan (of Madame Mallarmé)], written in 1887 (p. 57).

Avec comme pour langage	With nothing but a skyward
Rien qu'un battement aux	fluttering
cieux	As language
Le futur vers se dégage	The future verse slips
Du logis très précieux	Out of the very precious home
Aile tout bas la courrière	The wing the whispering
Cet éventail si c'est lui	messenger
Le même par qui derrière	This fan if it is the one
Toi quelque miroir a lui	The same one by which behind
	You some mirror has shone
Limpide (où va redescendre	
Pourchassée en chaque grain	Limpid (to which will sink back
Un peu d'invisible cendre	Pursued in every grain
Seule à me rendre chagrin)	A bit of invisible ash
	Which alone grieves me)
Toujours tel il apparaisse	
Entre tes mains sans paresse.	May it always appear
	Between your never-idle hands.

At first one might say that this is a conventional subject in a conventional form. The Shakespearean sonnet, although rarely used in France, is conventional. So is the subject, a lady's fan; the *poésie galante* of earlier centuries loved it. But *what* is expressed in this form, *why* this insignificant, almost negligible fan was chosen, and, finally, *how* this object is welded with the ideal theme could not be less conventional. The reader is confronted, not with convention, but with incomprehensibility. The latter is present in the very diction. The poem is devoid of punctuation. The only typographical hint at an articulation of the sense is the pair of parentheses in the third stanza; however, they contribute little to the understanding and do not interrupt the dreamlike murmur of the language. The beginnings of the first and second stanzas are so compressed as to be almost insoluble. The second stanza contains apostrophes; even the adverbial *tout bas* is boldly handled as an invocation. This second stanza is exemplary of Mallarmé's mature style: words, rather than speak by means of grammatical relations, convey a multiplicity of possible meanings. Furthermore, it is difficult to work out the sentence structure, at least from the second stanza on. "Cet éventail . . ." belongs to "toujours tel il apparaisse. . . ." But the curve linking these two word groups contains so many involutions that the sentence sounds elliptic. The syntax is distended, becoming as ambiguous as the content.

The title mentions the fan, but the poem immediately retreats from this precise object, registering only one thing within the semantic scope of the fan: *battement*, which is itself a fragment (*battement d'ailes* ["beating of wings"] would be verbally complete). The vestigial fragment connotes something more general, far beyond the range of meanings of the word *fan*; *battement* no longer refers to the fan but — metaphorically — to poetry, which is conceived of as future, i.e., ideal, poetry ("le futur vers"). Thus the very first stanza, rather than graphically describe an object, withdraws from it. The object does not become clear or definite; only the process of deobjectification is clear. The theme of the first stanza can be recapitulated as follows: Future poetry has no language in the usual sense, only a quasi language which, however, is almost nothing, the nugatoriness of merely a skyward fluttering of wings, upward, toward ideality; and this poetry abandons home and familiar things ("se dégage . . ."). Mallarmé, in his quiet fashion, repeats more or less what Rimbaud said: "A blast [of air] pierces gaps in the partitions, . . . blows away the limits of homes" (see above, p. 50).

From the second stanza on, the poem confronts the fan. After the opening line, whose words are difficult to place syntactically, a corporeity is hazily delineated — only to be rejected. The fan is mentioned by name, but its name is followed by a restrictive "if it is the one," which makes the fan indefinite and hypothetical. A variation of this occurs with the mirror: the fan *has* shone through the mirror, which is thus no longer present. Furthermore, the mirror is referred to as *quelque miroir* ("some mirror"). Mallarmé often uses *quelque* as a third article, the article of indefiniteness. And in this mirror that the poetic voice absents, something occurs to create . further nonpresence. Invisible ashes *will* sink back into the mirror. We never find out what the ashes are — possibly the gray hair of the woman addressed? The question is deliberately left unanswered. The linguistic presence of the ashes suffices. Objectively they are not present: they are invisible; they *will* come, "pursued in every grain." As is usually the case with Mallarmé, we should not heed the primary sense of the words but rather the categories used by the language to treat objects and corporeity — in this case, past, future, absence, hypothesis, indefiniteness. These categories dominate the last lines. The fan shall always remain thus: a skyward fluttering, a hypothetical thing, mysteriously involved with the past mirror, the past shining, the future ashes.

The poem addresses a "thou." But this mode of address is as unimportant as any other trace of human presence, for example, "ash" and "grief." Here there are no tender feelings or courteous compliments. Even the grief is devoid of emotion. The atmosphere is one of calm coolness that removes objects and anything human. Here, too, the absence of things has priority over their presence. Here, too, objects exist only in language. They are removed from their homey familiarity. Thus the poem carries the intention voiced in the opening stanza, to slip from the home. *Eventail*, like almost all of Mallarmé's poems, is about poetry. The ontological schema pervades the lines: objects are impure, nonabsolute, insofar as they are really present; only when annihilated do they permit the generation of their pure essential energy in language. Such diction, compared with normal parlance, can only be an "as if" speech, a transcending language that guards against any definite meaning, a language that can only be a fluttering of wings, a multiradiating atmosphere of meanings, of which there is no delimitation and in which everything is movement.

Poetry has always enjoyed the privilege of letting a word quiver with its multiplicity of meanings. Mallarmé forges ahead to the utmost limits of this license. He makes the infinite potentials of language the actual content of his writings. And he thereby attains a mysteriousness which not only liberates from confining reality (as was true of Baudelaire and Rimbaud) but also allows an empty transcendence, henceforth interpreted ontologically, to express itself in language by means of a total alienation of the familiar.

The third poem is an untitled sonnet composed in 1887 (p. 74):

Surgi de la croupe et du bond
D'une verrerie éphémère
Sans fleurir la veillée amère
Le col ignoré s'interrompt.

Surging up from the crest and
  the leap
Of an ephemeral glass
Without blooming in the bitter
  evening vigil
The ignored bottle neck stops
  abruptly.

Je crois bien que deux bouches
  n'ont
Bu, ni son amant ni ma mère,
Jamais à la même Chimère,
Moi, Sylphe de ce froid
  plafond!

I believe that two mouths have
  never
Drunk, either her lover or my
  mother,
At the same Chimera,
I, the Sylph of this cold ceiling!

Le pur vase d'aucun breuvage
Que l'inexhaustible veuvage

The pure vase with no beverage
Except inexhaustible widow-
  hood

76

Mallarmé

| Agonise mais ne consent, | Is in agony but does not |
| | consent, |

Naïf baiser des plus	Naïve and gloomiest of kisses!
funèbres!	To exhale anything announcing
A rien expirer annonçant	A rose in the darkness.
Une rose dans les ténèbres.	

This sonnet has a rigorous form insofar as the syntax is divided according to the rule of classical sonnet structure: each quatrain is composed of a single sentence, and the two tercets are joined in a single sentence. This construction coincides with the progress of the statements. But despite the traditionally correct form, despite the only slightly abnormal syntax, the poem offers a highly opaque content. The language passes by as if it were expressing the most natural things — and yet it states enigmas. We have to decipher carefully until the deciphering fuses with our hearing and until things mentally cognized start singing again and vanish in the uncognizable.

The poem may be approached by studying its acts of motion. The first stanza contains the movement of emergence abruptly halted. Emergence from where? From a *croupe* ("crest," "curve") and a *bond* ("leap," "bound"). The language puts a spatial value and a dynamic value (*croupe* and *bond*) on one level, thus bringing heterogeneous things together. Both things are still unknown. They belong to the "ephemeral glass." The latter may be an object, but its designation is so general that, at first, unable to identify it, we take it likewise as something unknown. This method is deliberate. The poem begins in vagueness and the unknown so far as objects are concerned. On the other hand, the movements are precise; and they involve the object by transforming its static line into a "leap." It is only later, in the third stanza, after the deobjectification is complete, that the poem reveals the precise name of the glass object: "the pure vase." The object emerges from behind the veil of motion, but only for a moment. And the vase is barely palpable. The adjective *pur* (which, characteristically ambiguous, can mean "mere" or "only," as well as "pure"— i.e., devoid of any form-destroying admixture) is simply a formal qualification, contributing little to the visual impression of the vase. The text moves slightly closer to objectiveness, but does not seize it.

Mallarmé often spoke of the "hocus-pocus" of art (*prestiges* in the sense of the Latin *praestigia*; p. 649). He meant, among many other things, verses created by a mysterious combination play of language; even if the reader figures out the trick, the dignity of the verses remains intact, since such poetry is a great game anyway. A line of this kind can be found in *Le Tombeau d'Edgar Poe* (p. 70): "Calme bloc ici-bas chu d'un désastre obscur [Calm block fallen down here from some dark disaster]." The line refers to Poe, to his tomb, and to poetry in general. The more obvious image would have been *astre obscur* ("dark star"), especially since Mallarmé says something quite similar about Poe in his prose. Yet the verse eschews the obvious word, uses an exact antithesis, and achieves a meaningful statement on the art of poetry. The rejected word (*astre*) is the origin of the accepted one (*désastre*). Hocus-pocus and language magic!

This technique is present in the very first line of our sonnet. *Croupe* and *bond* may possibly describe the volume of the vase and the dynamic line of its silhouette. But in French the words are unusual in this context. We suspect that they come from beyond the object itself. The semantic field of *vase* includes *coupe* ("cup") and *fond* ("bottom"). Both words, although rather obvious, never occur in the text, yet Mallarmé uses them as impulses to find near homonyms — and thus produces the desired effect of abnormality with *croupe* and *bond*. The hocus-pocus has a deeper meaning, veiled by Mallarmé's ironic smile. This practice is analogous to all the methods of his poetry in which he experiments with numerous abnormalities to arouse the dormant spirits in language. The use of word impulses would not be possible if Mallarmé were not fundamentally striving to get away from normal objective description or if this striving were not perfectly appropriate to an eschewal of normal objectivity. When the painter Degas, who occasionally wrote verse, complained of having so many ideas that they threatened to spoil his poems, Mallarmé answered: "Poems are made of words, not of ideas." Valéry, relating this anecdote in his book on Degas, adds: "Here resides the entire mystery." Mallarmé, like most modern poets, is obsessed with the old conviction that words are more powerful than thoughts.

But let us get back to our sonnet. What leaps up and stops abruptly? "The ignored bottleneck." Perhaps this is the neck of the vase, but it could be something else. Once again we are confronted with linguistic hocus-pocus, this time in a different form. An early letter written by Mallarmé includes comments on one of his poems: "The meaning, in case the poem has any, is conjured up by an inner reflection of the words themselves" (Mallarmé to Cazalis, July 18, 1868). Mallarmé means that a word can let its meaning overlap other words that essentially have nothing to do with it. One example is *fleurir* ("to bloom," "to adorn with flowers"). It evokes, albeit marginally, the idea of blooming — and mirrors it in the "neck": the neck of a blossom, i.e., the stem. We can readily assume that this association is intentional, since the final verse contains a "rose," which in turn harks back to the neck. The intention is probable, but not definite, since here there is no deliberate definiteness in objectivity.

There is something unequivocal in the poem. One need only observe words like *ephemeral, without, bitter, ignored, stops abruptly*. They name negatives. The strongest is the ignoring of the neck: the flower stem, if it is one, does not exist. These negativities spread as persistently as they do in *Sainte* and *Eventail*. The speaker is a sylph — a mythical being (derived from Paracelsus). All we learn about him is that his parents (note the reversal of the normal sequence, "her lover . . . my mother") have never loved. Anyone whose ears are attuned to Mallarmé will understand this statement: not even the sylph exists. The vase contains only emptiness and is close to death; it will not allow anything to be exhaled that might announce "a rose in the darkness." The rose, like any flower, is Mallarmé's symbol for the poetic word. The conclusion signifies the following: the empty vase, all aspects of which are failure, will not permit a word of salvation, which would be salvation even if it came in the dark.[2]

This sonnet is a poem of negativities. In the foreground they remain objective: the nonexistent blossoms, the nonexistent sylph, the emptiness of the vase. But, all in all, the negative is meant as a categorial entity whose scope is greater than that of any of its empirical bearers. Such a poem is possible only because something as abstract as the entity of the negative must weigh upon the word. The poem speaks in words and thereby in vestiges of ideas, but in such a way that it transforms them into tokens of the entity of the negative. The negative is present in the word, which speaks of the objectively absent. Yet the presence of the negative is incomplete, for the word cannot attain the "rose" of salvation, the absolute linguistic manifestation of nothingness — pure ideality. Only the failure of absolute linguistic manifestation becomes verbal, transformed into this poem. Something which fails to meet an ontological demand succeeds as a poem.

The depths of Mallarmé's poem are governed by clarity. But the language is a singing mysteriousness which shields the ontological thought, preventing its deterioration.

STYLISTIC DEVELOPMENT

Mallarmé took his time. In dogged resistance to a job he disliked (teaching high school), to poverty (occasionally extreme), to neurasthenic insomnia

---

2. The use of *flower* to stand for the poetic word goes back to an expression used in ancient rhetoric for an artistic figure of speech (*flos orationis*; e.g., Cicero *De orationis* III. 96). Mallarmé is aware of this sense (p. 828).

that lasted for many years, he managed to accomplish his work. For the sake of this work, he accepted toil and hardship equal to those of ethical discipline. A few of the poems took twenty or even thirty years to finish. His main themes, like Baudelaire's, were introduced quite early. Mallarmé's later work consisted of multiple revisions of first drafts. It was the development of an inner rather than an outer dimension. A letter written in July, 1866, reveals that Mallarmé was convinced that he already held in his hands all the lines of his future work. And, like Baudelaire, he wanted this work to become an architectural whole. This wish did not come true. The carefully structured and articulated themes of his thinking and writing never resulted in anything as integral and well rounded as *Les Fleurs du mal*. But the individual parts of his work are based on a solid plan, and the torso that Mallarmé left behind is a unity and not a conglomeration. It is incomplete, not because of any personal failure, but because of the superhuman goal. One cannot say that Mallarmé was less prolific than Baudelaire, considering the creations that surround the major works. Mallarmé's lesser writings include *Contes indiens* (ca. 1893), a still-neglected miracle of French prose (in which Mallarmé temporarily forsakes dark verse for the bright world of fairy tales); many occasional poems; the rhymed addresses in letters; and, finally, the practice sentences he made up for his English classes, malicious aphorisms in a twilight of scurrilous profundity. Although he dismisses the last as incidental, they are actually examples of the waggish ebullience of his imagination, of his playfulness which disarranges all reality. The aphorisms have the same source as the obscure gravity of his chief writings.

Mallarmé was certainly prolific, and, in his poetry, the flowing, the blossoming, and the breathing of his productivity are compressed into a high tension of energy within the narrowest of language fields. We can trace this method through the different versions of his poems. Every tone that sounds too loud or hints at oratory vanishes. Clichés give way to rare words. Syntactical curves dissolve into atomized sentences, so that the words, syntactically as independent as possible, become their own sources of light. An object originally named at the start of a poem is shifted to a later point so that the beginning is left free for a statement removed from the object. Or else, if an object first appears in its simple and usual whole, later versions shred it into multivocal, isolated details. The range of themes grows smaller and smaller, the world of objects lighter and lighter, and, in reverse proportion, the contents become more and more abnormal. Originally the verses narrate, describe, feel — that is, focus on a limited content; but later they center on themselves, on the abstract autonomy of language.

One can liken such revision to similar habits of independent stylists in painting. Thus there are three versions of El Greco's *Christ Casting the Moneylenders out of the Temple*. Whereas the first two bear a certain kinship to nature, the third is fully dominated by a style that has transmuted figures and objects into exaggerated elongations, rigidities, and sallownesses, thereby directing the eye away from the theme and toward the very penmanship of the artist. A more recent example is Picasso's set of eight lithographs of bulls (1945–46). They start with a natural depiction, lead to an anatomical and then a cubistic reduction of the animal, and end with a sketchy, totally disembodied linear structure. Here, too, the target of study is primarily the transforming style rather than the transformed object. And this is true of Mallarmé's poetry as well.

DEHUMANIZATION

A basic feature of modern poetry is its increasingly pronounced divorce from natural life. Together with Rimbaud, Mallarmé brought about a radical withdrawal from personal and confessional poetry, a genre that was still being cultivated on a high level by Verlaine. Older poetry, from the troubadours to the preromantics was hardly ever an experiential or diarylike communication of private feelings; only the misconception of a few literary historians infected by romanticism made it appear as if it were. But, on the other hand, this poetry, stylized and artistically varying the universal, remained within the range of the human and the familiar. Modern poetry excludes not only the private person but also normal humanness. None of the above-mentioned poems by Mallarmé can be explicated biographically — although for reasons of curiosity or laziness some critics have repeatedly tried to do so. But no poem by Mallarmé can be interpreted as an expression of a joy that we all know or a melancholy that we all experience and therefore comprehend. Mallarmé wrote from a center of gravity that would be difficult to name. "Soul" might do, but only if it is understood to refer not so much to discernible feelings as to a total inwardness that comprises both prerational and rational forces, dreamlike moods, and steely abstractions, and whose unity is perceptible in the vibratory currents of the poetic diction. Mallarmé continued along the route that Novalis and Poe had recommended, the road leading the poetic "I" to a suprapersonal neutrality.

Mallarmé often discussed this new conception of poetry. He once said that poetry is completely different from enthusiasm or delirium; it is a precise molding of words into a "voice that conceals both the poet and the reader" (p. 333). This definition is a tenet of absolute poetry, whose sound no longer seems to emanate from any human mouth or needs to reach any human ear. Elsewhere Mallarmé calls the verse-making intellect "a center of vibrating expectancy" (*centre de suspens vibratoire*) — a formula with a patent lack of any normal concept for the soul (p. 386). However, there are simpler statements. "Literature consists in doing away with the Gentleman who writes it" (p. 657). Writing poetry means "destroying a day of one's life or dying slightly" (p. 410), "devoting oneself to a unique task, different from anything striving to become life" (p. 552). Contemporaries describe Mallarmé as a kind person, gentle, courteous, sympathetic to the problems of others, extremely capable of suffering. His poetry reveals only his gentleness, the famous quiet speech he used in everyday conversation — but nothing of his humanity or his capacity for suffering. Once, when a visitor naïvely asked him, "Then you never weep in your verse?" the poet adroitly replied, "Nor do I blow my nose."

Even the early writings give evidence of this dehumanization, e.g., the prose piece *Igitur* (first draft, 1869). The title (a Latin conjunction) refers to an artificial phantom who, although not human, can, like a human being, perform a spiritual act: the act of self-abolition in the absoluteness of the Void. The dialogue scene *Hérodiade*, which Mallarmé worked on from 1864 until just before his death, and which remains a fragment, transfers a spiritual process into the biblical Salome. The girl, terrified of her body, of her drives, of fragrance and stars, grows aware of her destiny to become a creature of pure ideality. She rejects nature, atrophies as a girl, becomes part of a "white night of ice and cruel snow," a life-killing spirituality whose only pain is the inability to strain even higher. "Du reste, je ne veux rien d'humain [Moreover, I want nothing human]." This line, spoken by Salome, could stand as a motto for all of Mallarmé's poetry. Dehumanization tallies with self-isolation from vegetative nature (as in Baudelaire). The few objects in Mallarmé's late poems are nearly always artificial ones, such as things in a room. Flowers do occur, but they function as cultivated, unnatural symbols of the poetic word.

LOVE AND DEATH DEHUMANIZED

Mallarmé, too, knows the basic theme of all poetry: love. But, for him, the situation of love is an excuse to place spiritual acts on a level with such pretexts as an empty vase, a drinking glass, a lace curtain. Even a poem like the splendid sonnet *O si chère de loin* (1895; p. 61), closely resembling the conventional homage to a lady, is spirited away from natural feelings of love by its difficult language. In its subtle wisdom that a mute kiss expresses more than a word, it hints at Mallarmé's basic experience that only at the frontier of silence does the word realize its destiny — to become *logos* — as well as its insufficiency. The most explicit surmounting of a love situation by a spiritual one occurs in the sonnet *La Chevelure vol d'une flamme* (1887; p. 53). It exists on a zenith where words have left their earthly purpose of speech and communication in lucid syntax far below. An "I" appears quite casually, at a totally incidental point. There is no "you," only hair upon a forehead. The hair is metaphorically transmuted into a flame, which then releases a whole chain of images of burning; this is the sensuous event in the poem. But, behind it, the real event is totally different: hope for supreme ideality, failure, doubtful resignation to the finite. The metaphors deprive objects — namely, the hair — of their being; the inner stratum of the senses deprives the love sentiment of its being. The result is unfamiliarity.

We can clarify this process if we compare Mallarmé's sonnet with a thematically and artistically similar poem by the early-seventeenth-century Italian Marino, *Mentre che la sua donna si pettina* [While his lady combs her hair]. In accordance with baroque style (to which Mallarmé is unconsciously related), Marino decks the objective act (named in the title) with an abundance of complicated metaphors. The complex structure is soluble, however, because the elements derive from familiar reserves of metaphor (especially "sea" = "hair"; therefore, "ship," "shipwreck," etc.). The seventeenth-century reader (and today's educated reader) can find his bearings in this initially difficult poem because of the frame of reference provided by familiar imagery artfully combined and varied only on the surface. On the other hand, the metaphors in Mallarmé's sonnet are comprehensible, not in terms of a tradition, but only within Mallarmé's *œuvre* itself, in whose context they turn out to be far-reaching symbols of ontological circumstances. They detach themselves from their objective origin, become independent, and reach realms that no longer have anything to do with the beloved's hair. There is a further difference: Marino describes a purely external act (combing), while Mallarmé presents pseudoaction on the surface (hair falling over a forehead), behind which an abstract process of tension, unconnected with any human contact, takes place. The meaning of Marino's poem is simple: the lover, watching his beloved comb her hair, becomes conscious of his painfully happy love. A complete explication of Mallarmé's sonnet is impossible. The author prevents total interpretation for the sake of that remnant of ambiguity which keeps us from returning to the realm of the natural and the human.

We will obtain similar results if we compare one of Mallarmé's death poems with that of another poet: Mallarmé's *Toast funébre, à Théophile Gautier* (final version, 1887) and Victor Hugo's *Tombeau de Théophile Gautier* (1872; published posthumously in *Toute la lyre*, 1888). Hugo's poem mourns a man who, although dead, remains close by, cherished in the poet's memories of their friendship, and embellished by images of the beyond that are oratorically effective and intellectually unassuming. Mallarmé's poem, however, shifts the dead man to a remote, inaccessible place. The deceased has been consumed by mental processes; and, at his death, the soul died, too, while his *esprit* ("spirit," "intellect") survives in his poetic works. As soon as the man is gone, this legacy becomes free to assume a desirable impersonality — therefore, a double dehumanization. Mallarmé's first version (thematically identical to the last) was composed at the same time as Victor Hugo's poem. Neither author is conceivable without romanticism. Hugo, at the time of this poem a very old man, helped to found romanticism and perfected it. Mallarmé is its renegade heir. No bridge is possible between their contemporaneous poems.

POETRY AS PROTEST, AS WORK, AND AS A GAME

Mallarmé was thoroughly convinced that poetry is an irreplaceable language, the only area in which the adventitiousness, confinement, and indignity of reality could be totally wiped out. At times, this conviction assumed ritualistic form. But the poet had enough taste to chide any youthful admirer whose praise became too fulsome. Moreover, Mallarmé's cultlike isolation must be understood as an effort to preserve within the "torrent of banality" an island of gratuitous, spiritual purity: ". . . in the eyes of others, my work remains essentially like clouds in gloaming or stars: futile" (p. 358). Mallarmé continued the process which, ever since the beginning of the nineteenth century, had been leading poetry to a protest against the commercialized general public and the scientific expulsion of universal mystery and secret. It would be unfair to dismiss such protest as a literary affectation. It is simply a dissatisfaction with the world, a discontent that appears in the tension of modern form and which has always been a hallmark of superior minds.

Mallarmé was not fond of controversy. Yet every so often even he would lose his temper over the clamor of the general public. Along with many of his contemporaries, he recognized the power and the dangers of journalism. He abhorred newspapermen, who are "trained by the mob to give everything its vulgar character" (p. 276) and whose hack work, aimed at daily consumption, brings down the unique to their own level of scribbling. For Mallarmé, the book (i.e., the intellectual, spiritual opus, pure and simple) was an opposing creation that "conquers chance, word by word" (p. 387). "Chance" (*le hasard*) is Mallarmé's key word for mere reality and the contrast to that necessity which exists only in the spirit insofar as it obeys its own law. "Qui songe a les mains simples

[The man who thinks (dreams, imagines) has simple hands]'' (p. 412). This line proclaims simplicity to be uncompromisingness. Naturally, it is the simplicity of abstraction which, in withdrawing from the commercialized world, simultaneously leaves natural man behind. Modernity is extreme, even in the claim to power of the mind alien to nature. Therefore, and for other reasons as well, Mallarmé subscribes to the dictatorship of modern poetry as described earlier, in connection with Rimbaud.

For Mallarmé's own work, all this implied hard, dogged labor: experimentation toward that verbal ambiguity which, meant as a cogent sign of unreal tensions, can paradoxically be called precise. He rejected inspiration, which he regarded as poor subjectivity. He spoke of his "laboratory," of the "geometry of sentences"; he kept watch over his highly specialized verse-making with a technician's sense of responsibility — a technician of intellectuality and language magic. His song is a labor of cold perfection. It functions under conditions that, being difficult and unpopular, are labeled "hostile" (p. 535). The verse issuing from such work uses several vocables to create "a new, total word," securing in the latter an "isolation of language" (p. 368) — an insulation from all speech that serves a specific purpose, the "revolving of the heavenly body of poetic diction around itself," as Schelling had put it in similar, albeit less extreme, terms. The speaker of such a word, the poet, is also isolated. To ordinary eyes he is "lamentable," the chosen "sick man"; but for this very reason he is able to handle highly explosive material which he comes upon during his solitary labor over the word (p. 651). We can see that all this is a far-reaching continuation of the road traveled since Rousseau: poetry is seen as abnormality that rejects society.

On occasion, Mallarmé would wax ironical and talk about the meaning of poetry in terms that an ordinary mind might consider a death verdict: "What good is all this? / It's a game" (p. 647); or "the splendor of lying." But the joke is in the unpopular connotations of such concepts. *Game* refers to pointlessness, aimlessness, absolute freedom of the creative spirit; *lie* refers to the goal of unreality in creative products. Both terms advert to the provisional character of the accomplishment as compared with the difficulty of the task. These concepts play; they play deceptively with truth.

NOTHINGNESS AND FORM

Mallarmé's poetic labor also strove for the formal precision of the verse. His poems obey conventional laws of meter, rhyme, and stanza, but this formal rigor contrasts with the ethereal contents. "The further we stretch our contents and the thinner we make them, the more we have to bind them in clearly marked, palpable, unforgettable lines," he wrote in a letter to R. Ghil on March 7, 1885. The contrast between "thinned" (incorporeal) content and binding form is the contrast between danger and salvation. We established something analogous for Baudelaire. Mallarmé, in a letter to Cazalis (July, 1866), wrote a line indicating the ontological background for the function of form in his works: "After finding nothingness, I found beauty." This concept of beauty includes the beauty of metrical perfection. Mallarmé's ontological schema (hinted at in the above letter and clarified later) sets nothingness (the absolute) and *logos* in relationship to one another: the *logos* is where nothingness is born in its spiritual existence. According to old ideas of Romance culture, poetic forms are phenomenal manifestations of the *logos*. This intellectual context helps us to understand Mallarmé's statement. His lyrics, destroying reality, call all the more strongly for "beauty," the shaped beauty of language. Beautiful diction, insofar as the metrics satisfy the highest demands, will thus become a vessel for the salvation of the Void (in an objective sense). Subsequently, Mallarmé dropped his ontological motivation of form. What remained among modern poets (e.g., Valéry, Guillén, and others akin to them) was the fact that utterly abstract and multivalent verse demands a binding form as a frame of reference in space devoid of objects, as a direction and a measure for its song. Gottfried Benn, in 1921 and frequently thereafter, spoke of the "form-demanding power of nothingness." Mallarmé's explanation of form confirms the fact that the divorce of beauty from truth (an estrangement begun in the eighteenth century) has become definitive. Yet this very beauty of absolute form guarantees that even in the presence of nothingness, the splendor of the *logos* and of the dignity of human existence cannot be extinguished.

SAYING THE UNSAID: A FEW METHODS OF STYLE

Few readers are patient enough to decode Mallarmé's unusual language. He reckoned only with this minority — so far as he reckoned with any readers at all. Whatever we may think of this abnormal difficulty of language, we must realize that — albeit extreme — it is no isolated hallmark of modern poetry. Mallarmé strove to justify his special diction in a number of reflections. These focus on the idea that language has regained that freedom by means of which it remains exposed to the "primal lightning of logic" (p. 386), unspent by purposes of communication, and safe from the *rigor mortis* of clichés that would prevent thought and poetry from alleging themselves to be something entirely new. For Mallarmé, verse-making means renewing the primal act of linguistic creation so radically that speech is always the articulation of what was hitherto unspoken. Although

86

such ideas had often been expressed before, he carried them further, theoretically and practically: the initial utterance of the unuttered should preserve its primariness so that, in an almost immortalized nonassimilability into delimiting understanding, that utterance may be kept from returning to the treadmill of the commonplace. Mallarmé desires the poetic word not just as a higher, more festive degree of intelligible language, but as an insoluble dissonance with regard to normality.

The technical elements of such poetic diction must be unusual. We can merely adumbrate here. We find verbs in the infinitive — instead of the expected conjugated form — participles modeled after the Latin ablative absolute, inversions contrary to French grammar, a removal of the distinction between the singular and the plural, adjectival use of adverbs, reversal of normal word order, new indefinite articles, etc. Instead of following temporal or logical sequences in objects and themes, Mallarmé makes an impossible attempt to state, by means of the inevitably temporal unfolding of language, something simultaneous or even beyond all time. Every preposition has several concurrent meanings. His foremost technique is to tinge the meaning of one word with that of its neighbor: "Words . . . are lit up by mutual reflections," as he puts it programmatically (p. 366). In a quatrain composed for a library, we find the words *livres* and *délivres* (p. 162); in accordance with this philological technique, *délivres* is to be construed simultaneously as being derived from its rhyming word *livres*, so that the verb combines "books" and "liberate" to mean "liberate from books." [3]

A far greater accumulation of such technical elements occurs in the prose of *Divagations*. It is a contrapuntal writing, full of mysterious subtleties and capable of interweaving two, and sometimes several, trains of thought so that they speak at once. This process is rather similar to music, especially in that the simultaneity of multiple strands of thought produces a dynamic synthesis, imposing itself as a separate entity on the individual strands, and comparable to the synthetic effect of a phrase of polyphonic music.

No one was able to adopt these stylistic elements (a proof of Mallarmé's nonassimilability). Only a few of them crop up in subsequent poetry, and mainly those serving the reversal or intersection of thematic systems and the deobjectification of reality. Mallarmé's stylistic technique, a protest against modern reading haste, aimed to create an area in which the word recovers its originality and its permanence. Characteristically, the poet succeeded only by disintegrating the sentence into fragments. Discontinuity

3. See D. Steland, *Dialektische Gedanken in Mallarmés "Divagations"* (Munich, 1965), pp. 9 f.

in lieu of connection, adjacency instead of construction: these are the stylistic marks of an internal discontinuity, a speech on the brink of the impossible. The fragment becomes a symbol of approaching perfection: ". . . fragments . . . are nuptial evidence of the Idea" (p. 387). This idea, too, is a prime constituent of modern aesthetics.

THE NEARNESS OF SILENCE

Mallarmé knows and wants the nearness of the impossible. It is the nearness of silence. His poetry is imbued with silence in the form of "silent" (i.e., annihilated) objects and a language whose vocabulary shrinks over the years and whose tone grows softer and softer. In Mallarmé's reflections, "silence" is one of the most frequent concepts. Thus he calls poetry a "tacit flight of abstraction" (p. 385), and the written page a "fading" (p. 409), a magic perceived in full only when words sound back into the "silent" concert from which they emanated (p. 380). The ideal poem would be "the silent poem of pure white" (p. 367). In statements like these, mystical thoughts recur, attributing the insufficiency of language to the experience of transcendence. But now we are confronted with a mysticism of nothingness, just as we found a mysticism of empty transcendence in Baudelaire and Rimbaud.

Mallarmé realized that the nearness of the impossible was the boundary of his entire work. The introductory sonnet in his *Salut* names the three basic forces of his poetry: "solitude," the fundamental situation of the modern poet; "reef" (*récif*), on which he founders; and "star" (*étoile*), the unattainable ideality, which is at fault for everything. He once admitted in a conversation, "My work is a cul-de-sac." Mallarmé's isolation is complete and deliberate. Like Rimbaud, although in a different way, he drives his work to the point at which it abolishes itself and even announces the end of all poetry. Oddly enough, this action was repeated in the poetry of the twentieth century. It must therefore express a deep-seated urge of modernity.

OBSCURITY: COMPARISON WITH GÓNGORA

Mallarmé's isolation is also confirmed when he is compared with earlier poets of a kindred style. Critics have often likened him, because of his obscurity, to one of the most obscure of earlier European poets, the Spaniard Góngora. The two of them resemble one another in many details, as well as in the goal of their poetic technique (which is why Spanish translations of Mallarmé sound — and deliberately try to appear — Góngoristic). Góngora, too, abolishes reality and normal linguistic expression by means of a remote world of created conceptions and an arabesque structure of richly curved, complicated sentences, farfetched metaphors and vocables, hidden allusions, and cryptic associations. Yet we should not overlook the differences. No matter how enigmatic the syntax in Góngora's poetry, no matter how veiled the periphrasis, he still uses familiar symbolical and mythological material. His poetry is written for an elite whom the poet can assume to be aware of recherché stylistic charms and who will welcome his dark lyrics as a pleasurable opportunity to solve esoteric enigmas and exercise the mind. Góngora said so himself, employing arguments that have always been advanced by authors and theoreticians of obscure poetry: obscurity shields against vulgar eyes; it increases the intrinsic value, confirms the link with a social or intellectual aristocracy. Thus Góngora's poems imply a contact with an admittedly tiny audience.[4] The illumination of his obscurities requires in essence a correct rearrangement of his syntax and the reduction of his periphrases to whatever they circumscribe.

In this respect, Mallarmé's poetry is totally different. It was only in his early writings that he viewed obscurity as a shield against unwelcome popularity (1862; pp. 261 ff.). His mature poetry, to a more extreme degree than Rimbaud's, is directed toward no actual reader. At best, it has to create its own reader, a specialist for its specialized texts. The dehumanization destroys the author-work-reader triangle and dissociates the work from this double human relevance. "Impersonalized, the volume, as soon as the author separates himself from it, demands no approach from the reader. . . . It takes place all alone: created, existing. . . ." (p. 372). Moreover, Mallarmé's symbolism is all his own. The few symbols that are not his — e.g., swan, azure, hair — belong to a recent tradition (Baudelaire); but most of them are his alone and can be understood only as such — e.g., glass, glacier, window, dice. Here, as in other aspects, no tradition can aid in unraveling the syntax or the semantics. This factor, too, constitutes an enormous distinction between him and the earlier obscure poets. Modern symbolism, which transforms everything into a token for something else without fastening that something else in a binding sense structure, must inevitably work with self-sufficient symbols beyond the confines of understanding. And, finally, Mallarmé derives obscure poetry from the darkness that lies at the rock bottom of all things and "stirs faintly only in the night of writing" (pp. 382 ff.). In other words, obscurity is not poetical arbitrariness but an ontological necessity. The meaning of

4. A letter of his explains this in detail. See Góngora, *Obras completas*, ed. Mille y Jiménez (Madrid, 1943), p. 796.

a Mallarmé poem may be, must be, explicable, but only at the cost of reducing the multiplicity of relations and references in which the poem exists. The expounder of Mallarmé must remain in this space between understanding and reduction.

Diderot, Novalis, and Baudelaire had voiced a demand for obscure poetry. Their demand, when compared with the radical results attained since their time, is rather innocuous, even though they launched the development that began with Rimbaud and was brought by Mallarmé to a level of deeply meditated obscurity such as no twentieth-century poet could strive for or even desire.

Such poetry can be travestied, and by the poet himself. Mallarmé's rhymed letter addresses (pp. 81 ff.) are his self-parodies. When a journalist impatiently requested a manuscript from him, he replied, "Just wait until I've added a bit more obscurity." A visitor, asking whether a sonnet alluded to dawn or evening or the absolute, was squelched with "It refers to my bureau." Self-parody (of which only sovereign intellects are capable) reveals a forte of this obscure poetry: its playful freedom and the realization of its provisory character. But all this does not lessen isolation.

SUGGESTIVE, NOT INTELLIGIBLE, POETRY

In such poetry, language is no longer communication. Communication presupposes a mutuality between two people. But Mallarmé's diction is exclusively self-utterance. We have frequently mentioned the role of the absurd in modern poetry. The absurd is present in Mallarmé, too, and we can sum up its presence in the following way: the poet speaks so that he will not be understood. This fact appears less absurd, although not less abnormal, if we reject the ordinary concept of understanding and substitute the concept of infinite suggestiveness. The ambivalence of Mallarmé's poetry exerts a compelling effect on the reader, the unusual tone of its language transfixing the reader's ear. Mallarmé is thinking of a reader "open to multiple comprehension" (p. 283). And, in point of fact, Mallarmé's poetry provokes the reader to continue the unfinished productive act occurring within, and to continue that act by his own further production — which avoids any settled conclusion, just as the poem avoids one. The endless potentials of this language affect the reader only insofar as they inspire in him equally endless potentials of interpretation. The reader should not so much decipher as enter the enigmatic, where he dimly senses but does not prematurely stop deciphering, and where he may even come upon meanings not intended by the author. Mallarmé's greatest disciple,

Paul Valéry, subsequently described this situation: "My poetry has whatever meaning anyone ascribes to it."

For this very loose contact with the reader, Mallarmé used the concept of "suggestion." This notion derives essentially from Baudelaire, who had employed it in connection with the concept of magic. Mallarmé acknowledged in an essay (1896) that the common basis of modern styles resides in the fact that their "idealism avoids natural objects and, as too brutal, a precise thought that would arrange them" (p. 365), preferring instead to be pure suggestion. This conception, if we read further, is the reverse of objective description: "evocation . . . allusion" (p. 366). "Naming an object will spoil three-fourths of the enjoyment of a poem, the enjoyment being meant to be divined gradually: suggesting the object is the ideal" (p. 869). It is significant that for Mallarmé, and for most later poets as well, the suggestive effect of a poem is the only bridge to the reader. But no union with the reader materializes. The suggestion simply offers the reader the possibility of some sort of sympathetic vibration. This does not mean that the reader cannot recognize the decipherable basic themes in Mallarmé's poetry or pursue them to the very edge of inexplicability. If that were the case, interpretation would be senseless. But recognition is no longer forced. The isolation of obscure poetry deliberately refuses to terminate itself.

THE ONTOLOGICAL SCHEMA

(a) Estrangement from Reality

We have made frequent mention of Mallarmé's ontological schema, which forms the actual background of his mature poetry. This schema pilots the poem, almost by remote control, and in such a way that the progress of the poem turns into an ontological event. We are aware of the schema because in the most diverse lyrics the same basic acts recur, giving the simplest themes, words, and images a dimension that cannot be explained by those themes, words, and images. The theoretical rationale is to be found in the *Divagations* and in a few of his letters. We need not criticize the schema; our job is to evaluate it as a symptom of modernity, not as a philosophical accomplishment. Its eminently original content resides in its ontological interpretation and poetic reintegration of the basic experiences of modernity: the abortive passion for transcendence, the discrepancies, the dichotomy. And yet the poetry, despite all these possibly exorbitant demands, never sacrifices its lyrical being. Mallarmé's great artistry manages to join the ontological schema and the poetic word in that vibrating sonority and bewitching mystery which have always been, albeit to a more limited extent, the basis of poetry.

Our discussion at the beginning of this chapter revealed that one of the fundamental acts in Mallarmé's poems is the ejection of objects and objectivity into absence. This ejection denotes, first of all, the same striving away from reality as is found in Baudelaire's theories and Rimbaud's verse. Furthermore, it is linked to the same historical factors (which we have examined in the previous chapters). An additional factor was the growing pressure exerted by naturalistic writing. Yet Mallarmé increased all these factors in depth. His negation of reality appears as the consequence of an ontological discrepancy between reality and language.

A number of programmatic statements reveal Mallarmé's artistic goal. "Exclude [from your song] reality for being base" (p. 73). A prose passage contains ideas which can be summed up as follows: nature is present; we can add only material inventions, cities, railroads; true freedom, however, consists in seizing hidden relationships owing to an inwardness that, in accordance with its own judgment, extends across and simplifies the world; and that is the way of poetic creation; "[produce] the notion of an object . . . that fails to appear." The elimination of positive reality and the introduction of the creative imagination belong together. In poetry, this leads to a complex process, including the symbolic use of inorganic things. For Mallarmé, as for Baudelaire, metals, jewels, and precious stones become emblems of a spirituality superior to nature. This explains the part they play in *Hérodiade*, as equivalents of the level of life-extinction toward which the virginal girl develops. It explains Mallarmé's loving descriptions of sumptuous apparel and jewelry in *La Dernière Mode*, a fashion magazine he edited. However, the strongest negation of reality was the above-mentioned absenting of objects, together with the avoidance of unambiguous language. One way of achieving ambiguity is periphrasis. This device is a point of contact between, on the one hand, Mallarmé's stylistic intention to blot out reality and, on the other, certain peculiarities of baroque literature and its French variety, *préciosité*. For Mallarmé, too, periphrasis is meant to unburden an object of its brutal materiality and the effeteness of the customary word for the object. In addition, he uses periphrasis to unravel the word into qualities belonging to inner realms. A sentence from *Hérodiade* goes: "Light . . . those torches where the wax in weak fire and among vain gold sheds some alien tear" (p. 48). This is a circumlocution for candles. Yet these delimited objects are overwhelmed by multiple symbolic allusions: weeping, vanity, alienness. The allusions are the true content of the passage; no longer part of the candles,

92

they belong to Herodias' inner situation and constitute some of Mallarmé's fundamental themes.

(b) Ideality, the Absolute, Nothingness

The withdrawal from reality is accompanied by a striving toward ideality. At times, Mallarmé seems to be touching on Platonic thoughts. A line in an essay asserts: "The divine transposition for whose achievement man exists goes from the fact to the ideal" (p. 522). This upward movement, however, has a rather un-Platonic character: the "ideal" (a vague word) has no metaphysical existence. All the other positive terms for ideality remain equally imprecise. It is only the negative expression that creates a more precise concept: *le néant*, "nothingness," "the Void." This is a further step, and the most extreme one, along the path of empty transcendence which we have been tracing from Baudelaire.

We cannot go into the details of how Mallarmé arrived at this concept. Nor can we examine the possible and entangled impulses from German philosophy (Hegel, Schelling, perhaps Fichte) and negative theology. We will only indicate a few salient points. As of 1865, Mallarmé very conspicuously uses the word *néant* in passages whose themes were expressed earlier by such words as *azure, dream, ideal*. He writes in a letter (January, 1866), "The Void is truth." A major text consists of the already mentioned fragments of *Igitur* (1869). They show the complementary roles of the two concepts, "the absolute" and "the Void." The former expresses an ideality in which all "adventitiousness" of the empirical has been wiped out. Progress toward the absolute leads through the "absurd" (notice Mallarmé's recurrent use of this cardinal word of modernity) — the abandonment of the habitual, the natural, the living. The absolute, so called because it has to be detached from time, place, and object, is termed, when completely detached, the Void; pure being and pure nonbeing become identical (as in Hegel). Igitur, the allegorical character of the text, goes down to the seaside graves, taking along a vial of poison which "contains the drop of Void that the sea still lacks." He throws dice, and, when the dice stand still, time and everything in time, both life and death, have stopped; all that remains is empty, absolute space: the Void.

Mallarmé is careful enough not to indulge in any speculations on the Void. Consequently, we must likewise refrain from any speculation. But we must appreciate the part played by this concept in Mallarmé's poetry, and we must underscore the fact that the most negative of all concepts occurs at a peak of modern poetry.

The reader should not, however, think that Mallarmé intends a qualified

THE STRUCTURE OF MODERN POETRY

nothingness in the manner of moral nihilism. For him, the Void is an ontological concept of idealistic origin. He is concerned with the inadequacy of all reality. And only idealistic thinking can experience this inadequacy. But when the ideally adequate, by which data are measured, has soared so high that no definition can attain it, and when it remains as pure indefiniteness, then it must of necessity be called the Void. Borrowing from Baudelaire's sketches of empty ideality, Mallarmé gives his own Void the characteristic of the force of height, a compelling force that overwhelms the spirit like a visitation. The universal modern fate of having no original belief or tradition generates the desire not only to leave the height empty (as Baudelaire and Rimbaud did) but also to radicalize it into nothingness. Mallarmé's nihilism may be understood as the condition of a spirit that has removed all reality for the sake of creative freedom. We can speak of an idealistic nihilism, the result of an almost superhuman decision of abstraction to think of the absolute as the pure (i.e., detached from all contents) essence of being, and to approach the absolute tentatively, with a poetry in which the language itself makes the Void present to the extent that the destruction of reality permits.

(c) The Void and Language

Mallarmé's chief ontological question, however, involves the relationship between the Void and language. It is the poet's existential question. His answers include vestiges of the Greek idea of *logos*, although no contact with Greek antiquity is discernible. It is quite possible that Mallarmé's thoughts which carried impulses of romantic linguistics to a conclusion were original, that he did not realize that his theories very faintly echoed Greek ideas on language. In May, 1867, in a letter to Cazalis, he wrote:

> I am now impersonal. I am no longer Stéphane as you knew him. Now I am a faculty of the spiritual universe to see itself and develop by means of that which was my ego. I am able to take upon myself only such development as is absolutely necessary so that the universe may find its identity in this ego.

The wording is a bit careless. But, all the same, its meaning is clear: the empirical "I" is superseded by an impersonal "I," the place where the "universe" achieves its spiritual identity. We can add a statement made in 1895: "A race, ours, . . . was allotted the honor of giving viscera to the fear of itself suffered, other than as human conscience, by metaphysical and cloistral eternity" (p. 391). The abstruse imagery of this sentence veils the supplement to the epistolary utterance above. Both contain the idea that man, so far as he is intellect and thus language, is the self-consummation of absolute being; for being finds its spiritual birth here and only here, where the absolute, understood to be the Void, calls upon language — *logos (le Verbe)* — to find the place of its pure manifestation.

This idea, which Mallarmé articulates occasionally, if not frequently, unravels many enigmas of his poetry, especially the removal of all objects, all reality, into absence. This removal signifies a good deal more than artistic rejection of reality. It is meant to be an ontological process by means of which language gives an object absence that categorially assimilates the object into the absolute (the Void) and makes possible the purest presence (detached from all objectivity) in the word. Things materially demolished by a language that proclaims their absence attain in that same language — because it names them — their spiritual, intellectual existence.

Thus, ontologically, the modern power of the word and of unlimited imagination is established. The word, grasped in this way, is the creative deed of pure intellect. In its absoluteness, it ignores empirical reality and is left to its dynamics. The crucial point was that Mallarmé saw these dynamics not as adventitious subjectivity but as ontological events containing their own intrinsic necessity. Nevertheless, he, too, can call the absolute *esprit* ("spirit," "intellect") "imagination" as well as "dream." Both terms had been used synonymously for creative freedom long before Mallarmé. Their appearance in his works is important for us insofar as it indicates the development of the concept of imagination since the late eighteenth century and the scope of that concept when it was passed on to the twentieth century. We can compare the concept with what we have said about Rousseau's, Diderot's, Baudelaire's, and Rimbaud's ideas on imagination. These writers came to view imagination more and more as a force superior to reality and even dictatorial. Mallarmé, placing imagination on even a higher level, regards it as the home of his spiritual existence, a home demanded by absolute being. The consistency with which all these ideas join earlier ones is astonishing and reconfirms the structural unity of modern poetry and modern thoughts on poetry. Furthermore, Mallarmé's concept of imagination legitimizes the basic feature of such poetry: destruction of reality. Even before discovering an ontological rationale, Mallarmé claimed this feature for himself. In a letter to Lefébure (1867), he writes that he has produced his work only by expunging, that he has been forging deeper and deeper into the experience of "absolute darkness." And then, alluding to Dante, he adds: "Destruction became my Beatrice."

One of Mallarmé's favorite words for the removal of objectivity is *abolition*. It is surrounded by similar words: *vacuum, white, emptiness, absence*. These are the negative key words of his ontological poetics and poetry. Another key word, apparently positive, is *fleur* ("flower," "bloom"), and often specific flowers — *rose, lily. Fleur* symbolically designates language as an essential characteristic of mankind. "Worship of the vocable . . . is simply . . . the glorification of the innermost being of the race, in its flower, speech" (p. 492). The cardinal virtue and power of language, however, is poetry. And now the key passage:

> What good is the wonder of transposing from a fact of nature to its vibratory near-disappearance by the playing of speech, for all that; unless so that, without the constraint of a close or concrete recall, pure notion may issue forth. . . . a flower! . . . rises musically . . . absent from all bouquets [p. 368].

After the preceding discussion, these phrases require no exegesis. Once again, Mallarmé interprets poetry as the annihilation of objectivity but adds that such annihilation occurs because, in the word, the object is to become a "pure notion," a spiritual entity. Yet this notion or idea can exist nowhere but in the poetic word, which is why the flower is "absent from all bouquets." (This remark, together with Rimbaud's quoted above, on p. 57, was printed in the catalogue of the Picasso exhibition at Paris, in 1955.) Poetry turns into an activity that, in lonesome resplendence, shines its dream playing and its magical music into an annihilated world. And, on its ultimate levels of meaning, it expresses abstract figures and tensions in inconclusive ambiguities. For this reason Mallarmé employs the concept of the arabesque — as Baudelaire did — expanding it into a "total arabesque," which instantly turns into a "ciphering grown silent" (p. 648).

SES PURS ONGLES

In 1887, Mallarmé edited the final version of an untitled sonnet which begins, "Ses purs ongles . . . [Its pure nails . . .]" (p. 68). It can serve to illustrate his poetic practice of negating objectivity and creating language. In the original form (1868) the wording was different, but the themes and the subject matter were the same. Mallarmé commented on this initial version in a letter to Cazalis (July 18, 1868):

> I've taken the sonnet from a study I'm planning on the word. . . . It consists as far as possible of white and black, and is suitable for an etching of dream and emptiness. For instance: an open window at night; a room with no one inside; a night made of absence and inquiry; no furniture; at most, a hint of indefinite sideboards, with a dying mirror in the background,

astrally and incomprehensibly reflecting the Big Dipper and thereby linking the deserted home with the sky.

These comments hold equally for the latter version.

Ses purs ongles très haut dédiant leur onyx,	Its pure nails highly consecrating their onyx,
L'Angoisse, ce minuit, soutient, lampadophore,	Anguish, as a midnight lampadephore, holds up
Maint rêve vespéral brûlé par le Phénix	Many a vesper dream burnt up by the Phoenix
Que ne recueille pas de cinéraire amphore	And not received by any cinerary amphora
Sur les crédences, au salon vide: nul ptyx,	On the sideboards, in the empty parlor: no ptyxis,
Aboli bibelot d'inanité sonore,	An abolished knickknack of sonorous inanity,
(Car le Maître est allé puiser des pleurs au Styx	(For the Master has gone to draw tears from the Styx
Avec ce seul objet dont le Néant s'honore).	With this one object the Void is proud of).
Mais proche la croisée au nord vacante, un or	But near the vacant north window, a gold
Agonise selon peut-être le décor	Is dying, perhaps along the decoration
Des licornes ruant du feu contre une nixe,	Of unicorns rushing fire at a nix,
Elle, défunte nue en le miroir, encore	She, a deceased nude in the mirror, while
Que, dans l'oubli fermé par le cadre, se fixe	In the enframed, enclosed oblivion, soon
De scintillations sitôt le septuor.	The sevensome of scintillations settles.

We hear rhymes of a weird and jarring fascination. The odd vocabulary (which no translation can reproduce) derives partly from the Greek; the poet uses it not for the sake of local color but to imbue the text with an astonishing linguistic potency. What do we have here? First of all, Anguish, with several attributes. Although appearing as a kind of allegorical figure, it has no life. As an entity, it haunts the entire poem. Also present

97

are the night, an empty parlor, a vacant window, a dying gold. There are other things as well, but they exist only in language. The "vesper dream" is "burned up" and not received by any urn; the ptyxis is "no ptyxis." And then comes the significant line that describes this abolished object as unimportant ("knickknack") and existing only in sounds — albeit vain, inadequate sonority. The "Master" (which?) has gone off, taking along that object which "the Void is proud of": the Void achieves pride precisely in the eradicated object, which, since it does not exist, has only verbal being in the word that labels it. The nix of the third stanza is "a deceased nude." Of the things remaining present, the window and the looking glass are Mallarméan symbols for a view into the endlessness of transcendence. The other objects are annihilated and simultaneously are reborn in language. Throughout the sonnet, a dying occurs, accompanying the transition from presence to absence. Finally, we hear that the starry twinkle will "soon" settle: time, a barely stirring present in the octave, will change into timelessness — *will* change, future tense. The poem can and is meant to graze the absolute only later and hypothetically, just as it can touch absences (the Void) only by ciphering meanings. If it wanted to fully absorb the absolute of timelessness and thinglessness, it could not survive as a poem; it would be merely a silence, an empty spot. The language halts at the outermost bound at which it can still, by obliterating objects, create in the negative word itself a space to admit the Void. The entry of the Void is accompanied by Anguish, which is able to expand and which impregnates the remaining objects, rendering them uncanny, its own uncanniness intensified by the absence of the other things. All this is the doing of the language; whatever occurs in it can never take place in any real world.

THE ONTOLOGICAL DISSONANCE

At this point we must remark that in our effort to approach this difficult author we have made his temper seem more harmonious than it is. His mind is actually slashed by a dichotomy, the same one that was discernible in Baudelaire and Rimbaud: the dichotomy between language and ideality, desire and ability, striving and attaining. Yet even this dichotomy has ontological causes. Mallarmé's struggle to find such causes may be viewed as indicative of how deep and wide the gulf really is. Thus, the corresponding idea and its appearance in a poem turn out to be further symptoms of the modern Zeitgeist — more specifically, of a hallmark that we have repeatedly labeled the domination of dissonance. Mallarmé made it an ontological dissonance.

The poems are haunted by such words as *reef, shipwreck, plunge, night,*

98

vanity, key words for failure. Yet failure can forgo these words and speak in the symbolic texture alone. There are two types of failure here: the failure of language before the absolute (for the sake of simplification, we may call this type subjective failure) and, conversely, the failure of the absolute before language (objective failure).

We have offered several illustrations of the former, but we can supplement them briefly. A sentence in *Igitur* reads: "I utter the word in order to plunge it back into its inanity" (p. 451). Another essay claims that ". . . anything, any vehicle or placement, now offered to the ideal is contrary to it." And immediately Mallarmé speaks of "the mutual contamination of the work and the means" (p. 371). Precisely because of its acme, the ideal plan for the work allows the eternal lowness of language to emerge, thus preventing the consummation of the lofty plan. Transcending *Igitur*, the late poem *Un Coup de dés* (printed with a contrapuntal arrangement of the syntax) has the following theme: even the Void is unattained because the mind cannot escape "hazards" (language and time); man is the "bitter prince of the reef" (p. 469). A poem feared as a peak of incomprehensibility, *Prose pour des Esseintes* (p. 55), poetics in verse, can be grasped in connection with this theme of the inadequacy of language.[5] The first ten strophes address poetry that strenuously aims at an unreachable goal, and they focus on the possibility of the creation of poetry. Then the curve descends: a work can merely smile at the goal but will not attain it; the "spirit of struggle" inherent in the poem (the discord between desire and goal) must endure as painful knowledge that "that country exists" (the land of ideality), and that it will always force poetry to raise itself to that realm and to fail as well, but with the benefit that failure guarantees the invisible presence of ideality.

This is still along the lines of Baudelaire, albeit with an ontological twist. But now comes something very different. For Mallarmé, the dehumanization has become so extreme that he shifts the ultimate origin of poetry and thought from man to absolute being. Almost as if under compulsion, he had to think about and treat in poetry the dissonance of the modern mind as a characteristic of absolute being. More markedly than in his other themes, he replaced an attainable contact between man and transcendence with a total loss of contact. Not only is language insufficient when it is supposed to give a spiritual birth to the absolute; but the absolute, too, yields only inadequately to language. Both poles, language and absolute being, obey the law of failure. Although the highest possibility for Mallarmé's poetry remains within inadequacy, this poetry,

5. Since the title has puzzled most readers, we may note that *prose* goes back to church Latin *prosa*, which, among other things, denotes "hymn." Appropriately, the poem is composed of hymnal quatrains, and the word *hymne* occurs in the second stanza.

because of the ontological dissonance, achieves the greatest degree of disaster. What succeeds is the word for the abortive contact between the absolute and man. And the verses utter the word very quietly.

A brief discussion of two poems will demonstrate this. The first poem, *Autre Eventail* (p. 58), depicts a double action, objective and spiritual. The first action is as simple as can be: an open fan is moved and then folded together. Yet this act is identical to the spiritual one; we might even say that one symbolizes the other. For the fan contains "pure, pathless delight" upward, toward an unbounded, expanding ideality. But "space," representing ideality, "trembles . . . like a large kiss / That, insane at being born for no one, / Can neither shoot forth nor calm down." Even the absolute suffers from isolation; its "kiss" does not find a mind to receive it. And so the fan closes. The will, striving upward, fails also, sinks back upon itself, retaining nothing but "a shrouded smile," the awareness of double failure. Only one thing remains: ". . . rosy river banks stagnant on the evenings of gold"— the sheen of the absolute. The shimmer "remains" in both senses of the word: it stays where it is, never progressing, never becoming a full light; and it endures, immortalized in the word that has engaged the impossible. The word, despite its insufficiency, is an expedient home for the Void with its own isolation. The symbolism of the final strophe expresses it in the following way: ". . . this is it, / That white, closed flight that you lean / Against the fire of a bracelet." The dark, lovely poem is haunted by a deep resignation.

The second poem, the sonnet *Petit Air II* (p. 66), is written in a strained syntax contrary to the analytical sentence structure of the French language; the poet places adverbs, verbs, and appositives before the subject in order to point out that those parts of speech convey the important points. A first impression might be that the "ditty" is simply describing a painful idyl, for Mallarmé has completely succeeded in identifying the ontological act with the imagery. "Untamably," a voice sounds from high above, furious and silent, compelled and lost. It sounds at the very moment that "my hope" (the will to the absolute) surges up. It is the voice of "The bird you never hear / A second time in your life," the voice of the absolute. But, importunate as it may be, it remains silent, reaching no one — once again, the isolation of the absolute. And then a sobbing bursts forth, dying out in uncertainty as to whether it sprang from "my" breast or the bird's — whether it was my sob because I did not hear the voice, or the bird's sob because it could not reach me. All that is left after this double failure is the bird, "Torn apart . . . / Lying on some path": the absolute, incapable of attaining a complete spiritual existence. The statement wavers, however; it is more of a premonition that all this *could* exist than the knowledge that it actually does. At this utmost extreme of his poetry,

Mallarmé will not venture to make an unequivocal statement. He limits himself to symbolic action with a host of possible meanings. And this, too, is a failure, a deliberate one. For only a faint, allusive song can protect the almost incomprehensible tragedy of being from effeteness and oblivion owing to delimiting comprehension.

The German novelist Jean Paul Richter, in his philosophical *Vorschule der Ästhetik* (1812), speaks of the "current *Zeitgeist*," which, rather than copy nature, egomaniacally annihilates the world and the universe in order to create a full and free scope for itself in the Void." This statement, in the section on poetic nihilists, foreshadows modern poetry, including Mallarmé's — just as the character of Roquairol, in Richter's novel *Titan*, anticipates Baudelaire. There is a difference, however: in Mallarmé, "egomania" has given way to an ontologically motivated independence of the spirit. Whatever we may think of the motive, we must appreciate the sincerity with which this quiet, self-sacrificing man thought out and artistically realized, in all its consequences and implications, the negative condition assigned to modern poetry. Such verse must of necessity be difficult and obscure. But its right to exist lies in its intrinsic consistency.

OCCULTISM, MAGIC, AND LANGUAGE MAGIC

Mallarmé was keenly interested in occultist literature. Friends of his introduced him to the writings of Eliphas Lévi (Abbé Constant). In addition, Mallarmé corresponded with V. E. Michelet, who was promulgating the secret doctrines of late antiquity that were attributed to Hermes Trismegistus; Michelet used the term *hermeticism* for them and recommended their application in poetry. (Today, in France, *hermétisme* still means primarily occultism, alchemy, etc.) Mallarmé agreed with Michelet. In the essay *Magie*, the poet says: "[There] exists, between old practices and the sorcery that poetry will remain, a secret parity"; thus poetry is "evoking, in a deliberate darkness, the silent object, with allusive and never direct words. . . ." And the poet is an "enchanter of letters" (pp. 399 f.). Next he mentions concepts like fairy, magician, charm (in the Latin sense of a spell or incantation, the connotation meant in Valéry's title *Charmes* for his collection of verse). Mallarmé speaks of "the alchemists, our forebears." All this expresses his belief in a correspondence between poetry and magic rather than his actual belonging to occultist groups. Nevertheless, this belief, held by earlier writers, is stronger in Mallarmé. He, too, feels the need of modern poets to connect a highly intellectual poetry with magical, archaic levels of the psyche. The language magic of his verse, in conjunction with the obscurity of the contents, is the most suitable device to exert the suggestiveness described above, which he would like to substitute for simple intelligibility.

Language magic can manifest itself in the sonority of the lines or in the verbal impulse that guides the verse-making. A famous remark of Mallarmé's is: ". . . the poet . . . leaves the initiative to the words, which are mobilized by the clash of their inequality" (p. 366). Another sentence reads: ". . . the rhythm [of the infinite], among the keys of the verbal keyboard, yields, as if under the interrogation of fingering, to the use of apt, even everyday, words" (p. 648). Mallarmé admittedly based many of his poems on some linguistic impulse or revised his first drafts by strongly focusing on one such impulse. One poem begins: "O si chère de loin et proche et blanche . . ." (p. 61). This first line twice indicates distance (*loin, proche*) and, at the same time, a color (*blanche*). It is almost as if this onset were to grasp a further conception of space. But then something different happens, something unconnected with space. *Blanche* is not part of an objectively ordered series of concepts. The language itself is acting. The origin of *blanche* lies in the sound *ch* occurring in *chère* and *proche*, spreading forth as an independent sound and evoking a word that will do it justice. This is a minor example, one of many which need not be discussed here. But we should note that Mallarmé's sonorous verses, even when they work with jarring sounds rather than harmony, have an insistent power that lodges in the memory although the meaning itself may fade. Valéry confirmed this when he wrote that despite his miserable memory, which made it impossible for him to learn anything by heart, he could still retain Mallarmé's "strange poems." The same insistency characterizes the works of any number of twentieth-century poets and is often the only standard for measuring the quality of a poem.

POÉSIE PURE

At this point it might be useful to touch briefly on the concept of *poésie pure*, which appeared occasionally in Sainte-Beuve, Baudelaire, and others, and then cropped up in Mallarmé. In the twentieth century, the term refers to a theory of poetry based on Mallarmé (and the "symbolists"). We can understand its meaning with the help of the words *pure* and *purity*, which recur so often in Mallarmé's writings and always connote "purity *from* something." These are privative concepts for him, just as they are for Kant, who applies the adjective *pure* (*rein*) to ideas "in which nothing is found that appertains to sensation." When Mallarmé speaks of a pure object, he is referring to its essential purity, its freedom from any contaminating foreign matter. The meaning of *purity* in his poetry can be construed from

102

a phrase that appears in a letter written in 1891: "consuming and exhausting things for the sake of a central purity." The premise of poetic purity is thus deobjectification. And all other characteristics of modern poetry are assembled in this concept used by Mallarmé and passed on to his heirs: rejection of contents derived from everyday experience, of didactic themes, and of other themes aimed at any purpose whatsoever — practical truths, run-of-the-mill feelings, intoxication of the heart. By relinquishing such elements, poetry will be free to allow the sway of language magic. In the play of language forces lying below and above the communicative function, poetry will achieve the compelling, nonmeaningful sonority that gives a verse incantatory power. Mallarmé, like his predecessors, often spoke of the kinship between poetry and music. Some of his statements in this regard subsequently contributed to the definition of *poésie pure*. Thus, in 1944, A. Berne-Joffroy wrote: "*Poésie pure* is the sublime moment in which a sentence harmoniously forgets its content. It is the verse that wishes no longer to speak but to sing." [6] In regard to Mallarmé, however, music should not be construed merely as harmonious language. For him, music is, in addition, a vibrating of the intellectual substance of poetry and its abstract tensions, a vibrating audible more to the inner than to the outer ear. Furthermore, the concept of *poésie pure* fits in with the Gestalt of Mallarmé's poetry: in its privative meaning, this concept is the aesthetic equivalent of the Void on which it centers. Beyond Mallarmé, the concept is valid for all poetry that is not so much sentiment and reaction to worldly content as a play of language and imagination.

DICTATORIAL IMAGINATION, ABSTRACTION, AND THE "ABSOLUTE GAZE"

In earlier chapters we frequently spoke of dictatorial imagination. It exists in Mallarmé's writings, in which its images supplant a reality whose objective systems no longer interest the poet. Here the imagination proceeds more quietly than in Rimbaud's poems, but its quiet workings have the force of an ontological act. Its semantic range, as in Novalis' and Baudelaire's works, includes the concept of abstraction. "Strictly imaginative and abstract, therefore poetic," is a characteristic equation (p. 544), in which *poetic*, in accordance with its original Greek sense, means "making," "producing," "creating." However, a second concept occurs in close proximity: *regard absolu*, the "absolute gaze." Its meaning can be found in the essay *Ballets* (1891): ". . . the ballerina is not a woman

6. Berne-Joffroy, *Présence de Valéry* (Paris, 1944), p. 202.

dancing . . . she is not a woman, but a metaphor summarizing one of the elemental aspects of our form: a sword, a cup, a flower; . . . and she does not dance, but suggests . . . with bodily script [what a text could only duplicate and with a great deal more trouble]'' (p. 304). Thus, watching a dancer means viewing elemental forms beyond her empirical appearance. Such observation results from an "absolute gaze, impersonal or lightninglike" (p. 306). This seems Platonic. But the essay concludes: "[the dancer] brings to you, beyond the final and ever remaining veil, the bareness [= purity] of your concepts, and she will silently write down your vision in the manner of a Sign, which she is." The thought leads rather un-Platonically to the subject of seeing. The viewer perceives not so much objective elemental forms as the elemental forms of his own mind; and he projects them into phenomena by transmuting the forms into signs of that mind. Phenomena stripped of their empirical trappings are overwhelmed by the absolute gaze, which, aimed at the gazer himself, can use the bare phenomena only as a sign language, totally at his disposal, for his movements. The essay on ballet was the strongest justification of absolutely creative poetry that ever was advanced. The "absolute gaze" can thus be applied as a key term for the abstract poetry of Mallarmé and his heirs, as well as for abstract painting, which, eschewing objects, presents a structure of tensions composed of pure lines, colors, and forms.

Mallarmé's poetry touches the phenomenal world only insofar as he twists it about, withdrawing it from the normal objective system of space and time. And here, despite completely different premises, lies his structural kinship with Rimbaud. We can give a few more examples. Black hats fly down a street: the street is "subjected to the black flight of hats" (p. 65). The street comes before the event, and the event, in the generality of the black flight (plus the unreal contraction of color and motion), comes before the hats. Normal vision would perceive the hats first, yet here they appear only at the end, and as something quite incidental. Mallarmé, too, likes to merge mutually remote things in the manner of Rimbaud's crossfade technique (described earlier). The beginning of his essay *Plaisir sacré* (even his essays are poetry) contains a statement which, translated into normal speech (and thereby ruined, of course), would say: In autumn, the Parisians return from hunting, go to the theater, yield to the spell of the music. But the sentence actually says: The wind hunts down the people, from the horizon, back to the city; the curtain rises above the deserted magnificence of autumn; the scattering of the fingering exercises, suspending the foliage, is mirrored in the cymbals of the orchestra (p. 388). The autumn is expressed only in a metaphorical transferral, i.e., in the mention of the theater ("curtain") and the conductor ("fingering"). Both realms, the fall and the theater, interlock to form a unity that turns into something more than a mere metaphor. The visible priority of the detail over the whole, of the accidental over the object, is a further characteristic of the unreal style, a characteristic that will have a future. Describing an angel with a naked sword, the poet concentrates on the outstanding feature of the blade: "an angel . . . standing . . . in the nakedness of its sword" (p. 28). Describing a group of ballerinas, Mallarmé speaks not of the figures but of "evasive muslin pallors" releasing "a smile and open arms with the sad clumsiness of a bear" (p. 276). The dancers appear only in a partial quality which merges with the partial quality of another creature, and the blend is so thorough that it is difficult to identify the creature: a clown. The accidental qualities are detached from the figures and woven into unreal structures. A late poem by Mallarmé begins, very allusively, with a lace curtain; the second stanza goes:

> That unanimous white conflict
> Of a garland with its like,
> Fleeing toward the wan window,
> Floats rather than shrouds [p. 74].

The objectiveness is completely overshadowed by the sinuous movement into which it has been converted by the abstracting imagination. One should not, as some critics do, label this practice impressionistic. It is not so much the result of received impressions as the imprinting of invented figures on a material totally divested of reality.

ALONE WITH LANGUAGE

With these few illustrations we have returned to Mallarmé's artistry. They would suffice to bear out his contention that poetry is a remote edifice. His work, at any rate, is the most remote edifice ever built by a modern poet. Economically constructed with limited material, his poems try "to melodiously and silently cipher" (p. 648) the infinite empty space of the absolute into the language of earthliness. Once, in a conversation, Mallarmé claimed that ever since "Homer had gone far astray," poetry had lost its bearings. When asked what had preceded Homer, he replied: Orpheus.[7] Thus Mallarmé himself reached that far back, to a mythical figure, to the essence of a singing in which verse and thought, wisdom and mystery,

7. H. Mondor, *Vie de Mallarmé*, 3d ed. (Paris, 1951), p. 638.

are one. Mallarmé may have done so because he felt a kinship with Orphic poetry, or even because the primordialness for which he strove in his diction compelled him to make his language comprehensible by appealing to the most remote, most mythical, source of poetry.

Mallarmé's poetry embodies total solitude. It has no desire for Christian, humanistic, or literary tradition. It refuses to interfere with the present. It rebuffs the reader and imposes inhumanity upon itself. Even in regard to the future, it realizes its own solitude: ". . . the poet has only to work mysteriously with a view toward the future or toward never . . ." (p. 664). Mallarmé's poetry experiences reality as inadequacy, transcendence as the Void, and its own relationship to both as an unresolved dissonance. What remains? Speech containing its own evidence. The poet is alone with his language. This is his home and his freedom, at the price of his being just as readily misunderstood as understood. If this were not the basic situation of modern poetry, Mallarmé would not have gained such veneration.

V

EUROPEAN POETRY
IN THE
TWENTIETH CENTURY

REMARKS ON METHOD

The type of poetry that dominates the twentieth century was born in France during the second half of the nineteenth century. It was anticipated by the German poet Novalis and by Edgar Allan Poe, and was then outlined by Baudelaire and his successors. Rimbaud and Mallarmé staked the boundaries to which poetry can venture. Twentieth-century verse has brought us almost nothing fundamentally new, no matter how fine some of the poets may be. This statement does not detract from them in any way; but it permits and even compels us to recognize the stylistic unity of their texts, a factor linking them to their predecessors. Stylistic unity does not mean monotony. Common features span dissimilarities between different authors to form a consistency in linguistic practice, view, themes, inner curves. Goethe and Trakl do not evince stylistic unity; yet Trakl and Benn do, difficult as it may be to compare them. This comment is no slur on originality, which, being a matter of quality, is not determined by type. But the type, in this case the stylistic unity of modern poetry, makes the poems easier to approach. In fact, an understanding of this stylistic unity is the only approach to those poems that deliberately elude normal comprehension. The result would have to be a penetration of the artistic individuality of the poets. We can only outline this approach in the present context. By showing to what great extent the features that emerged in the last century are alive, we hope to clarify the confusing vista of present-day poetry.

Have these symptoms survived because of their influential power? This may be so in a few cases, but it is not decisive. In superior poets, literary

107

influence is not so much a passive process as the result of an elective affinity that has led them to confirm and strengthen their own artistic talents as they find them in some earlier poet. Even in the absence of any influence, a structural similarity between a modern poet and the above-listed forebears may be apparent. Such a likeness proves the — generally valid — fact that there *is* such a thing as a stylistic and structural pressure within a given era. In our case, the pressure is the one that has been shaping European poetry for nearly a hundred years. Thus, rather than go into possible influences, we shall employ a method that we have already used — the method of depicting the hallmarks of a common poetic practice.

At the same time, we have to omit literary programs and classifications. Literary manuals are wont to speak of "symbolism" and to date its demise around 1900. We have thus far avoided this scholarly term, because it conceals the fact that the writers referred to (Mallarmé heading the list) exhibit peculiarities that characterize twentieth-century poets such as Valéry, Guillén, Ungaretti, T. S. Eliot, Trakl. Either symbolism has not passed away, or the term is inadequate and must be supplanted by a description of the details constituting the poetic style in question. (Valéry pointed out that "symbolism" is useless as the name for a group simply because *symbol* has so many meanings.[1]) Any reader of historical studies or critical essays dealing with the past fifty years of European verse-making will discover how many styles, schools, and trends there have been, one following on the heels of another: dadaism, futurism, expressionism, unanimism, creationism, neo-objectivism, modernism, ultramodernism, surrealism, hermeticism, antihermeticism, ultraism . . . The Spanish writer R. Gómez de la Serna, in a series of essays entitled *Ismos* (1943), stowed all the modern trends that he could get hold of in such "isms." Such overrating of literary and artistic variants probably stems from the proclivity of Romance nations to adopt the fashionable "latest." A tendency of this sort is blind to coherent relationships. Factional politics and wrangles may have exerted some influence here. On the other hand, this picture of a supposedly rapid turnover of styles is symptomatic of the modern age in *one* respect: it fits in with a frequently expressed intention of the poets, who claim that they are not writing for eternity but, at most, for an unknown future; their work is meant to be only a provisional experiment, which, however, in order to aim at the future, must break with the past — even the most recent past. Such was Rimbaud's sensibility, and then Cocteau's. In 1953, in *Démarches d'un poète*, Cocteau professed his adherence to an art that is a continuous restlessness in search of something new, an obloquy of the past, a keeping up with the latest fashion and an outdistancing

1. Valéry, *Œuvres*, ed. J. Hytier (Paris, 1957–60), I, 1272.

of the previous one, whose manner has become "beauty," i.e., habit. This scramble has made the artistic conscience restless, and the reflex has been the rapid turnover of styles. But this turnover is an optical illusion. The diversity simply does not exist. There are nuances and variants that testify to the range of potentials in present-day verse, but they have little bearing on a critique of its stylistic structure.

"FESTIVAL OF THE INTELLECT" AND "COLLAPSE OF THE INTELLECT"

We must, of course, guard against oversimplification. Yet the over-all picture reveals two trends permitting an initial orientation. They are the very same trends instituted by Rimbaud and Mallarmé in the last century. Roughly speaking, one tendency is toward a form-free, alogical poetry; the other, toward an intellectual, stringently formalistic poetry. Both trends, contrasting sharply with one another, were formulated programmatically in 1929. One formulation was made by Valéry: "A poem should be a festival of the intellect."[2] (The amplification in the text adds a refinement that always signalizes Valéry's reflections.) The other formulation, the result of protest, was made by the surrealist André Breton: "A poem should be the collapse of the intellect." Another statement directly follows: "Perfection is laziness."[3]

The fact that such opposites prevail in twentieth-century versecraft, and that they are worded so radically, is part of the over-all style. It is not enough to look upon them as contrasts between two literary factions — which they are, but only on the surface. Their polarity recurs, although rearranged slightly, within each of the types themselves. (We established this point on several occasions in the foregoing chapters.) This is the general polarity of modern poetry, the span — present in almost every poet — between cerebral and archaic forces. Moreover, the innumerable congruities of the two polar types constantly indicate the "nonpartisan" structural unity to which they belong. Intellectual poetry and alogical poetry concord in their flight from a humane middle range, their aversion to normal objectiveness and everyday sentiment, their replacement of a confining comprehensibility with an ambivalent suggestiveness, and their goal to make a poem an autonomous, self-signifying entity whose contents are a result of its language, its unlimited imagination, or its unreal phantasmagoria, rather than a mimesis of the world or an utterance of emotions.

2. *Ibid.*, II, 546.
3. Breton, *Revue surréaliste*, 1929.

109

Interestingly enough, the study of modern painting has led to similar conclusions. Werner Haftmann, in his *Painting in the Twentieth Century*, cites Kandinsky's distinctions between the "great reality" and the "great abstraction" and, with the help of these distinctions, manages to raise the conflicting trends of twentieth-century painting to "a higher level." The artistic traits described under the heading "The Great Abstraction" coincide amazingly with our characterization of Rimbaud's sensory unreality and, likewise, with the pure tensions in Mallarmé's object-annihilating poetry. Furthermore, according to Haftmann, these two "provinces are totally opposite positions," whose viewpoints and procedures fuse in practice because they are related. Thus, the structural unity of modern verse, on which we will dwell here, is characteristic of the structural unity of all modern art. This fact explains the stylistic analogies between poetry, painting, and music. An external but nevertheless important confirmation is the active personal contact between poets and painters throughout the era described here, from Baudelaire's association with Delacroix and the group comprising Henri Rousseau, Apollinaire, Max Jacob, Picasso, and Braque, and the friendship between García Lorca and Salvador Dali. Manifestoes by painters and musicians employ the ideas and terminology of literary programs, and vice versa. Much earlier, Diderot gained revolutionary understanding from analyses of music. Measured in terms of later developments, this interart process turns out to be an anticipation of the structural unity basic to the daring poetic and artistic ventures of the modern age.

SPANISH POETRY OF THE TWENTIETH CENTURY

Hereafter we will frequently refer to Spanish verse. Ever since the turn of the century, and in the wake of the Nicaraguan-born Rubén Darío, Spain has been experiencing a flowering of poetry whose quantity, quality, and originality are so great that Spanish critics are speaking of a second Golden Age in their literature. Foreign critics can only agree. The works of Antonio Machado, Juan Ramón Jiménez, Jorge Guillén, Gerardo Diego, Federico García Lorca, Dámaso Alonso, Vicente Aleixandre, Rafael Alberti, and others form perhaps the richest product of European poetry in the first half of our century. The Spanish like to assert that their modern poetry is free of outside influence. But even if this were true, and it is debatable, we cannot overlook certain structural affinities with French and even Anglo-American poetry. Ortega y Gasset declared in 1925 that all contemporary Spanish poets were following in Mallarmé's footsteps. Although this was an exaggeration, it does indicate that even Spaniards feel that the writers to whom Ortega was adverting may draw extremely close to European, and particularly French, poetry without abandoning their Spanishness.

In 1900 a stylistic change began to take place in Spain. The initial cause was a satiety with declamatory, sentimental, and naturalistic verse. The change was further abetted by a native poet, Luís de Góngora (1561–1627). Unrecognized for centuries, he came to be appreciated for the very features which classicistic scholarship had adduced as proof of his worthlessness. The immediate spur for this return to Góngora was the celebration marking the tricentennial of his death; the underlying cause was his kinship with modernity. The Spanish discovered in Góngora his faculty for both cerebral and imaginative conceptualization of remote ties between things in nature and in myth; his language as a continual metamorphosis of phenomena into "metaphorical ellipses" (Diego); the allurement of his artistically dark style (which tirelessly erected poetic counterworlds to the real world); the rigor of his poetic technique (especially his practice of dislodging the syntax to produce high tension in the lines); and, last but not least, the reconciliation of his intricacies with the fascination of his sounds. These discoveries were made for the most part by poets. And the latter are known, in reference to the Góngora tricentennial, as the generation of 1927, which, in addition to the writers listed above, includes like-minded literary critics.[4]

Thus Spanish poets, under Góngora's influence, turned away from earlier styles. Nevertheless, the change occurred for the same reasons and with the same goals as in France. A poetry working with exquisite linguistic means wanted to regain the mysteries and psychic subtleties suppressed by cultural disenchantment. The outcome was a combination of technique and subject matter that had to resemble its French counterpart. Thus any number of modern Spanish lyrics were of a piece with verse by Rimbaud, Mallarmé, and their successors, and yet retained a specific Spanishness. In Spain, too, modern poetry has grown more obscure and more esoteric. But, for Spaniards, the esoteric begins elsewhere than it does for other Europeans. The borderline is more distant. The return to a native poetry

---

4. Considering the importance of this Góngora renaissance for modern Spanish poetry, a short bibliography is in order: Rafael Alberti, *Cal y canto*, 1927; Vicente Aleixandre, in "A Don L. de Góngora" (1927), in *Poesías completas* (Madrid, 1960), p. 612; L. Cernuda, "Góngora," in *Como quièn espera el alba* (Buenos Aires, 1947); Gerardo Diego, *Antología poètica en honor de Góngora* (Madrid, 1927); Federico García Lorca, *La imagen poética en Don Luis de Góngora* (1928). Literary history and criticism: Dámaso Alonso, "Góngora y la literatura contemporánea," in *Estudios y ensayos gongorinos*, 2nd ed. (Madrid, 1961); Jorge Guillén, *Language and Poetry* (Cambridge, Mass., 1961), pp. 41 ff.; Alfonso Reyes, *Cuestiones gongorinas* (Madrid, 1929), esp. "De Góngora y de Mallarmé." Many of these poems and critical works point out, in opposition to the strictures on poetic obscurity, that Góngora's darkness is actually a light which temporarily blinds us since our eyes are not used to it. For the comparison of Góngora and Mallarmé, see above, pp. 88–90.

led not only to Góngora but also to folklore, particularly the romances (ballads). This fundamental treasure-trove of Spanish poetry had always been characterized by an obscure style, full of laconisms and allusions, ominous, and chary of thematic and logical coherences. Modern poetry has borrowed this style. In certain enigmatic lines of a García Lorca or even an Alberti, a Spanish ear will catch the homey sound of popular ballads, whereas a foreigner will hear only a mysterious diction that sounds anything but folksy. The impression of esotery occurs at a much higher level for a Spaniard, in the out-and-out intellectual poets (above all, Guillén). These matters may be purely domestic. Yet it is significant that in the twentieth century, Spaniards drew from their folk poetry — including the gypsy songs of Andalusia — a range of hieroglyphs that veil and evoke rather than name. These hieroglyphs suit a modern poetic style which has many reasons for wanting to be obscure and bold.

TWO REFLECTIONS ON POETRY: APOLLINAIRE AND GARCÍA LORCA

Ever since Poe and Baudelaire, lyricists have been developing theoretical reflections on a par with their poetry. The reasons are not didactic. The real cause is the modern conviction that poetic activity is an adventure of the operating and simultaneously self-witnessing mind, which, by reflecting on its activity, actually heightens the poetic tension. The viewpoint that such reflections lead to an unpoetic state has as little validity as the quondam saw: "Work, artist; don't talk." Nearly all great poets of the twentieth century have put forth a poetics, a system, as it were, of their own poetry or of versecraft in general. These theories express as much about modern poetry as do the poems themselves. Furthermore, they have shored up an idea that emerged in the early nineteenth century, one that was supported by Verlaine and Mallarmé: the idea (uncommon in earlier poetics) that poetry is the purest and highest manifestation of literature. The modern isolation of the poet is mirrored in the thought that no roads lead from the lonesome summit of the lyrical down to the slopes of mere "literature." The poetics stress the endless distance separating poetry from narrative and dramatic writing based on coherence and logic. It is the distance between soliloquizing and communicative writing. "Poetry is an anachoristic art," declared Gottfried Benn.

It will be useful to give a brief account of two theoretical works, both of which reveal how many basic features of nineteenth-century poetics have passed into twentieth-century ones.

The first is a programmatic statement by Apollinaire: *L'Esprit nouveau et les poètes* (in *Mercure de France*, 1918). This somewhat confusing piece contains the following main ideas: The "new spirit" is the spirit of absolute freedom; freedom in poetry leads to an unlimited use of all subject matter without regard to its class; poetry is ignited in nebulae and oceans or in a falling handkerchief and a flaring match. From the most powerful and the most insignificant objects, it draws forth things never heard before, transmuting them into irritating surprise, into "new joys, even when they are a torment to endure." The most trivial of objects can send poetry into an "unknown infinity where the fires of multiple meanings blaze," or into the twilights of the unconscious. The absurd is on a par with the heroic. The new poetry also includes the new objects of technological civilization: the telephone, the telegraph, the airplane, and ."machines, the motherless offspring of mankind." The new poetry amalgamates such objects with freely invented myths, which are allowed to do anything — most of all, the impossible. The goal is the "synthetic poem," which should be like a newspaper page, where the most disparate things simultaneously strike the eye, or like a film, which swiftly reels off image after image. There should be no descriptive, ornate, or oratorical style, no country gewgaws, only sharp formulas that delineate the complex as precisely as possible. Versecraft is like the work of a fine mechanic. Poetry has to do everything in order to match the daring of mathematics. Then again: ". . . like the alchemists," poetry has to strive for "rare research and formulas" and it even becomes a "primevally lyrical alchemy." Like the new spirit, poetry is full of dangers and traps — a daring experiment, but one that must be dared, the courage being more important than the success. The poet must always be intent on surprise. And here, in surprise — in aggressive dramatics aimed at the reader — Apollinaire sees the real difference between the old poetry and the new. The poet, however, seeking the unknown in order to articulate it in abnormal diction, will be lonely, ridiculed, or outlawed.

We need hardly emphasize that these ideas (which the author had already put in practice in his own verse) owe much to Rimbaud. Apollinaire's piece is the most important theoretical link between Rimbaud and twentieth-century poetry.

To this forward-looking program, we can add García Lorca's backward-looking lecture, *La imagen poética en Don Luis de Góngora* (The poetic image in Góngora) (1928). This work is an important manifestation of the Góngora renaissance in modern Spain. And it is also an aesthetics of modern poetry. The rediscovery of Góngora in Spain (see above, p. 111) had fecundated the new poetry, which, in turn, brought about an understanding of the most difficult of all older Spanish poets. García Lorca calls him "the father of modern poetry." But he also cites Mallarmé, declaring him to be Góngora's best pupil, although the Frenchman did not know the Spaniard. García Lorca points out their differences as well as their affinities. The kinship between Mallarmé and Góngora resides in their poetic technique. This technique and its reasons are discussed in the above-mentioned speech, which can be taken as an indirect description of modern poetry. And the following summary may be seen in that light.

Góngora was convinced that the value of a poem increases in proportion to its distance from the normality of the external and internal world. He loved pure, gratuitous beauty, which emerges only when "communicable feelings" are excluded. He hated reality, but ruled absolutely over the realms that exist only poetically. His mental landscape allows only the autonomy of words, out of which he built an edifice that resists time. Nature is out of place here. For "nature, which comes from the hands of God, is not the nature that lives in a poem." Góngora's works are not to be measured against reality, but according to their own standards. He put objects and events "into the camera obscura of his brain, from which they re-emerge transformed in order to leap across the world." The transformational power resides in metaphorical imagination. The latter produces unreal images which are on the level of myths and which force together areas remote from one another. This imagery eclipses the content of his verse to so great an extent that it becomes insignificant. The "cold light of Rome" lies upon his poems. Inspiration may have sparked them, but they became a pure, hard substance only by a meticulous testing of the semantic and aural qualities available in the language itself. The result is a poetry that flees from the reader instead of looking for him. We must woo it with the mind. Its darkness is actually an excess of mental light.

The tone, the goal, and the level of the two programmatic pieces are very different. Yet both join forces in affirming a cerebral poetry independent of reality and normality, and dissonantly alien to the reader.

THE INCONGRUENT STYLE AND THE "NEW LANGUAGE"

The interpreter of a modern poem must always dwell much longer on technique than on content, motif, or theme. This is an understandable consequence of its structure. Goethe could transmit poems by Hebel and others to the public simply by relating the contents. Naturally, the poetic substance remained invisible, since it could not be conveyed in this manner. But nevertheless this kind of procedure was possible and useful for poets desirous of a reader's company in order to communicate intelligible objects and feelings in a language serving such objects and feelings and their natural order. A poem by T. S. Eliot, St.-John Perse, or Ungaretti cannot be

114

satisfactorily interpreted on the basis of content, although such poems certainly have their "contents," which may even belong to a set of themes highly revealing for each author. But the distance between the subject matter and the technique of language artistry is considerably greater than in earlier poetry. The summit of work and effect lies in that very technique. The energies are thrust almost entirely into the style. The style is the linguistic execution and, as such, the most immediate manifestation of the great metamorphosis of the real and the normal. Thus, the difference with regard to earlier poetry lies in the fact that the balance between content and form is destroyed by the preponderance of the latter. With all its disquiet, its fragmentation, its alienation, the abnormal style draws attention to itself. The reader cannot, as he did with older poetry, concentrate on *what* is said and neglect *how* it is said. Incongruence of the sign with what it stands for is a law of both modern poetry and modern art. A cloth rag on a painting becomes the incongruent token of the body of a mandolin. In a poem, a forest becomes a token of steeple clocks, blue a token of oblivion, the definite article a token of indefiniteness, a metaphor a token of objective identity.

With this preponderance of incongruity, the themes and objects touched upon within the form sometimes lose all significance. The modern poem refrains from the use of descriptive or narrative lines that would recognize the objective outer or inner world in its objective existence. Such lines would jeopardize the authority of the style. Any vestiges of the normal objective world that the style may absorb have only one function: to throw the transforming imagination into gear. This does not mean that today's poetry has to limit itself to the few and negligible objects on which Mallarmé concentrated. It may do so. But just as many poems are crammed with objects. In such poems the plethora of things is subject to new combinations of the mode of viewing and the stylistic means, and is material for the authority of the lyrical "I" — all of which confirms the deliberate reduction of meaning. This explains why modern poets are always talking about the paltriness of their subject matter. Reverdy wrote in 1948: "The poet has no subject; he consumes himself in himself. . . . His work is valuable simply because it will not recognize any reason for its discontinuity or its practice of riveting incompatible things to one another." For the Spaniard Salinas, the premise of "pure poetry" is that it remain as free as possible of things and themes, because only then does the creative motion of language have scope in which to move. The subject matter is the means to a poem. Gottfried Benn stated in 1950: "The style is kept going by formal tricks. . . . Bright ideas are driven in like nails, and gimmicks hung upon them. Subject matter and psyche are never interwoven; everything is planned; nothing is carried out."

The style of modern verse, as described in statements like those above, denies the claim that the content must have intrinsic value and coherence; this style thrives on its own dictatorial claims and exists in an unresolved dramatics between these claims and its content. It is always in search of "new language," a search that has been going on since Rimbaud. "Oh mouths, man is looking for a new language, which grammarians will have no say about," writes Apollinaire in his *Calligrammes*. But what shall this new language look like? Apollinaire's answer remains approximate, although it points toward a brutalized and dissonant, and then a deified, language: ". . . consonants without vowels, consonants that burst and bang, sounds like a top, like tongue-clicking, like scratchy spitting"; but also, "the new word is sudden and a trembling god." Aragon, in the preface to *Les Yeux d'Elsa* (1942), writes: "Poetry exists as long as there is constant reinvention of language. This implies breaking the set framework of language, the rules of grammar, the laws of speech." Note the negative definitions. The absolute desire for the new can express itself programmatically only as a smashing of the old. Yeats admitted about himself: "I have no language, only images, analogies, symbols." In T. S. Eliot's *Ash Wednesday*, the following lines burst in: "Speech without word and / Word of no speech." St.-John Perse speaks of a "syntax of lightning" and proclaims, "We are paving our new ways to words never heard before." All these poets are seeking a kind of transcendence of speech. Yet this transcendence remains as indefinite as the other one, the empty transcendence we discussed in connection with Baudelaire.

The notion of the "new language" grows more precise when emphasizing the aggressive intention. By breaking with the habitual, the new language becomes shocking to the reader. Ever since Baudelaire, "surprise" has been part of the terminology of modern poetics, just as it was in baroque literature. Valéry writes: "A study of modern art would have to show that every five years, for more than half a century now, a new solution has been found for the problem of shock." He admits his reaction of shock to Rimbaud and Mallarmé. The surrealists speak of the stunning effect that a poem should have; Breton calls poetry a "demonstration of protest." St.-John Perse describes "the luxury of the unusual" as "the first law of literary behavior." Seen in a larger context, such tenets reveal that the protest inherent in poetry since romanticism has greatly increased in strength. If modern poetry defines itself at all in relation to the reader, it is as an attack. The chasm between the writer and the audience is kept open by shock effects. They occur in the abnormal style of the "new language."

Flaubert, while writing *Madame Bovary*, defined style as "a way of seeing" — a definition that would have been inconceivable in any earlier

116

poetics rooted in humanism, and one that was practiced in Flaubert's novels, in most modern fiction, and more and more in poetry. The law of a style so defined does not derive from the theme, the subject matter, or even the traditional literary language. It comes from the author himself. The result is a phenomenon best known in painting. Since Cézanne, it has become customary for painters to return, over and over again, to an insignificant subject because they are interested not so much in the motif as in trying out the possibilities of their style. Picasso produced several versions of Manet's *Déjeuner sur l'herbe*, each one different from the others. Subject matter becomes less important than formal inventiveness, which is supposed to produce a self-sufficient organism created out of the imagery rather than the elements of outside reality. As a consequence, the number of themes is reduced, and each theme occurs solely as a practice piece for variations, each one manifesting the self-aimed style. This practice can be found in poetry, too. Valéry once wrote that in his opinion, poetry almost coincides with the attempt "to produce many variations on a single subject." Guillén published *Variaciones de una durmiente*, four different translations and adaptations of Valéry's *Dormeuse*. Guillén also wrote the pairs of *Variaciones sobre temas de Jean Cassou* [Variations on themes by Jean Cassou] (1951). P. J. Jouve offered double "variants" of several of his poems. A prose volume by Raymond Queneau, entitled *Exercises de style* (1947), varies a single theme ninety-nine times. The interest is in the transforming style in itself.

FURTHER REMARKS ON THE "NEW LANGUAGE"

Several peculiarities of the "new language" ought to be discussed. In doing so, let us bear in mind R. Caillois's remark at the beginning of his monograph on St.-John Perse: "I am not probing into abysses. I am reflecting on the use of the article or the adverb. This method is surer, although it, too, can gently lead into abysses." [5]

The syntactical and semantic difficulty of the modern poem seems to demand a rendering into a kind of normal parlance. And any interpretation can, and usually must, yield to this requirement in order to bring the reader to the poem (even if this is not the only goal). Yet an interpretive translation adulterates the poem. Although, this holds true for all poetry, in modern verse such a falsification is far greater for the reason touched on above: modern poetry strives to be different on the basis of the way it speaks, and in most cases its form is the cause rather than the effect of its being

5. Caillois, *Poétique de Saint-John Perse* (Paris, 1954).

THE STRUCTURE OF MODERN POETRY

different. The manner can be explicated, but the fact that it is different cannot be suppressed.

This difference is often revealed in the relationship of a poem to the sentence. The more untraditional a poem wants to be, the farther it moves from the sentence as a conventional structure consisting of a subject, a verbal predicate, an object, modifying words, etc. In regard to modern poetry, we simply can speak of a hostility toward the sentence, the ultimate result often being fragmentariness.

Several types of this hostility can be distinguished. The most common occurs in poems that have nominal phrases for several lines, and which finally, and almost casually, introduce a verbal predicate:

> From the far anxiety of dawn
> Uncovered masts.
> Painful awakening.
> Leaves, familiar leaves,
> I *hear* you in wretchedness.
> [Ungaretti; Friedrich's italics]

The first stanza (eight lines) of Gottfried Benn's *Nacht* [Night] consists only of nouns; in the next few stanzas, several verbs are added, but their semantic and syntactical importance is much less than the fragmentary nominal statements and exclamations:

Nacht. Von Himmel zu Meeren
hungernd. *Dernier cri*
alles Letzten und Leeren,
sinnlos Kategorie.
Dämmer. Aus Unbekannten
Wolken, Flüge des Lichts —
alles Korybanten,
Apotheosen des Nichts.
. . . .
. . . .
. . . .
Ach — Äonenvergessen!
Schlaf! aus mohnigem Feld,
aus den lethischen Essen
zieht ein Atem der Welt,
von acherontischen Zonen
orphisch apotheos

Night. Hungering from
sky to seas. *Dernier cri*
of everything final and empty,
category senseless.
Twilight. From unknown
clouds, flights of light —
everything Corybantes,
apotheoses of Void.
. . . .
. . . .
Oh — aeonian oblivion!
Sleep! from the poppied field,
from the Lethean food,
wafts a breath of the world,
from Acherontic zones
orphic-apotheosic

118

rauscht die Hymne der Drohnen:	*soughs* the hymn of the drones:
Glücke des Namenlos.	blisses of Nameless.
	[Friedrich's italics]

The reverse is also possible: Ungaretti's *Noia* [Ennui] begins with a short clause complete with a verb, but then come lines with open noun sketches that finally terminate in a verbal sentence; and yet the verbs, a total of three (one a mere infinitive), cannot, and are not even meant to, dispel the motionlessness of a nocturnal asphalt desolation. The static quality is most pervasive in the verbless middle lines:

> This night, too, *will pass*
> This life all around
> hesitant shadow of the trolley wires
> on the moist asphalt
> I *watch* the heads of the coachmen nodding. . . .
> [Friedrich's italics].

Poems with a greater number of verbs tend to introduce them as infinitives without subjects, or in conjugated form but relegated to a subordinate clause. A good example is Montale's *Meriggiare pallido . . . . :*

> *Taking* a siesta, pale . . .
> *Hearing* the chatter of blackbirds, the rustle of snakes . . .
> *Watching* the files of red ants
> *break* and *form* ranks. . . .
> [Friedrich's italics]

Guillén seems to have gone the furthest in ejecting verbs. He has even managed to write a poem of twenty lines without including a single verb — an extreme case, but consistent with his predominantly nominal style. The poem referred to is *Niño*.[6] The "child," promised in the title, seems to be missing from the poem. Instead of an empirical, physical child, we find certain basic phenomena of Guillén's world: a current, a rose, snow, the sea. Their possible relationship to a child is merely suggested by the title; they have withdrawn from this relationship in the form of noun apostrophes which are mutually incoherent as well.

"Above all, away from all verbs. To throw everything around a substantive, to erect towers out of nouns," wrote Benn in 1926.

6. Guillén, *Cántico* (Buenos Aires, 1950), p. 27.

The antisyntactic attitude of modern poetry, with its disabling of the verb, signifies that the nominally stated contents of the idea or of the abstraction are to remain entirely themselves rather than be embedded in any sort of temporality or flow of events; in fact, in the most extreme cases the contents are not even to relate to one another. The ousting of verbs not only increases, both formally and syntatically, the fragmentariness of this poetry; it also fortifies the isolation and thereby the high tension of whatever is stated nominally. The noun achieves greater intensity, transcending its usual importance. The next step is the obvious — and then frequent — manner of writing in single key words.

A few more instances of antisyntacticism should be mentioned. Words appear alongside one another, their function not clarified by relational words. Thus, a volume of poems by Eluard, published in 1929, was titled *L'Amour la poésie* [Love/Poetry]; the reader cannot tell whether the grouping of the words is causal (love is the mainspring of poetry), an equation of love and poetry, or something else. Proximity without relation effects whole clauses and even sentences. To cite an extreme specimen by Apollinaire:

> Three burning gaslights
> The cook she's consumptive
> If you're ready, we'll play backgammon
> A bandleader has a sore throat. . . .[7]

None of these sentences is derivable from a preceding one. Are they bits and pieces of conversation? The random collection of incoherent snippets of talk has become a modality of poetry, one that is not copied but which refers to itself and, as a self-centered poetry, produces its own poetic coherence.

Starting with Mallarmé, it became a rule for most poets to avoid punctuation and pointing out interpolations, thereby abolishing the syntax which they had secretly planned. Such antisyntactical stylistics (or should one say, stylistics that recast syntax?) always reveal the following: modern poetry circumvents or disturbs coherence and relationships, and aims primarily at a demonstrative and simultaneously stenographic, yet multiradiate, statement.

Closely allied with the syntactical ellipsis is the lexical or syntactical

7. Apollinaire, *Œuvres poétiques*, ed. M. Adéma and M. Décaudin (Paris, 1962), p. 180.

ambivalence peculiar to modern poetry. The last strophe of Elsa Lasker-Schüler's *Unser Liebeslied* [Our love song]:

Und von roten Abendlinien	And from red evening lines
Blicken Marmorwolkenfresken	Marble cloud frescoes look
Uns verzückte Arabesken.	Us entranced arabesques.

The reader might suspect a typographical or even a linguistic error. But obviously, akin to the practice in other lines, the *uns* ("us") of the final line is meant to be hazy. We could complete it as *auf uns* ("at us"), whereby "entranced arabesques" would be appositional to "us." Or we could construe *blicken*, in the penultimate line, as short for *erblicken* ("notice," "catch sight of").

Paisaje [Landscape], by García Lorca, ends:

Los olivos,	The olive trees,
están cargados	they are laden
de gritos.	with shrieks.
Una bandada	A flock
de pájaros cautivos	of captive birds
que mueven sus larguísimas	that move their long, long
colas en lo sombrío.	tails in the shadow.

The second — elliptical — sentence could be a metaphorical sequel to the foregoing metaphor about the shriek-laden olive trees; yet it might just as easily be a literal explanation of the "shrieks" in the olive grove.

A line in Quasimodo's *Vento a Tindari* [Wind at Tindari] goes: "Salgo vertici aerei precipizi [I climb summits airy precipices]." The adjective *aerei* ("airy") is placed in such a way as to refer, in accordance with Italian usage, to either *summits* or *precipices*, or to both; critics have rightly pointed out what they call Quasimodo's "adjectival divalency."[8]

Ungaretti composed a *Song without Words:*

> The sun left light to a dove . . .
> Cooing, it comes, when you sleep, in dreams.
> Light, it comes then. . . .

8. L. Aneschi, quoted in *Poeti del novecento*, ed. G. Spagnoletti, 2d ed. (Milan, 1965), p. 30.

The English rendering cannot retain the syntactical divalency of the original, which is all the more reason to stress it. It is debatable whether the verb *verrà* ("comes") in the second line belongs to *light* in the first line or to *dove*. We can construe it either way in accordance with Italian syntax, which does not require the use of the personal pronoun as the subject of a verb. The participle *turbando* ("cooing") obviously belongs to *dove*; and yet the third line unequivocally links the verb *verrà* with *light*. In line with the stylistic laws of modern poetry, we can infer that the first two lines are meant to have a double reference ("cooing, the dove *and* the light come"), and that this subsides to a single one in the next line. The light implied in the second line borrows from the dove an unusual and alien metaphor: "cooing." Or one might speak of a crossfade technique rather than a metaphor.

Modern poets like to emphasize the inherent ambivalence of human speech in order to elevate poetic diction beyond utilitarian language. And they do so much more often than earlier poets did. The blatant task of utilitarian speech is to communicate reliable information, which is generally followed by an action, an attitude, or an objective orientation. To remove these limitations, the modern age uses further means, for whose analysis normal grammar will not suffice unless we determine in what way the diction flouts the usual rules. Thus, we come across poems in which every line reads like a subordinate clause; for example, every line begins with the conditional conjunction *if*, and yet they never lead to the expected main clause (Benn's *Dann*). Construing the stanzas as subordinate clauses is therefore invalid. Other poems have lines containing a *but*, yet the opposite pole that this *but* suggests is never conceived or at least never articulated. And then there is the abnormal use of the copula *and* to indicate not so much a sequence of contents as an unexpected turn in the language. (Countless examples will be found in Apollinaire, Eluard, St.-John Perse, and in English or German poems with a style reminiscent of that found in the King James or the Luther Bible.) Furthermore, we should note such phenomena as functional changes of prepositions, adjectives, adverbs, and temporal and modal verb forms; substantives used without articles (especially noticeable in German and the Romance languages); demonstrative pronouns used not for spatial, temporal, or objective organization, but for the emotional heightening of the substantive; and so forth.

A stylistic practice, syntactically correct but semantically unwonted, and increasing in its own way the modern ambivalence of poetic language, is contraction. Ungaretti writes, "And in your eyes you have a quick sigh." The sigh of the mouth and the lamenting gaze of the eyes are compressed into one. To quote Ungaretti again, "The dark beauties, clothed in water." He actually means the dark-skinned women *near* the Nile, yet the line turns great proximity of two images (women and Nile) into near identity. Marie-Luise Kaschnitz: "... before the morning crows." The contraction is produced by the omission of the rooster, with whose job of crowing before daybreak the morning is identified. Jules Supervielle: "The gold-wind of their pinions." The flight of birds in early-morning wind and in the gold of the morning sun is concentrated into three nouns.

Whenever language, limited to a purely objective, unequivocal, and nonatmospheric communication, fears a loss of poetry, it will strive toward silence rather than toward speech. In the chapter on Mallarmé, we pointed out the function of silence in both his poetry and his theories (see above, p. 88). Max Kommerell, in *Gedanken über Gedichte* (1943), wrote: "It cannot be denied that in the utterance of the lyrical poem, which blissfully discloses to us the magnitude of possible speech, the unsaid and the unsayable are also present in what is said, a silence in speech." Of course, "silence" here is an auxiliary concept for that which language alone makes perceptible and poetically acute. Kommerell is referring to the utter delicacy, the amazing strangeness, in the combination of words, a suggestive echo within the reader, a hush concealing the future, as well as a speech implying that its next step is silence. This concept of "silence in speech" can be applied to much of recent poetry. But it must be applied even more indispensably to the poetry that we have been calling "modern," and the poets have made frequent statements to that effect. Jimènez seeks, as the acme of expression, the "silent word." Reminiscent of Mallarmé are two sentences in a lecture Ungaretti gave in 1941: "A word that lets silence echo in the sanctum of the soul — is it not a word that would fill itself with mystery? It is a word of anxious hoping, the hope of regaining its original purity." [9] Valéry, in a late epilogue to *La Jeune Parque*, wrote: "A silence is the strange source of poetry." Hilde Domin, in the preface to her book of lyrics, *Hier*, gives a poetic definition of poetry: "The non-word / suspended / between word and word." And in her poem *Linguistik*, she cautions: "Learn silence in speech." The reader might also refer to Gerardo Diego's sonnet *Callar*, whose emotional theme is silence, and which fears words as the betrayal of inwardness.

The longing for potentially unadulterated silence can often explain the poet's preference for a short poem. At any rate, the terseness and "throttled speech" (Karl Krolow) of such poetry fits in well with that desire. Thus some modern poems have as few as two or three lines. A number of these poems have become famous; e.g., Jiménez: "Touch it no more, / for thus is the rose" (he means, as Mallarmé does, poetic perfection, which must no longer be touched); Ungaretti's *Eternal*, "Between a picked flower and

---

9. Ungaretti, with J. Lescure, *Les Cinq Livres* (Paris, 1954), p. 22.

a given one / inexpressible nothingness,'' which is found at the beginning of *L'allegría*; Ezra Pound's *In a Station of the Metro*: "The apparition of these faces in the crowd: / Petals on a wet, black bough.'' [10] It almost seems as if only such brevity, and the silence that makes it possible, can let the poetic intensity of the poem erupt.

A separate study of the titles of modern poems would be invaluable. As a linguistic element or, rather, as expressing a relationship (or even a nonrelationship) to the other parts of the poem, the title, too, can be a conveyer of the "new language.'' It was always customary for the title to name the theme, the subject, the emotion of the poem, with the verses developing or fulfilling whatever the title announced, just as, conversely, a rereading of the title would sum up whatever had been revealed in the poem. Naturally, this convergence exists in modern poetry, too, but less often than a dislodging of the relation between the title and the poem. Countless variants exist: A single line from within the poem is randomly selected to be the title, when any other line would do as well. Other titles are so intrinsic to the poem that the text would be more than puzzling without them (for example, Pound's *In a Station of the Metro*). Or else the title is so abstruse that it contributes little to the understanding of the poem (for example, Guillén's *Niño* [see above, p. 119]). This is true of the title *Arbre* [Tree] and the very remote content of this poem by Apollinaire.[11] Such incongruity adds further levels of ambivalence. A number of Jiménez' titles are interrogative, two of them even limited to a question mark. Benn's poem *Dann* contains three lines, each commencing with "If a face . . .'' without a sequent to the conditional *if*; and the syntax is completely fragmented in other respects as well. The title is the word that is missing from the poem: *Then*. The conclusion ensuing from the condition precedes the lines as a verbal fragment — a technique of reversal, numerous subspecies of which, not necessarily involving the title, occur in modern poetry. The features common to all these titles are probably the diminution of linguistic and semantic coherency and, more generally, the need to invent abnormalities here, too.

THE FUNCTION OF DETERMINANTS TO PRODUCE VAGUENESS

A stylistic feature of modern poetry, one that is linked to the basic trait of alienation of the familiar, is the "vagueness function'' of determinants, which we can explain as follows.

10. Compare W. Iser's interpretation in his *Immanente Ästhetik: Lyrik als Paradigma der Moderne* (Munich, 1966), pp. 368 f.

11. Apollinaire, *Œuvres poétiques*, p. 178.

Benn's poem *Welle der Nacht* ends with the line "The white pearl rolls back into the sea." In accordance with one's normal sense of language, one may ask, Which pearl? None was mentioned in the foregoing lines — only a blowing, a rolling, lightly borne by beings and things or, rather, by their magic names. The pearl, too, is such a conveyer. What it bears is more significant than the pearl itself: a spoken sound and the absolute motion of rolling back. The definite article does not define the noun that it modifies; it merely introduces the noun in order to make it the phonic counter of an absolute movement that turns back and concludes the whirling and approaching movements of the preceding lines. The object named by the noun, the pearl, was not anticipated by anything; and, because the definite article coincides with this unfamiliarity, the pearl is vague and mysterious. The *in*definite article (*"a* white pearl . . ."*) would have evoked a different atmosphere.

In normal usage, the definite article defines, points out, an object that is known or has been previously mentioned. It linguistically confirms what is known, or an object introduced beforehand, or even a person, and, as such, it contains a vestige of the demonstrative. In modern poetry, however, the definite article is used in such a way that, as a determining means, it elicits attention, which it then instantly disorients by introducing an entirely new object. This practice, as well as the similar use of other determinants such as personal pronouns, adverbs of place, etc., was employed by nineteenth-century poets, especially Rimbaud. In our century this practice has been spreading immoderately, becoming a chief stylistic feature. A poem by Jules Supervielle, *L'Appel*, contains fantastic things: "The ladies in black . . . , the mirror . . . , the marble violin. . . ." All the elements of the action are expressed with the definite article as if we were quite familiar with them. Yet they refer to nothing we know, as is often the case in true fairy tales. The most frequent use of this practice can be found in T. S. Eliot, St.-John Perse, and Guillén. The determinants, together with the vagueness of speech, usually create an abnormal tension of diction and the device of lodging unfamiliarity in things that sound familiar. Modern poetry, which is fond of incoherent contents, introduces anything new with startling suddenness. The determinant, by making the "new" seem familiar, heightens the disorientation and makes the isolated, rootless "new" even more enigmatic.

APOLLO INSTEAD OF DIONYSUS

Modern poetry is cool in the normal sense of the word, and reflection on it is cool, also. The poems are judged with a thorough technical knowledge accompanied, however, by the realization that poetry is mysterious, a border strip wrested from the ineffable, a miracle, and a power. But one studies its power as if it were an experimental explosion of almost atomic word forces, and its mysterious diction as if it were the surprising result of chemical combinations attempted for the first time. The poet is an adventurer in hitherto untrodden language fields. He is equipped with the measuring instruments of his concepts, which allow him to check himself at any time, and which safeguard him from ambush by banal emotion. The spell of modern poems is curbed by manly restraint. Even the dissonances and darknesses are under the sway of Apollo, the lucid artistic conscience. Inspirational transports are no longer the sole indication of artistic quality, as they were before the nineteenth century. They did have their aftermath, however, and public opinion adhered to them for a long time. The much-admired model was a twentieth-century German poet, Rilke, who had artistic stature but remained sexless. His poems were "dictated" to him in "night storms"; they leaped into his "wide-open feeling," so that his "hand trembled and the tissue cracked." Afterward, to princesses, contessas, noble ladies, "very dear and worthy gentlemen," he gave detailed accounts of his "being flung," with many *somehows* and *somewheres*, and with the noblest genitives. The consequences were odious; one result was a sorry confusion of this one brand of verse with poetry per se.

Almost all leading European poets are distrustful of inspiration and carefully discriminate between excitation and energy, and between personal agitation and intellectual validity.

> Poetry is a deeply skeptical art. It presupposes an extraordinary freedom with regard to our ideas and our feelings. The gods graciously give us a first line; but then it is up to us to produce the second one, which must harmonize with the first and be worthy of its older, supernatural brother. All the energy of experience and of the mind just barely suffice.

Valéry wrote the preceding lines in an essay on La Fontaine's *Adonis*.[12] "Sighing and elementary sobbing" have no function in poetry until they become "spiritual figures," he writes elsewhere.[13] García Lorca, in his speech on Góngora, praised Valéry for ideas of this kind and carried them even further. Recoiling from the oratorical and overly dramatic poetry of D'Annunzio, the Italian poets are following a similar course; they prefer the well-measured "naked word" (Ungaretti) to smitten speech. Basically,

12. Valéry, *Œuvres*, I, 482.
13. *Ibid.*, II, 20.

all these views are old. Their frequency in the Romance countries is connected with Latin cultural foundations. Yet their emphatic recurrence from Baudelaire to the present indicates that modern poetry is still involved in a process of deromanticization.

Such views have been formulated in other countries as well. Novalis anticipated them. T. S. Eliot spoke of the depersonalization of the poetic "I," whose action becomes similar to that of science; he stressed the "intensity of the artistic process" and desired to look not just into the heart but "deeper, into the cortex of the brain and the nervous system." In Germany, Gottfried Benn made up for lost time with striking formulations that cleared the air. His lecture *Probleme der Lyrik* (1952) became a midcentury *ars poetica*. Benn restored the honor of the German word *artistisch*, which refers more to the formal aspect of art. He applied it to the stylistic and formal will, which has its own truth, superior to that of the content. "For only in the area of shaping does man become perceivable." A very Latin statement! Inspiration does not lead; it *mis*leads, leads astray, seduces. It "hurls forth a few verses," but then man in his formative power steps up, "immediately takes hold of these verses, put them under a microscope, studies them, dyes them, hunts for pathological points. . . ."

Modern poets often speak of their "laboratory," of "operating," of "algebra," of "calculating" a verse. Valéry, in his book on Degas, does not describe the cozy disorder in artists' studios of the past, but instead, a "painting laboratory," with a man dressed in severe white and wearing rubber gloves, working according to a precise schedule and surrounded by special instruments. Valéry had the irony to offer this as an image of the future. But it had long since come true. The reader of Werner Haftmann's *Painting in the Twentieth Century* has the impression that modern art is like a gigantic laboratory filled with highly intellectual people who discover "formulas," "define" space, try out "acoustic constructions." Poetry is no different. Its leading representative is the "thinking poet" (Elisabeth Langgässer), for whom oranges and lemons become an "algebra of ripe fruits" (Krolow), and who can join Benn in saying: "I'm an optician; I work with prisms." Characteristically, Valéry, mindful of the original Greek sense of "poetry," circumscribes it as "fabrication," adverting not so much to the work itself as to the act of making, in which the mind heightens and perfects itself.

We should be careful not to misinterpret this attitude of modern poets as a cold surrogate for absent creative powers. In point of fact, we can observe that the intellectual reflectiveness of the language leads to poetic triumph whenever it has to cope with a complicated, dream-hazy material. The extraordinary sensitivity of the modern psyche has sensibly consigned

127

itself to an artistic expertise of Apollonian clarity, which ensures that the poet's desire for ambivalent, magical poetry demonstrates its own necessity in a lengthy trial before finally speaking.

The part played by the awareness of form in modern poetry is in line with the above. In poets like Mallarmé, this awareness manifests itself in practice as metrical precision; and even the accompanying theory follows in Mallarmé's footsteps without, however, adopting his ontological foundation. The most prolific observer of practical and theoretical formal rigor is Valéry. His statements are a zenith of Romance formalism. He realized the mysterious unison of skepticism and formal rigor: "Doubt leads to form." Doubt is aware of how dubious the mere ideas of content are; poetry, however, seizes upon metrics as a set of rules that, as in a game, are to be followed to the letter, and which transcend crude spontaneity and the chaos of chance ideas. The special feature of metrical precision in modern poetry is its contrast to the dark, dream-hazy content — analogous to that other tension between lucid syntax and intricate statement.

Yet even poets with little or no formal rigor — and they constitute a majority — have a reflective attitude toward their formal devices. Claudel meticulously calculated the correlation of his free verse and the periods of respiration. Aragon minutely analyzed the innovations of his rhyming system. These concerns bear out the consciousness of modern poetry, a consciousness totally different from traditional technical knowledge by means of which earlier poets found their specific diction in varying given material. García Lorca, who exhausted all possibilities of form to the point of total dearticulation of the verse, once admitted in a conversation: "If it is true that I am a poet by the grace of God — or the devil — then my being one is due also to technique and effort, and because I try to be absolutely aware of what a poem is." T. S. Eliot saw artistic practice as precision work similar to producing a machine or turning a table leg. Although his own metrical forms are free, his precision work is evident in the subtle repetition of lines and in the planning of longer poems which, like musical compositions, comprise several movements. In good poets, formal freedom is not anarchy but a carefully measured multiplicity of significative tokens.

Finally, we would like to point out that the situation in contemporary music is parallel, that the structural unity which we have been discussing is common to all of modern art. Stravinsky's *Poetics of Music* (a counterpart to Valéry's *Introduction à la poétique*) contains the following as its main ideas: every artistic operation must take place in the "shadowless light" of the poetic, i.e., in the knowledge of how to make; the artist is the highest type of *homo faber*; his God is Apollo, not Dionysus; inspiration is of secondary importance; of primary significance is the operating discovery that replaces improvisation with construction, and chaotic freedom with "the realm of artistic restraint," in which only melody finds its smile again; the poetic is, ultimately, an "ontology."

DUAL RELATIONSHIP TO MODERNITY
AND THE LITERARY HERITAGE

Since Baudelaire, poetry has been turning to the modernity of technological civilization. A peculiarity of this development is that it can be both positive and negative. Apollinaire fuses the very real world of the machine with the dream images of the absurd. The machine becomes magical; at times, it is hallowed. But the attempt leads to dissonance. Apollinaire's *Zone*, the long opening poem of his *Alcools* (1913), puts airports and churches on the same level, makes Christ "the first pilot," and has him set an altitude record. A variant is Jacques Prévert's *Le Combat avec l'ange* [The struggle with the angel], in *Paroles* (1949): the struggle is a boxing match that takes place in a ring, under magnesium light; man, beaten, sinks down upon the sawdust. It seems as if technology and the life of metropolitan masses entice as they torment, stimulate as they provide new experiences of desolation. Poetry reacts to them in this twofold manner. The phenomenon is hard to disembroil. Poetry is haunted by the suffering from lack of freedom in an age dominated by planning, clocks, collective constraint, an age in which the "second industrial revolution" has reduced man to a minimum. He has been dethroned by his own machines, the products of his power. The theory of cosmic explosion and the reckoning with billions of light-years have depreciated him to an insignificant accident.

These things have been described often enough. Yet there seems to be some connection between such experiences and certain characteristics of modern versecraft. The flight into the unreal, the abnormal imagination, the deliberate mysteriousness, the hermetic isolation of language: all these can be understood as attempts of the modern soul, trapped in a technologized, imperialistic, commercialized era, to preserve its own freedom as well as the miraculous in the world, something far different from the "miracle of science."

Nonetheless, this poetry is marked by the era to which it opposes its extreme freedom. The coolness of its craftsmanship, its tendency to experiment, its hardness of heart, and other features as well, are immediately derived from the *Zeitgeist*. Poetry attempts the "synthetic poem," in which primal poetic images — stars, seas, winds — mix with technological entities and scientific jargon. "I see a thick spot of machine oil and think for

129

a long, long time of my mother's blood" (Jouve). For the Italian Cardarelli, the hour before death is like waiting below a clock in a railroad station and counting the minutes. In T. S. Eliot's and St.-John Perse's poetry, such cool and sober states are made into song without a loss of dissonance. However, we have to observe something else. As in Rimbaud and Mallarmé, present-day poetry has often reached the point of self-destruction. This is perhaps the most violent conquest attained by modernity, analogous to mankind's efforts at blowing up the globe.

A similar double aspect is evident in the attitude toward the literary heritage or to history in general. The norm is a deliberate rupture with tradition. Because of the historical disciplines, the comfortable availability of all literatures, the museums, the highly advanced methods of reproduction and interpretation, etc., the nineteenth century developed such an overabundance of historical wealth as to generate a counterpressure, an aversion to anything belonging to the past, a dislike that had been brewing in the crumbling of the humanist mentality and which could assume any form from weariness to abuse. "Any writer worthy of the name has to write against everything written before him" (Francis Ponge). Even among those who were more restrained, the memory of bygone literature turned into a call for writing differently from one's predecessors under any circumstances. Valéry, in his noble and ironic manner, explains; "Reading is a burden to me. . . . I sometimes congratulate myself on being so poor and so unfit for the hoards of accumulated knowledge. I am poor, but I am king . . . of my inner monkeys and parrots." [14]

Insofar as the practice of modern poetry is symbolic, we can observe a fact recurrent since Mallarmé: the symbols are self-contained rather than taken from a familiar body of material. Valéry and Guillén seem to be exceptions; yet even their symbols reach back no further than to Mallarmé, thereby constituting a modern stylistic type and not part of an extensive traditionalism. When St.-John Perse converts limestone, sand, reefs, and ashes into symbolic counters, no literary training will help the reader to grasp them, especially since the poet is not striving for any precise meaning. It suffices that these symbols suggest fleeting semantic possibilities. The meanings of symbols vary from author to author and must be gathered from each writer separately; a frequent result is that the symbols are completely unintelligible. The extent to which this self-contained symbolism has spread to music is apparent in Hindemith's preface to his *Marienleben* (1948).

On the other hand, the open break with tradition is countered by a

14. *Ibid.*, I, 961.

receptiveness to all literatures and religions, and by the desire to immerse oneself in the psychic depths of Man, where Europe and Asia, magical and mythical primal images, meet. This was evident in Rimbaud long before C. G. Jung developed his influential psychology of the collective unconscious and archetypes. Modern poetry is rich in verses echoing universal poetic, mythical, and archaic material. The heritage of folklore appears. Medieval subjects and legends are touched upon, and the result can be as enchanting a work as Claire and Yvan Goll's continuation of the *Fioretti* of Saint Francis of Assisi (*Nouvelles petites fleurs* . . . [1943]). St.-John Perse's poems are full of allusions to older painting, ancient myths, exotic places of worship. Ezra Pound weaves into his poems patches of Provençal, Old Italian, Greek, and Chinese poetry. T. S. Eliot's *Waste Land* borrows symbols from the legend of the Holy Grail as described in a scholarly work, plus a number of themes from the Upanishads and the Bible, and uses, in a new context, fragmentary or veiled quotations derived from Richard Wagner, Baudelaire, Shakespeare, Ovid, Dante, Augustine. The poet provides the necessary explanations in a self-commentary in which the reader finds it difficult to tell how much is meant ironically. Eliot's practice inspired many imitators, including the Italian Montale and the Spaniard Diego.

Nevertheless, methods of this kind do not issue from a genuine traditionalism, which presupposes that a poet feels at home in a unified and closed period of history. Such borrowings, references, and quotations are wraithlike disorganized remnants of a disrupted past. They may be meant as a synthesis, yet their effect is helter-skelter and chaotic. Like the unbounded absorption of a world in which all objects are put on the same level, they belong to a style of haphazardness, incoherence, the telescoping of everything. They are — and this can be observed particularly in Ezra Pound — devices for making the poetic persona a kind of collective "I" that appears in a startling succession of masks. Or else, as in St.-John Perse and Gottfried Benn, they derive from an intention to use the most farfetched words to elicit a magic of tone and imagery of great lyrical fascination. Such poems anachronistically crisscross historical fragments and linguistic tokens, or else place them beside words typical of the modern world. "The cycles erupt: age-old sphinxes, violins, and a gate from Babylon, and a jazz combo from the Rio Grande, swing music, and a prayer . . ." (Benn). Such lines are the privilege of a poetry that can rove about anywhere as long as it sings. But this fusion and this removal of barriers spell the death of history. Modern poetry makes historical space as homeless as objective space. We mention this tendency simply for the sake of description, not to place judgment upon it.

DEHUMANIZATION

In 1925, Ortega y Gasset published his essay on the dehumanization of art (*La deshumanización del arte*). The title has become a formula, demonstrating that an observer of modern art must make use of a negative concept; the application, however, is descriptive rather than condemnatory. Ortega's essay stems partially (this is unspecified) from Kant's and Schiller's aesthetic views, especially the theory of gratuitous beauty. The emphasis of the essay is on the idea that the human sensation evoked by a work of art distracts from the aesthetic quality. Ortega applies this idea to every period of art and advocates any style that transforms objects and deprives them of their essence. "Stylization means deforming reality. Stylization includes dehumanization." Thus, once again we run across the concept of distortion. Although this utterance implies a universal aesthetic principle (and is valid within limits), it is specifically modern in that it includes deformation and dehumanization.[15] But it is only in light of the circumstances prevailing since the mid-nineteenth century that such a negative definition of style has become possible. And Ortega's comments passed imperceptibly over to modern art. He views as its prime constituents the devaluation of organic structures, the theory that the work of art has no meaning other than the one inherent in its deforming style, the self-irony that is a reaction to the overly dramatic demeanor of past art. The most important feature, however, is the dehumanization. It manifests itself in the elimination of natural feelings; in the reversal of the earlier superiority of man over object, with man reduced to the lowest order of the hierarchy; and in the depiction of man from a viewpoint that makes him seem as nonhuman as possible. "The aesthetic pleasure of the modern artist arises precisely from this triumph over the human." The concordance of this essay with poetic programs and methods since Baudelaire is striking.

The category of dehumanization encompasses many features peculiar to modern poetry. The "I" is an anonymous, indefinable mood in which the potent and open elements of feeling have given way to a hidden vibrating, and which, whenever it threatens to turn sentimental, is hardened and alienated by astringent additions. The difference between this "I" and a more human one is evident in the development of Ramón Jiménez. Prior to World War I, he wrote a deeply personal poetry of melancholy, dream, tears, and exquisite gardens. As of the twenties, his verse became harder. In one poem, he called the soul a "column of silver." The metaphor is lovely but, like the rest of the poem, indicates a soul from which a

---

15. Dehumanization does not signify "making inhuman." If Ortega had meant this, then Guillén's criticism of him in his autobiographical work would have been correct (*Language and Poetry*, p. 245).

cozy melancholy has vanished, a soul that has become an indefinable tension between above and below. Ungaretti's poetry, particularly that which followed *Sentimento del tempo* (1935), speaks from a situation devoid of both joy and pain, and vibrating in a neutral contemplation. Thus, in a poem on the dawn (*Nascita d'Aurora* [1925]), he totally avoids the jubilation with which he used to celebrate this theme. The movements in the poem are exclusively those of the diction and the unreal imagery; they have no "soul" values. The suspicion that intimate feelings may be expected has made the very name of poetry suspect. The results are titles like H. Pichette's *Apoèmes* [Nonpoems] (1947), Georges Bataille's *La Haine de la poésie* [Hatred of poetry] (1947), and Francis Ponge's *Proêmes* [Proems] (1948). Even the aristocrat Paul Valéry comments that artistic work, like scientific work, has "something inhuman" about it. Calling a poem a "festival of the intellect," he adds that it contains the image of "that which one is usually not," for in the poem human "trivia" are silenced. By way of comparison, we may note that they were anything but silent in Verlaine's poetry.

An example of poetry devoid of an "I" or any human presence is García Lorca's *El grito* [The cry] (in *Poema de cante jondo*, 1922); the poem contains only about a dozen lines.

> The ellipse of a cry
> goes from mountain
> to mountain.

The space is not primary here, nor even the cry, but rather the ellipse, a geometric figure, the initial subject of the action. Everything else derives from the ellipse in secondary objectification: space, mountains, olive trees, night. The ellipse, half literal and half metaphorical, turns into a black rainbow, then into a violin bow "beneath which the long strings of the wind quiver." We never find out who uttered the cry. Only the cry exists. A human utterance is completely separated from any human being — does it really come from a human being? The closing lines mention some people who probably heard the cry:

> The people in the caves
> hold out their lamps.

But this human presence fails to humanize the poem. And, besides, these last lines are parenthetical. The poem glances back at the perplexed cave-

133

dwellers, from a great distance, and perplexed, as it were. *El grito* is verbalized anonymity; its event is the sonorous line that reaches the mountains, the olives, the wind, today, tomorrow, yesterday, but whose source is not human. García Lorca is a master of that great domain of modern poetry: the anonymous.

An anecdotal poem by Krolow, *Der Augenblick des Fensters* [The moment of the window], has a "someone" as subject at the beginning. He is not named more precisely, not even when, after acting ("pours light out of the window") and after the tender and gentle consequences of this action, he is mentioned again. We cannot even tell whether the "someone" in the first line and the "someone" in the penultimate line are identical. If two different people are meant, they have one thing in common: anonymity. The intimate, familiar words within the poem do not relieve the anonymity. It is stronger than anything else, stronger even than the question as to whether there are two "someones" or just one. The anonymity has a disturbing effect, however, as it projects the small, familiar events into the spectral, into a dreamy dehumanization.

Occasionally there are more familiar, more human themes, such as the theme of unhappy love. Its modernization is demonstrated in a poem by Alberti, *Miss X, enterrada en el viento del oeste* [*Miss X, buried in the west wind*] (1926). It is not the speaker who is weeping: "Hairdressers weep without your hair." A nightclub is mourning because Miss X is no longer with us; "The sky no longer sends your wireless." Quick evocations of ships, seaplanes, closed banks, casinos, consulates. Toward the end, the language chokes. "Sun killed by an electric shock. Moon charred." There is no personal pain. Pain exists only in objects. They are a mixture of the grotesque, the banal, of civilization and cosmos, with pain hardening into an unsentimental fact. Marinetti's *Futurist Manifesto* (1909) contained the following challenge: "The suffering of a human being is not more interesting to us than the suffering of a short-circuited lamp."

There are poets who protest against sadness, but, on the other hand, they have not regained the human joy of older poetry. "Do not open your bed to sorrow," writes St.-John Perse. Yet his verses move in inner peripheral zones almost beyond empathy, especially since time and place, which might enable orientation, are withdrawn from the outer world. He calls for a love of life, and his appeal is reckless and violent. His poetry conveys the reader to strange spiritual territories to which he cannot react with "joy"; they are magnificently artificial. Alberti's collection *A la pintura* (1948) contains a hymn to white, which is meant as the color symbolic of merriment. Chaotic imagery is strained to refer to this white. Yet the latter has a synthetic nature; it is an insistent call of language, the product of an imagination intoxicated with light, but which is deforming. Guillén's poetry has been praised for its lack of tragedy and bitterness. "Suffering is offensive," he writes in one of his poems.[16] Yet his lack does not dehumanize his works any the less. Things and people are transformed into abstract categories. The poet stares impersonally into the pure figures of space and light. His intellectual happiness never overshadows a deep-seated dissonance. It makes no sense to quiz modern poets as to when they evince sorrow or joy. Such contents, which certainly occur often enough, soar upward or withdraw into a zone in which the soul is wider, cooler, but also braver than the sensitive human being.

One of the many variants of dehumanization is a poetry whose contents consist exclusively of objects. And the choice of extremely insignificant objects is as characteristic as the omission of any sort of qualification. Such poetry is almost a continuation of what Flaubert once did in the novel. A typical practitioner is the French poet Francis Ponge. Picon said that Ponge shows what poetry can be like when one has stopped believing in it. The object-subjects of his free-form poems are bread, a door, a shell, pebbles, a candle, cigarettes. They are captured in such objectivness that Sartre spoke of "poetic phenomenology." The capturing "I" is fictive, a mere conveyer of language. And the language is anything but realistic. It does not really warp the objects but either paralyzes them or imbues naturally numb objects with such a bizarre life that a ghostly unreality springs forth. And the human element is also omitted.

Yet it is precisely this pseudo-objective poetry which points out that man *is* present in all of modern poetry, but in a different way — as creative language and imagination. The dehumanization of the contents and the spiritual reactions comes from the unlimited authority arrogated by the verse-making intellect. Even in poetry, man becomes his own dictator. He annihilates his own naturalness, bans it from the world, and expels the world itself in order to satisfy his own freedom. This is the strange paradox of dehumanization.

ISOLATION AND *ANGST*

Musil, in a posthumous text, defines the poet as "the man most strongly aware of the irrecoverable solitude of the ego in the world and among human beings." This thought, which had existed in romanticism, survived the nineteenth century to become a modern idea resembling the concept of the *poète maudit*, and attained a grimacing form in Apollinaire's prose tale *Le Poète assassiné* (1916). In this work the allegorical and absurd plot

16. Guillén, *Cántico*, p. 72.

leads to the murder of the poet, who is assassinated by all countries; a sculptor dedicates "a statue of nothing" to the murdered hero. Trakl's late poems elicited the apt remark that in his verse the individual exists only in relationship to himself. St.-John Perse's lengthy poem *Exile* (1942) describes his language, which he summons into the unknown, as "the pure speech of exile." Rumor has it that we are living in an "age of anxiety": W. H. Auden uses this phrase as the title of a poem (1946). The universal proclamations of anxiety, or *Angst*, contain a good deal of fashionable chitchat. Anxiety is an obligatory component of "topical" adolescent verse, superseding the earlier moons and moonings. The best and most virile poems, however, show the authenticity of anxiety as a basic experience.

Goethe's poem *Meeresstille* [Ocean stillness] tells of the paralyzing spell of the terrible, of the enormous motionless expanse. Yet a second poem of his belongs with this one, *Glückliche Fahrt* [Happy journey]; the terrible subsides, the "anxious fetter" dissolves, the boatman takes heart, and land looms in the distance to save him. Poetry of this sort tolerates anxiety and the terrible only as a transition to clarity and hope. We will come across few texts in modern poetry that begin in *Angst* only to escape it. A certain thematic similarity to Goethe's poem can be found in a short poem by Ramón Jiménez, *Mares* [Seas]. He tells of a voyage in a boat. The boat bumps into something, but nothing results. There is only stillness; there are only waves and something "new" for which no word is available. This voyage is the reverse of Goethe's: we move from hope to paralysis. García Lorca followed his above-mentioned poem about the cry with another one, *El silencio*. Yet the second poem does not remove the uncanniness of the nonhuman cry; instead, it produces new uncanniness, a sinister silence through which "valleys and echoes glide, and which presses foreheads against the ground." He often makes silence the soundless presence of *Angst*, as in his *Elegia del silencio*, in which he calls silence the "ghost of harmony, smoke of lament," for its bears "age-old suffering and the echo of cries forever extinct." Then, again, he writes of a superanxiety. One of his late poems is *Panorama ciego de Nueva York* [Blind panorama of New York]; it is written in free verse, and the content has little to do with the title. Where is the great and absolute pain? Not in the megalopolises with their blood and misery, not on the "earth with its unchanging doors that always lead to the redness of fruits." The voice has no pain, only teeth, "but teeth that must remain silent in the black fury." This is *Angst*, afraid of not receiving the food of pain, which it hungers after. *Angst* speaks a different language in Eluard's poem *Le Mal* [Evil] (in *La Vie immédiate* [1932]). He never mentions anxiety. Yet the

136

poem exudes a hypnotic spell deriving from the reiteration of "il y eut [there was]" — a practice of Rimbaud's — from the litany-like *single* sentence that carries the poem, and from the statements themselves. "There was the door like a saw . . . , the aimless waste land, there were the broken panes, the dramatic flesh of the wind was lacerated on them . . . , there were the borders of swamps . . . , in a deserted room, in an abortive room, in an empty room." The incoherent objects, quickly glossed over, are not meant to be viewed in themselves. They are tokens of negation, refusal, demolition, a sawing-up, and thus — although the language is reticent — they are tokens of *Angst*, which perceives or, rather, produces everything that the tokens represent.

Colloquially, one may say that an indigent room has its own poetry. Jacob Burckhardt called the "miraculous spectacle" of history "poetry." In both cases, *poetry* signifies the spiritual habitability of sensory phenomena, whether indigent or miraculous, and presupposes a contact between the individual and the world. Modern poetry, however, shows a different countenance. It deliberately alienates the familiar and puts near-by things at a distance; it seems to be propelled by a compulsion that upsets the contact between the individual and the world, as well as the contact between human beings. In Flaubert's late novels, the derangement of contact has become the law of inner and outer style; the behavior of objects is contrary to that of an individual human being: when he suffers, they glow and flourish; when he goes to his beloved, bleak slums line the street. A basic situation in these novels is the failure of people to meet as planned, either spatially or psychically; none of them reaches his goal. The paratactical sentences mirror the splintering of the plot into an aggregate whose individual events rarely have a causal relation. Later novels have even increased the derangement of contact (Camus, Hemingway, Butor, and others). In the twenties, Bertolt Brecht used *Verfremdung* ("alienation") as a key word in his poetics; he said that alienation could be achieved by omitting all the orientating motivation of an event. Shortly before his death, Apollinaire spoke of the "alien domains" toward which his poetry was heading. A poem by Max Jacob, *Jardin mystérieux* (1928), is full of waiting and listening; but the discontinuous sounds of a chaotic outer world never appease the waiting; they go beyond the poem and become part of an eternal wait for something that never comes.

Musil continues the above-quoted statement on the poet with the following (likewise unintentionally modern) idea: "Even in friendship and love, the poet feels a touch of the antipathy that keeps every creature away from others." The thought that human nearness is actually distance is a frequent theme of modern poetry. Ungaretti's *Canto* flows into unsentimental sorrow; the beloved woman is "remote as in a mirror," love discovers the "endless tomb" of inward loneliness. García Lorca: "How far away I am when I'm with you, and how near I am when you're away!" A love poem by Karl Krolow (1955) contains these lines: ". . . Will you hear me from behind the bitter-herbs face of the moon that crumbles? . . . And the night shatters like sodium, blue and black." The harsh imagery, the crumbling and shattering, betoken the frustration of fervently attempted closeness as well as salvation by means of creative language — the only salvation possible.

Even the natural absence of the dead turns into absolute distance. A famous example is García Lorca's cycle about the dead bullfighter Sánchez Mejías (1935). The final poem is *Alma ausente* [Absent soul]. Little mention is made of the dead man; the poem emphasizes that no one knows him anymore: not the bull, nor the horse, nor the ants in his home, "nor the child, nor the evening," nor the stone beneath which he lies. He is so far away that not even thought can reach him. "But I celebrate you" — yet even this attempt fails; the singer, too, becomes distant from the unreachable dead man and can sing only of the mournful breath that blows through the olive trees.

In 1929, Alberti published his collection of poems *Sobre los ángeles* [About the angels]. These angels, like those in Rimbaud, have no Christian significance. They are vestigial symbols of something metaphysical, legendary creatures invented by a lonely man, and "mute as the rivers and the seas." A dramatics takes place between them and mankind, leading to a total removal of contact. Man knows that the angel is here; yet man does not see him, nor does the light see him, "nor the wind and the panes." And, likewise, the angel does not see man, either, does not know the cities he himself passes through, is devoid of eyes and shadow; he weaves silence into his hair, is "a lonely moist hole, a dried-up well"; living in our midst, he is dead; he has lost the city, and the city has lost him. The basic symbolism of the poems (which critics have superfluously labeled "surrealistic") is clear, no matter how difficult or incomprehensible individual lines may be. Angels once brought light and grace to mankind, even appeared as God's avengers to wreak terror. In Alberti's poems, however, the angels no longer know man; they are tired of him, so tired that man can only picture them as ugly and dead.

In Kafka's *Das nächste Dorf* [The next village], an old man says: "I can't understand how a young man can make up his mind to ride to the next village without fearing that the time span of an ordinary, happy life will barely suffice for such a ride." This parable expresses a seminal situation of modern writing — a failure to arrive at even a near-by goal. A poetic example is García Lorca's *Canción de jinete* [Riding song]. The

138

rider knows the roads leading to his destination, the city of Cordova, but he also knows that he will never arrive. Death is staring at him from the towers of Cordova. He will never come home again; he will meet death on the wide, windy plain. Once again, a glance at older poetry will clarify the position of modern poetry. First of all, in Du Bellay's *Heureux qui comme Ulysse* [Happy the man who like Ulysses], written in the sixteenth century, the speaker, staying in Rome, is homesick for his faraway village on the Loire. His nostalgia summons up homey images: the wall surrounding his house, the smoke from the chimney, the slate on the roof. Faraway things exist clearly in his soul, emanating a familiar calm despite the distance. Even the reason for his absence is a familiar human experience: his work has forced him to live abroad. Then, in Goethe's posthumous addenda to the *Western-Eastern Divan*, there is a poem that begins: "Lasst mich weinen [Let me weep]." Here, too, the speaker is far away from his goal. He spends the night in the endless desert, musing about the many leagues that separate him from Suleika, and he weeps. Du Bellay's poem and Goethe's have a common element: a man is thinking of a faraway goal to which he is drawn. For him, it is not faraway. He possesses it as the object of desire; it remains familiar and attainable. Du Bellay is homesick; Goethe weeps over the "road-lengthening, aggravating windings"; and, for both poets, pain leads to solace. Further solace is provided by recalling mythical characters. Du Bellay thinks of Jason and Ulysses; although the poet envies these long-ago homecomings, the envious memories remain within the realm of humane brotherhood. Goethe recalls Achilles, Xerxes, Alexander, and is unashamed of his tears because these great men once wept.

At the very beginning of García Lorca's *Canción de jinete*, Cordova is called "remote"; this adjective is not to be construed in its spatial sense alone. The rider already sees the city before him; but, although relatively close, it has moved to an absolute distance. An enigma, represented by death, has made the city unattainable and has turned the short route into an endless and mortal one. No distinct emotion — neither homesickness nor tears — responds. The soul abides in a shapeless mood. A few fitful calls to the pony, to the road, to death — nothing more. And then the elliptical sentences, their lack of verbs creating the proper diction for the motionless acceptance of the alien. We can see the vast differences. For the older poets, the spatially remote destination remains spiritually close by. For the modern poets, spatial nearness becomes inner remoteness. García Lorca's *Canción de jinete* is the poem of impossible homecoming, impossible because an unknown spell has placed the near-by home beyond all reach.

OBSCURITY, "HERMETICISM," UNGARETTI

Modern poetry compels language to take on the paradoxical task of simultaneously expressing and concealing a meaning. Obscurity has become the predominant aesthetic principle, outlawing the customary communicative function of language and letting the poem hover in such a way that it withdraws rather than comes closer. Poets like Ungaretti or Aleixandre may claim, in statements about themselves, that their writings are elementally human and natural; yet their poems seem to derive from a single process of encodement, or at least they have that effect. Obscure poetry tells of events, creatures, or objects without informing the reader of their cause, their time, or their place. Utterances are interrupted rather than terminated. Often the content is made up of changing language movements, abrupt or hasty or smoothly sliding ones, for which the objective or emotional events are merely material without attainable meaning. No wonder that some modern poets have been going back to the most enigmatic of the old Provençal troubadours, Arnaut Daniel, whom Pound has translated and whom Aragon admires. It sometimes looks as if modern poetry is simply a notation of inklings and blind experiments garnered for some future date to incite clearer inklings and more successful experiments. Things are made available but cannot yet be availed of. Ever since Rimbaud and Mallarmé, the potential addressee of a poem has been the vague future. There have always been poets who set themselves vatic goals and spoke of them in sublime obscurity. But modern prophecy is not sublime. It has no clear vision of the future. Its dark lyrics revolve restlessly around indeterminable possibilities.

Poets have made any number of utterances programmatically demanding and sometimes even justifying obscurity. A few of these poets were mentioned in the first chapter. The drive toward obscurity brings up the problem of comprehension; the poets' answers are along the same lines as Mallarmé's, although without his mental thoroughness. Yeats wants a poem to have as many meanings as it has readers. For T. S. Eliot, the poem is an independent object existing between the author and the reader, with the relationship between the author and the poem distinct from that between the reader and the poem; the reader draws the poem into a new play of meanings with their own justification, even if these meanings lead away from the indeterminate intention of the author. The Spanish poet Salinas writes: ''Poetry depends on the higher form of interpretation that resides in misunderstanding. When a poem is written down, it ends but it does not stop; it seeks another poem within itself, within the author, the reader, and in silence.'' The concept of understanding has given way to the concept of

140

further versification — not only by the reader but also by the anonymous poetic powers, of which the author himself was totally unaware and which slumber unused in his language as well as in silence. This idea is laden with significance and is as cryptic as the poetry accompanying it. (Salinas subsequently changed his mind, but his later opinion does not invalidate the earlier one.) "The darkness with which the poet is reproached derives from the very night it explores: the darkness of the soul and of the mystery in which the human creature is submerged" (St.-John Perse). Other poets write that it is poetic precision itself which demands a new use of words, a new vocabulary, and abnormal metaphors, the resulting poetry being inevitably obscure.

Guillén's *Cántico* contains the poem *Cierro los ojos* [Close the eyes], a poetic apologia for poetic obscurity reminiscent of Mallarmé (a line from whose *Surgi de la croupe* serves as an epigraph). The content, half described and half translated, is as follows: I close my eyes, and the darkness strikes sparks; they are a joyous destiny. Night breaks its seals and brings up from the abyss the splendors that oppose death. I close my eyes, and a great world persists, dazzling me, empty of tumult. I found my certainty upon the dark; the darker the lightning, the more it is mine. In the blackness arises a rose.[17]

The sense of the text can be explained as follows: Darkness comes from seclusion from the outer world. The inner world opens; free from the noise and mortality of life, it turns the darkness (absence of reality) into light, becomes the birth of the rose that blossoms only in the light of darkness ("rose," as with Mallarmé, is the symbol of the poetic word, but here it is linked to the theme of failure). It is only in the unreality which poetry needs in order to be dark that perfect poetry succeeds. This idea expresses a crucial decision of modern poetry.

Some time ago the Italians came up with a word for obscure poetry: *hermeticism*. At first derogatory and suggestive of confusion and occultism, the term soon became positive. Thus its etymology, like that of most terms for literary groups, has been an ascending one. The main Italian poets considered by their countrymen to be hermeticists were Ungaretti, Quasimodo, and Montale (also celebrated for his translations of T. S. Eliot). This grouping is a convention of criticism and could just as easily have included other poets. The interesting thing is that hermeticism became a definite concept in literary criticism, which, by accepting the word, accepted an essential characteristic of modern poetry. "Hermetic" poetry

17. [Based on a translation by J. M. Cohen, in *The Penguin Book of Spanish Verse*, rev. ed. (Harmondsworth and Baltimore, 1960), p. 370. — *Trans.*]

is the Italian version of *poésie pure* and the most violent reaction against the declamatory writing of twentieth-century Italy (D'Annunzio).

Ungaretti, whom we shall discuss briefly, was influenced by Mallarmé, Apollinaire, Valéry, St.-John Perse, and Góngora. Since the 1920s his lyrics have been marked by an extreme concentration of language. The word, he says, should be a quick burst of silence, as it was in Mallarmé. The word is a fragment; it exists trembling between the fleetingly grazed but highly enigmatic world and the silence that instantly closes in again upon the word. All of Ungaretti's poems reveal this hallmark of the fragmentary. The most powerful effect is in the short poems, of which Ungaretti is as much a past master as is García Lorca. These poems should not be read for their contents, which at times are amazingly trivial or else totally unfathomable. The reader should, instead, absorb their words as formulas of lyrical sound with a spellbinding resonance beyond any translation. Nor do the longer poems offer contents with an objectively logical sequence. The movements (for example, opening, lighting up, sinking, trembling to a halt) are clearer than the moving objects and yet, in themselves, are multivalent and easily rearranged in a different sequence.

Ungaretti's obscurity is demonstrated in the free-verse poem *L'isola* [The island] (in *Sentimento del tempo*). In vibrating and sonorous but utterly simple sentences devoid of any "I," it tells of an incident. The agent is a "he." Who? There is no answer, only the indefiniteness of the determinants — specifically, the personal pronouns, which, in accordance with normal Italian usage, remain elliptical and are represented only in the verb forms. Thus, the vagueness is more effective than in an English translation and is increased by the string of disconnected statements. Bucolic objects constitute the material of the action: an island, woods, a nymph, a shepherd, and sheep.

> To a shore . . . he came,
> And went on
> And a fluttering of wings called him
> Which had unfurled from the shrill
> Heartbeat of the torrid water
> And he saw a ghost . . . a
>   nymph . . . ;
> In himself, from pretence to the true
>   flame
> Roaming, he arrived at a meadow
>   where
> The shadow thickened in the eyes
> Of the virgins . . .

Which virgins? Here the action stops. It remains a fragment devoid of cause or goal. The end is a standstill. The groupings of words become more and more abnormal:

> The branches dripped
> A lazy rain of arrows, . . .
> . . . .
> sheep . . .
> . . . nibbled on
> The luminous blanket;
> The shepherd's hands were a glass
> Polished by weak fever.

Where is the one who arrives? The static image terminating the poem has forgotten the initial action as if neither the action nor its agent had ever existed. And the agent himself is more insignificant than the action. The content of the poem resides in the line of motion: arrival, encounter, inaction. The movements are abstract; they signify themselves alone and are imbued with the mystery of the inexplicable action which they constitute. Nor does the ending solve the mystery; instead, it adds a new one. The stasis may terminate the dynamics, yet the dissonance of the image (hands like glass) reaches a higher level, the level of absolute and despotic language, to move into obscurity.[18]

The hermetic verse of some poets leaves the reader with the impression that the works end with the "slamming of a door," as Gustave Picon once remarked. But when hermeticism is merely faddish gesticulation, a charlatanry prospers, chattering away at random — and eliciting great admiration. Avant-garde writers, who are filled with enormous self-respect, excel in statements of arrant nonsense. Even Rimbaud was occasionally guilty of this. One consequence of fashionable hermeticism is the helpless-

18. Leo Spitzer interprets *L'isola* as a straightforward love poem in the tradition of pastoral poetry (see his review of the first [German] edition of this book in *Modern Language Notes*, November, 1957, as well as the appendix to Ungaretti's *Il taccuino del vecchio* [Milan, 1959], p. 120). The indefinite "he" supposedly has the same function as the "I" or "you" generally used in poetry and is identical with the "shepherd" of the penultimate verse, who would thus be the subject-agent of the poem. Even if this identity is deliberate, one must nevertheless admit how unusual and even disorienting it is to narrate an action whose bearer is not mentioned until the very end. And as for the "he," there is a considerable difference between its indefiniteness and that of the "I" or "you," which is common in poetry and which, even without any precise reference, turns a poem into a monologue or a dialogue. In order to regard Ungaretti's poem as clear and straightforward, one would have to have a set of coordinates; yet the poem does not hint at any points of reference. Furthermore, the gentle hermeticism does not in any way detract from its beauty.

ness of the critics. A few years ago, in Australia, some pranksters published a volume of totally nonsensical verse, which, they claimed, was the posthumous work of a miner: critics were deeply moved by the "profundity" of this *Nachlass*. An American edition of Yeats's poems contained the words *soldier Aristotle*, a typographical error for *solider Aristotle*. A young poet, not realizing that this was a typographical error, voiced his amazement at the mystery of the "soldier Aristotle." There are utterances that verge on the unbearable, such as Rilke's pretentious remark on his sixteenth sonnet to Orpheus: "You ought to know, or guess, that this sonnet is addressed to a dog; I don't care to *gloss* it." Mallarmé used to dispatch such remarks with a certain self-irony.

LANGUAGE MAGIC AND SUGGESTIVENESS

Ever since Rimbaud and Mallarmé, modern poetry has become increasingly a matter of language magic. (We explained this term in earlier chapters.) Poetics of the twentieth century constantly mention the idea of "suggestion" and "suggestiveness" when touching upon the question of poetic effect. Bergson made this concept part and parcel of his aesthetics in his *Essai sur les données immédiates de la conscience* (1889). The same concept is used by painters and musicians. "Suggestion" occurs when cerebral poetry releases magical psychic forces and emits rays which the reader is unable to resist, even though he may not "understand" anything. This suggestive radiation derives mainly from the sensory powers of language: rhythm, sound, tonality. They function in unison with so-called semantic overtones — connotations on the periphery of a word or sparked off by an abnormal linking of words. The poetry of suggestion and language magic grants to the word the authority of the prime authorship of the poetic act. For such poetry, only the word, and never the world, is real. This is why modern poets are constantly emphasizing that a poem does not mean, but *is*. The numerous discussions of *poésie pure* revolve around this idea.

Poe's principle of drafting a poem from the sound energy that precedes the sense in language, and then, and only then, inserting a secondary meaning, survives to this day. Benn writes: "The poem is finished before it even begins; the author simply does not yet know his text." Elsewhere, with an astounding reminiscence of an utterance by Novalis (see above, p. 14), Benn says: "There exist only verbal transcendences: the mathematical theorems and the word as art." Benn's own poetry reveals the aforementioned principle of the authorship of the word, particularly in the primacy of the sound, which can lyricize even the driest contents. His poem *Chopin*

144

is sonorous biography.[19] The content consists of allusive fragments of action, reflection, inner monologue, spoken in broken sentences. The sequence within the poem does not correspond to the chronology of life and death; it moves in the opposite direction. There are names of concert pianos; there is mention of a fee, an address, and precise information on Chopin's technique; there is even a medical diagnosis ("with hemorrhages and scar tissue"). But even these dry, matter-of-fact statements vibrate; and the vibrations gloss over the fragments and breaks, making the poem haunting and unforgettable. We can see to what extent the poet can neglect conventional poetic motifs without destroying the lyrical substance, which, although seeming to verge on prose, is now open to new, meditative tones.

At this point we might again mention Ramón Jiménez. His later period includes poems having a hypnotic effect. Certain lines consist of a burden-like repetition; others are framed as questions that require no answers. Reiteration and unanswered questions make the communication as pressure-less as possible, allowing it to pass into a sonorous enchantment with a dying fall, an enchantment that emerges as the true master of the verse. Poetry that stems from the impulse of the words or pure sound leads to the countless possibilities of the kind described at the end of the chapter on Rimbaud. Thus Henri Michaux writes, "dans la toux, dans l'atroce, dans la transe [in the cough, in the atrocious, in the trance]"; the language, obeying its own drive, produces an inexplicable meaning but pierces deep into the ear; a persistent group of syllables (*dans la*) arouses a varied, but nearly homonymous, cluster of sounds. At the close of Eliot's *Waste Land*, there emerges abruptly the meaningless syllable *Da*, recurring several times, preceding fragments of a Hindu tenet which alternate with other lines; only at the very end are the fragments combined to form a group of Sanskrit words. This entire process is musical and is possible only in a poetry that handles language as primarily a potency of sound.

PAUL VALÉRY

The relationship of poetry to the sovereign power of language was probably dealt with most thoroughly by Valéry, in a clarifying elaboration of some of Mallarmé's ideas. Poetry, Valéry continually reiterates, is a penetration into the primal strata of language, strata that once yielded formulas of magic and incantation and might still be yielding them. Furthermore, poetry is a testing of the combinations of changing areas of meaning and changing effects of sound until the *one* combination succeeds, and with the inevitabil-

19. Benn, *Gesammelte Werke*, ed. D. Wellershoff (Wiesbaden, 1962–63), III, 188.

ity of a mathematical formula. Valéry knows that in such poetry the "meaning" will suffer most of all. A poem has "no true meaning," that is, no single meaning that might exhaust it. Valéry's own poetry always permits multiple interpretations. A poem such as *Les Pas* seems to depict a tender love scene (which is how Rilke translated it into German). Yet the poem speaks in a diction that hints at something else, a spiritual scene of poetry itself, with the expectation of the Muse a greater blessing than her arrival. Both explanations are possible; neither can be isolated without a loss of the twilight in which the poem was artistically submerged.

Valéry's ideas are founded on an epistemological nihilism, which we can only touch upon here. Because no cognition is possible, poetic speech acquires the total freedom of projecting poetic creations into the Void. Valéry calls such creations "myths": "*Myth* is the name for everything that exists and subsists with only the word as its cause." [20] And the word is "the means by which the spirit multiplies in the Void." As for reality, which exists only as chance and accident, poetry continuously transforms it, reaching the unreality that Valéry labels "dream." In poetry, the spirit catches sight of its own powers and perfects them by overcoming the self-imposed resistance of rigorous form. Only the acts of the spirit are necessary and are thus superior to reality, which is always accidental. We can see how close these ideas are to Mallarmé's. The greatest French poet of the twentieth century justifies poetry on the basis of pure (nonpersonal) subjectivity, whose domain is not the world but language and "dream." Such poetry possesses the skeptical lucidity of recognizing, in both the insignificance of the real and the nothingness of transcendence, the condition of its own single possible perfection — namely, artistic perfection. One of Valéry's most revealing utterances goes: "[A poetic figure] is a perfectly wrought fragment of a nonexistent edifice." [21] "Nonexistent" means that the poem exists only as language; "fragment" means that the poem always remains inadequate when compared with the goal. Note that once again negative definitions (in this case, two) are necessary to support something that can be stated only positively: the poetic act. A further utterance goes: "Nothing is as beautiful as something that does not exist." This phrase is blatantly similar to one of Rousseau's (see above, p. 11). The completely different, unsentimental justification that marks Valéry's ideas indicates the difficult route that thinkers about poetry have taken since Rousseau.

At one point Valéry defines the poem as a "marvelous and highly sensitive balance between the sensual and the intellectual power of

20. Valéry, *Œuvres*, I, 963–64.
21. *Ibid*., p. 1490.

language." One may say that Valéry's own lyrics possess this equilibrium. He frequently explains that some of his poems sprang forth from a meaningless play of rhythms and sounds to which words, images, and ideas were subsequently added. The finished poem retains the genetic degrees as a scale of values: the poem is primarily song and only secondarily content. There are lines of fascinating sonority: "Dormeuse, amas doré d'ombres et d'abandons . . . ," ". . . Puis s'étendre, se fondre, et perdre sa vendange, / Et s'éteindre en un songe en qui le soir se change."[22] The vowels and nasals rise and fall between heights and depths, eventually returning to the medial level of the beginning.

The initiative that the words provide can, however, reside in their meanings. The poem *Intérieur*, whose action unfolds in both an outer and an inner space, starts with the lines: "A narrow-eyed slave girl, her glance heavy with soft chains, / Changes the water for my flowers, submerges into the near-by mirrors."[23] The metaphor of the chains has its source in the slave girl, and the immersion in the mirror is suggested by the water. An early poem, *La Fileuse*, with pure image-studded symbolism, echoes Mallarmé's theme of lack of contact between man and the world. A girl, sitting at an evening window, sinks into sleep and dream; a rose in the garden futilely greets the sleeping girl. As the connection between the girl and the flower is broken, the language weaves them together in an unreal mesh, with words that detach themselves like ghosts from the leitmotiv of spinning:

> But the sleeper spins an isolated
> wool;
> Mysteriously the frail shadow braids
> itself
> Into a spun object along the thread
> of her long, sleeping fingers.[24]

And the outside world, turning into twilight, becomes part of the "spinner."

Naturally, we cannot limit an interpretation of Valéry's lyrics to the function of language. His poems also have a law of inner style. This law resides not so much in the themes as in the fact that the poems make spiritual acts perceptible in the image material; and these acts are acts of artistic conscience. Valéry speaks at one point of the "intellectual

22. *Ibid.*, pp. 122, 123.
23. *Ibid.*, p. 147.
24. *Ibid.*, p. 75.

comedy" that forms the nuclear event of a poem. One of the most tangible examples is found in *Au platane*. We hardly need to say that the plane tree of the title is not treated as an object of nature. In its entire phenomenality, the tree is pure dynamics, tensed between the lure from above and the fetters from the deep. The tree hears the call of the "winds," which want to become language in the tree; it also hears the request that it deny language. And these events occur in accordance with artistic experiences such as we have found in Mallarmé. In Valéry, too, the tension is never resolved. A dissonance speaks in the abstract tension of powers within the poem and in the resistance of the unresolved content to the resolved singing.

It is obvious that in Valéry's poetry neither the themes nor the solutions are uniform. This very fact points out that he is primarily interested in the intellectual dramatics, the *comédie intellectuelle*. The intellectual events themselves can change frequently. At one point there may be an awakening from chaotic dreaminess into lucid consciousness and then again, vice versa, a submersion into sleep. No matter how close Valéry may be to Mallarmé, the older poet's rigorous, albeit hidden, fidelity to his themes is replaced by a mutability of themes. In Valéry's *Cantique des colonnes*, the pure lines in architectural bodies sing a silent song for the eyes that perceive stone-static being regulated by numbers; the intellect and spirit harmonize with this being. The renowned poem, *Le Cimetière marin*, has Lucretian breath, and not only in the themes and images taken from Lucretius. It is a poem about a spiritual crisis. The conscious tries to become identical with static being, with the "roof" of the sea, with the diadem of lofty light, then with the nonexistence of the dead. But dynamic life is a more powerful lure; although fully aware of the speciousness of such life, the conscious ultimately surrenders. The previously static and then dynamic metaphors for the ocean subside; the sea regains its natural names (*waves, water*) as a sign that the conscious is now open to natural reality. This process is like a revocation of the extreme deobjectification taking place in Mallarmé's poetry, and counterbalances *Cantique des colonnes*. Yet we can find totally different solutions in other poems. The solutions are not as important as the fact that the intellectual and spiritual act turns into song in which cerebralness and sensuality, clarity and mystery, harmonize.

JORGE GUILLÉN

From here, we can proceed to the Spaniard Jorge Guillén. His poetry is in the same class as Mallarmé's and Valéry's. He even was a friend of Valéry's and translated his poetry. In his early years, Guillén explicitly advocated *poésie pure* (*ma non troppo*, as he added);[25] subsequently, he rejected it.[26] These two stances signify neither contradiction nor development, but merely show how vague the outlines of *poésie pure* are. Guillén is the most mature and most consistent practitioner of intellectual poetry. Most of his poems are parts of a uniform work, *Cántico* [Song of praise], first published in 1928, frequently expanded, and completed in 1950. *Cántico* has an architectural composition like that of Baudelaire's *Les Fleurs du mal*, with a numerical order of almost Dantesque rigor. Guillén's verse is, in every particular, poetic ontology and ontological poetry. It floats between the simplest phenomena and the most complex abstractions. Its self-justified obscurity (see above, p. 141) makes it the most difficult product of modern poetry. There is no personal "I" speaking in *Cántico*. Its subject-voice is the "spiritual eye"; this recalls Mallarmé's "absolute gaze." The absolute eye detaches itself from the vital material to mirror the fullness of the world and the pure structure of being that shines through that fullness. *Cántico* is imbued with a quiet, yet alien, jubilation, the intellectual jubilation of a visual power which, gazing at objects, perceives in them the stillness of their primal forms, and which is fully aware that it can endow all things in existence with a permanent spiritual being in the Word.

Guillén has been called "the most Eleatic poet," which characterizes his relationship to transcendental being. Yet his poetry is not so much a statement on being per se (which would make it impossible as poetry); it is a movement: a movement toward being, a movement from chaos to light, from disquiet to calm. Its highest value is light, the immaculate manifestation of being; the poems most filled with light are formally the most precise. One line reads, "Always there is light." But the real event in this poetry is the *fiat lux*, the "bliss of transition." The poetic energy derives from an intensification toward "beyondness," which first raises an object to its natural completion, makes a garden "more garden," a bridge "more bridge," and thus releases a categorial entity (as in Mallarmé) that is ultimately bathed in the light of existential perfection. This process comprises the total realm of life and sensuality, in which "matter was given the grace of becoming phenomenon." However, Guillén transforms and alienates matter. Objects yield, "weeping," to pure ideality. The language never adorns them; it strips them down to their naked essence, which is inserted into completely unreal contexts.

25. See Gerardo Diego, *Poesía española contemporánea (1901–1934)*, 4th ed. (Madrid, 1962), p. 328.
26. Guillén, *Language and Poetry*, p. 244.

The first line of *Ciudad de los estíos* [*City of summers*] calls the city the "city of chance."[27] Silken light descends upon it, smoothing and clarifying the lines; the city becomes "drunk on geometry"; "delights of exactness" take control; the city becomes an "essence city" (*ciudad esencial*). Landscapes turn into nonmaterial webs of tension. Snow and cold symbolize the absolute, where the fatality of life is transcended, where life itself is transcended — although Guillén occasionally seems to pay homage to life in a kind of panvitalism. The visible dematerializes. A vacuum, characteristic of Guillén's imagery, comes into being and then is filled with certain static primal phenomena (circles, lines, volumes) or dematerialized symbols thereof (a rose, a torrent, snow). Or else pure lines precede the dynamics: the sea consists, at first, of curves rather than waves. The poem is virtually a stereometric light-filled model of Being, attributing no natural humanity to man.

Guillén's love poetry, like Mallarmé's, is an ascending cognition of Being. In the body rather than the soul of his beloved, the lover, whose gaze is cerebral, perceives the phenomenal manifestation of Being; she, however, fails to realize that she is "a view of lucidity."[28] The splendor of spring is not meant for the human heart; "a call passes over the chaotic murmuring, a remote, fading, gentle call from no one to no one."[29] Children play on the beach, but they are not the actors; the sun, the seashells, and even the hands of the children are the true dramatis personae, turning into independent creatures; and the poem terminates with a final transition to the music of concepts: "Red fetters, shells, shells. Harmony, end, circle" (*Playa*). For, from the circle, "invisible within the block of air," the secret of Being speaks, superior to life, and, like poetry, manifest and at the same time concealed in refulgence (*Perfección del círculo*).

A mere recapitulation of such poetry will hardly convey the musical quality, a metallic singing in the harsh and violent sounds of Spanish. Even the abstractions are musical. In accordance with its themes, this poetry works with a rich vocabulary of the abstract and the geometric: curve, abundance, presence, infinity, substance, void, center. There is no linguistic line of demarcation between such words and others for simple, nongeometric things, just as there is no objective line between the conceptual and sensory contents of this poetical world. One line goes, "The plumage of the swan delineates a system of fateful silence."[30] In poems depicting a scene, abstractions are the active subjects. The language, however, uses further devices to complement its themes. There is a prevalence of nearly

27. Guillén, *Cántico*, p. 146.
28. *Ibid.*, p. 103.
29. *Ibid.*, p. 119.
30. *Ibid.*, p. 147.

verbless nominal statements to isolate phenomena and concepts, to withdraw them from time, or to invoke them hymnally. There is no torrent of language, only hesitancy and discontinuity, a blocklike construction, and then again brief, unanswerable interrogation or tentative stroking. Guillén is a virtuoso in the art of evoking from utter terseness echoes reverberating on and on, in a mysterious space. Like so many modern poets, he produces a seminal contrast between very simple syntax and obscure contents. The latter, whether as images or as concepts, appear as adjacent fragments, none developing from the preceding. Even the most minute links of association are broken. Something is always happening. But the transitional phases, so long as they remain in the empirical, evince no visible necessity and seem beyond the law of cause and effect. Necessity obtains only in the sequence or exchange of abstract tensions. Only one thing is unequivocal: the absence of natural humanity. (Natural humanity appears more emphatically in Guillén's poetry after 1957.)

The poem *Noche de luna* [Moonlit night], subtitled *sin desenlace* [without solution], exemplifies what such poetry can do with an old motif. The landscape is one of concepts: height, whiteness, expectancy, will, thinness. These notions form a network of supraobjective entities, encompassing a nonhuman event in the bright, nocturnal coldness. The few vestiges of the visible float wraithlike through the unreal action. The order is one of movements: a descent while "the plumages of the cold hover"; a brief stay on a plain while "silently the expectancy of waves spreads out"; an initial ascent from the depth, an "ascent to whiteness," while "splendid shores implore mercy from the wind"; and a second ascent that takes place only as a question, but which interrogatively raises the world to a "white, total, eternal absence." The poem is constructed of pure fields of tension, which remain unresolved because of the final unanswered question. There is no "I." Only the language speaks, identifying things seen with things thought, and relegating the latter to the coolness of an almost mathematical formula. Yet the formula sings.

ALOGICAL POETRY

The opposite of this type of verse, whose lineage goes back to Mallarmé, is the poetry in which alogical, hallucinatory, somnambulistic contents well up from the semiconscious or the unconscious — or at least are meant to do so. Alogical poets like to cite Rimbaud and Lautréamont, as well as occultism, alchemy, and the cabala. Alogical poetry is meant to be dream poetry. "Dream" has the psychological sense of the dream created in sleep or the artificial dream induced by drugs and the like, as opposed to the poetic dream, which, particularly in accordance with modern Romance usage, designates the creative imagination. The borderline between these two kinds of dreaming is vague, especially in their artistic realization; it is a borderline between a psychological principle and an aesthetic one. Yet both principles coincide in justifying a subjectivity beyond reality and in explaining that man, by virtue of his capacity to dream, is lord of the world.

Alogical verse, like intellectual verse, makes use of the imagination's power to create unreal imagery, albeit such imagery as is received passively and in an unsystematized form from the profound strata of dreams in sleep and in waking. This power, pitted against man insofar as he remains a "cerebral monster" (André Breton), equates him with the force prevailing over his prepersonal, anonymous depths. Man is not deprived of power; his power merely has another basis. Quite characteristically, Tristan Tzara, a theoretician of alogical poetry, lauded the "dictatorship of the intellect." The emphasis was on "dictatorship"; but the fact that the "intellect" was seen as the ruling force in the innermost alogical recesses made the dictatorship all the more violent — a fact that we have witnessed in Rimbaud. Meanwhile, the teachings of Freud and Jung had taken effect. Jung traced poetry back to the impulses of dark *Urvisionen*, "primordial visions," with the poet functioning merely as a medium who lets the materials of the collective unconscious flow through him, creative formation being of secondary importance. This theory has had its consequences for the surrealists.

The immediate precursor of the surrealists was Apollinaire; in fact, it was he who coined the term *surrealism*. In 1908, he wrote a prose poem *Onirocritique*. The title transmogrified the multivalent French notion of "dream" into a scientific term, influenced in all likelihood by a late-classical book of dreams, Artemidoros' *Oneirokritika* (second century A.D.). Parts of Apollinaire's text were allegedly copied; in line with the fundamental character of the text, the selection of passages can be as random as anything we omit.

> The coals of the sky were so near that I was afraid of their smell. Two unequal animals mated, and the runners of the rosebushes became vine leaves, heavy with the bundles of the moons. Out of the throats of the ape came flames, and decorating the world with lilies. The monarchs were entertained. Twenty blind tailors arrived. Toward evening, the trees flew away, and I multiplied one hundredfold. The herd that I was, set out to sea. The sword slaked my thirst. A hundred sailors killed me ninety-nine times. A whole nation, pressed in the wine presses, bled singing. Irregular shadows lovingly darkened the scarlet of the sails, while my eyes increased in the rivers, in the towns, and over the snow of the mountains.

The alert connoisseur will catch echoes of Rimbaud's voice and reminiscences of his poetic practice. Apollinaire's piece sounds like an apocryphal addendum to *Les Illuminations*. The tone of sequential narrative derives from the succession of unreal images and fragmentary events which are devoid of reciprocal contact and which could just as easily have been set in a different sequence. The only connection between the various events is one of absurd metamorphosis, as in a dream (a head becomes a pearl, sounds turn into snakes). There are no individuals, only masses. Both the imagery and the mode of expression approach dreaming. Yet this dream world is one of insanity, ugliness, grimace, and murder. And it is these hallmarks, and not just the experimental dream style, that make the text modern.

In comparison with the output of the surrealists since the twenties, the poetry of their forerunner, Apollinaire, remains the most inventive and imaginative example of this style. The most interesting thing about the surrealists is their set of programs, which constitute a semischolarly confirmation of poetic practice since Rimbaud: the conviction that man in the chaos of the unconscious can expand his experience unlimitedly; the belief that the mentally ill, no less than the poet, are "geniuses" in producing "suprareality"; the conception of poetry as a formless dictation from the unconscious. The surrealist programs confuse artificial retching with artistic creativity. No poetry of a high order has resulted. The poets of quality who are considered surrealists — Aragon and Eluard — owe their verse not so much to such programs as to the general stylistic compulsion which, effective since Rimbaud, has made poetry the language of the alogical. Surrealism is a result, not a cause; it is one of the many forms of the modern "yearning for mystery" (Julien Gracq).

Likewise, Italian futurism and German expressionism can be seen as indigenous phenomena without our having to seek possible influences. Their word explosions, their "demolition of reality," their somnambulisms, their collapsing cities, their grotesque jokes, are merely confirmations of the stylistic structure that first emerged in France several decades earlier and soon appeared in other countries.

The penetration of poetry into a dreamlike, somnambulistic twilight is evident all over Europe. This new penetration is different from romantic dream poetry in that it probes much deeper beyond a threshold before which a few vestiges of the waking world might permit a final anchorage. Benn's poem *Der Traum* is a pure dream melody. Strange names reel through it; unreal mixtures bloom, dissolve, graze: "the self-lusting breath of named flowers," "kneeling women, barely in the context of figure, their heads hanging high into the twilight." The poem itself is exactly what it says about dreaming: "Its names refer to nothing on earth. . . . The worlds of this dream are simultaneous and also form a single space; they waft and fall. . . .''

GARCÍA LORCA'S *ROMANCE SONÁMBULO*

At this point, a discussion of García Lorca's famous *Romance sonámbulo* [Somnambulistic ballad] (written prior to 1927) is in order. So that we may orient ourselves to its ''content,'' let us consider the following synopsis: a girl is standing on a moonlit balcony; somewhere else two men are conversing; later the two men come up to the balcony; subsequently the girl is floating dead in a cistern. But this summing up of a crime of passion annihilates the poem. Something entirely different happens: a somnambulistic interweaving of barely suggested remnants of action and an unreal magic of word and image. The poem begins with a color, green. The color has no connection with the action or the objects. It comes *to* rather than *from* them: ''green wind, green flesh, green hair.'' The color is a magic force haunting the poem, a veil of sound. (A preliminary stage can be found in Ramón Jiménez' poem *La verdecilla*, also about the unreal expansion of green. Yet here there is causality: the green originates in a girl's green eyes. No such source is present in García Lorca.) Vague, disconnected areas of landscape appear, and, in between them, shreds of action and outlines of people. A boat on the sea and a horse on the mountain are juxtaposed in two successive lines that become a recurrent sound force. The procedure is lyrical rather than narrative; there is no spatial, temporal, or causal framework. The theme — love and death — is never specified yet it wells up as an unspoken force from the sketchiness of actions and objects. Great metaphors occur: the fig tree rubs the wind with the sandpaper of its branches; the mountain, a thieving tomcat, bristles its sour agaves; an icicle of the moon bears the dead girl over the water. There is no clear-cut action; only the occurrences in the sovereign domain of word and color are clear. The green, before appearing one last time, is joined by black — the sign of death. Everything is invoked, and everything remains open. We are no longer really on earth. Just as there is no space between individual places (only the unreal metaphors constitute space), so also time stands still. First there is night, then morning ''wounded by a thousand glass tambourines,'' and, at the end, night again. These time stages are not those of narrative. They are lyrical perspectives of motionless time (as in Valéry's *Fileuse*, in which evening light turns into darkness and then back into evening light). The ending, an echo of the opening lines, seems to close a circle. And yet, ''Perhaps there was no motion here; perhaps a fan opened in the middle of a second at the speed of a kindling

154

light — a fan of images unfolding between the many *greens* that contain them like staves."[31] This ballad of García Lorca's is great and bold poetry. It needs no justification in the psychology of dreams.

THE ABSURD; "HUMORISM"

Modern poetry, with all its dissonances, has a proclivity for the absurd. Baudelaire was one of the first to laud the ability of dreams to invent absurdity, a triumph of released subjectivity. In 1939, Eluard, like Rimbaud before him, demanded of poetry a "disturbance of logic to the point of absurdity." Breton had gone even further, declaring that only the absurd was possible in poetry. A reply from Spain was Aleixandre's poetry, which — at least until the late forties — was tied to surrealism. Their metrics free and even formless, their syntax often incomprehensibly ambivalent, Aleixandre's poems deliberately and disorientingly juxtapose things that never find or even seek one another in nature or in logic. The term "poetry of the absurd" may barely cover the complete poetic scope of his verse; yet the term urges itself upon us, and there is no reason to eschew it. Just what is absurd about Aleixandre's poetry? Probably the haphazard way he dovetails vestigial aspects of the outer world and the inner world, rebuilding each of these worlds with elements and occurrences that, instead of awaiting explicating paraphrase, appeal to associative guesswork. His poems have a secret center which the reader becomes aware of only when hearing the flow of sound. But we are never far from the threshold of chaos.

The label "absurd" might also be applied to grotesque verse in the style of Alberti, and to all the verse known in France as "black humor" (*humour noir*), a somber, shivery humor, remote from the cheerful absurdities of Christian Morgenstern and Hans Arp, whose linguistic devices are related to all the experiments of modern poetry.[32] Black humor is a radicalization of Victor Hugo's theory of the grotesque. A fragmented world, the bizarre, and the scurrilous are special cases of a deforming style à la Rimbaud. Gómez de la Serna set down the theory of modern "humor," calling it "humorism" (in *Ismos*). The interesting thing about this theory (and similar theories of the French) is that it encompasses all the characteristics of such a deforming style and thereby of a major portion of modern poetry. "Humor," according to Gómez de la Serna, smashes reality by inventing the improbable, forcing together separate times and

31. Gerda Zeltner-Neukomm, "Zur Lyrik F. García Lorcas," *Trivium*, 1949.
32. For Morgenstern, see J. Walter, *Sprache und Spiel in Christian Morgensterns Galgenliedern* (Freiburg and Munich, 1966).

things, alienating anything in existence; "humor" rips the sky apart to reveal the "enormous sea of emptiness"; "humor" is an expression of the discrepancy between man and the world; "humor" is the king of nonexistence. We can see that this description is nothing but a variant of modern poetics.

REALITY

Let us once again pose the problem of reality, as we did with regard to Rimbaud, and in the same heuristic form. In so doing, we sharpen our awareness of the authoritative way in which poetry either transforms, destroys, or totally rejects world matter. In the twentieth century, the relationship of poetry and art to the world is still marked by the same experience of confinement articulated in Baudelaire's lines: "The world, monotonous and small, today, tomorrow, always." The expansion of physical space due to increased knowledge and technology is considered a loss rather than a gain. Yet what we characterized as the dialectic of modernity (see above, p. 53) also holds true: the passion for the infinite, the invisible, or the unknown encounters an empty transcendence and boomerangs destructively upon reality. For, with regard to present-day poetry, insofar as it is not confessional verse (which presents its own problems), we may speak of an empty transcendence. In Guillén's works, the absolute is both lightness and geometrical perfection, but its contents are not defined. The moment poetry comes into contact with any sort of ideality, it uses expressions for total vagueness or symbols of pure mystery.

The relationship of twentieth-century poetry to the world is many-faceted, yet the result is always the same: a devaluation of the real world. In poetry, as in the novel, the real world has splintered into a set of individual phenomena meticulously comprehended and replacing the totality. Such phenomena can appear as brutal facts, as "reporting": for example, the poems of Blaise Cendrars, who put out a volume called *Documentations* (the original title having been *Kodak*). This "reporting" neutralizes the world to such an extent that it no longer belongs to mankind. Medial lyrics, which let a soul close to man speak via things or landscapes, are nearly extinct. Like the novel (Flaubert, and then Hemingway, Sartre, Butor, and others), poetry often treats the exterior world as an ineluctable opposition to man. Subject matter tends to be sought in the banal and the base, where its weight is even more oppressive and makes man even lonelier. Big-city garbage, hangovers on cheap booze, streetcar tracks, dives, factory yards, scraps of newsprint, and the like crop up; in superior texts, they are imbued with the "galvanic shudder" that Poe and Baudelaire desired in the poetization of the commonplace in modern life. Ugliness, a dynamic stimulus since Rimbaud, retains its sway. We might take a look at Benn's *Bilder* [Images]. It consists of a single compound sentence; the articulation is not syntactical (in the first, the thirteenth, and the fifteenth lines, "siehst du" is a disguised conditional clause; "du siehst" in the last line is a disguised main clause). It is the internal weights and the change of tone toward the end that articulate the poem. Various images of ugliness, disease, degeneracy, crowd through the long, single sentence leading to the punchline that all these phenomena are works of the "great genius." Is this comment derisive or an interpretation of ugliness as a token of some kind of supraworld? Probably the latter. The quietly ecstatic tone, the incipient, vague transcendence, the twilight of meaning — and all this in concentrated imagery of ugliness (which is something quite different from the opposite of beauty) — are features of the modern poet.

Even the choice of fauna and flora moves in a downward direction. "The laurel is tired of being poetic," writes García Lorca. We come across algae, seaweed, garlic, onions, and crows, snails, spiders. Trakl has angels from whose eyelids "worms drip." In line with all this, Sartre, in a novel, compares life to roots; for Goethe, roots were amorphous chaos incapable of exaltation. Montale calls a volume of poetry *Ossi di seppia* [Cuttlefish bones]; one of his favorite words is *raw*; he speaks of the "crooked syllable, dry as a branch," and prefers things that are cracked and breaking and callous. These latter things can also be found in Krolow: "Moon grabbed me in its claw." As in Baudelaire, the inorganic betokens a spirituality superior to life (Valéry, Guillén). Yet often it is juxtaposed to or merged into the organic without the exalting significance. An untitled poem by Montale, beginning "Addii . . . ," talks about a farewell; only an unidentified "you" remains as a vestige of the human; the weight of the statement lies on the automatisms which "loom, walled in, from the corridors" and on the "hoarse litany of the express train."

T. S. ELIOT

In both Mallarmé's and Valéry's poetics, the notion of the fragment is extremely important. The fragment is the utmost possible artistic realization of the invisible in the visible; precisely because of its fragmentary nature, it indicates the superiority of the invisible and the inadequacy of the visible. The fragmentary has remained a hallmark of modern verse. It is especially manifest in a practice of taking shards of the real world, working them

157

over again and again, and yet making sure that the broken surfaces do not fit together. In such poetry the real world seems like a confused network of major cracks — and is no longer real.

This brings us to T. S. Eliot. Critical interpretations of his works differ to the point of total contradiction. There is agreement on only *one* thing: that Eliot's poetry, with its wealth of peculiarities, casts a powerful spell because of its "tone." The sound is an unforgettable and in no wise harmonious mixture of many different tones. The language, always unpredictable, runs through the most dissimilar modulations: dry reporting, melancholy, contemplation, flutelike melody, occasional claptrap, and then again irony, sarcasm, casual conversation. This polyphony ties together every single one of Eliot's long poems more effectively than the basic cerebral, spiritual, or psychic situation — which lies so deep that no one can describe it precisely. Some of the themes may be recognizable: the desolation of man in the waste land of the metropolis; ephemeralness; reflections on the function of time and on the alienation of the world. But these themes waft through the poetry; they do not convey it. The real conveyer is what Eliot called the artistic emotion, something completely impersonal, that soars upward and plunges downward from the sublime to the base, "Going in white and blue, in Mary's colour, / Talking of trivial things . . . ," as two lines in *Ash Wednesday* put it. The emotion penetrates the "objective correlative" — that is, images as well as human and objective actions. But which images and which actions? Eliot remarks that the essential features of the present day are impermanence and extreme polarity; and these features are the inherent characteristics of his poetic technique. Admittedly, his practice fits in with modern civilization, which, with its complications, contradictions, and nervous sensations, demands a poetry that is comprehensive and yet that speaks allusively and indirectly and will thus inevitably be difficult.

Early in *The Waste Land*, we come across the phrase: ". . . for you know only / A heap of broken images . . ."; and, toward the end, "These fragments I have shored against my ruins." These lines may be taken as a profession of fragmentism, the law of Eliot's poetry. This law determines the statements, which may begin with a short narrative, break off, continue as an inner monologue only to be interrupted by an unrelated quotation, followed in turn by a shred of conversation between undelineated people. The content of one cluster of verses will crumble in the next group or be totally forgotten. The same holds for imagery and action, which form a montage of heterogeneous fragments devoid of spatial or temporal context: decaying furniture in a parlor, gas works, rats, cars, London fog, dry leaves, and then nymphs, Tiresias, precious stones, as well as an unshaven merchant from Smyrna, all mingled chaotically. Even cultural areas fade into one another: a waiter is juxtaposed to a flashing recollection of Agamemnon; the River Plate is simultaneously the Sacré Coeur. In *Four Quartets*, the second part of *East Coker* begins with a description of a November day, only to interrupt: "That was a way of putting it — not very satisfactory. . . ." Then the same motif follows in a completely different *ductus*, and a totally dissimilar content emerges; this practice derives from Lautréamont. The same part ends with a sententious line, ". . . the wisdom of humility: humility is endless," followed by two incoherent images: "The houses are all gone under the sea. / The dancers are all gone under the hill." The closing seems to signify a secret link between the content of the gnomic line and two objective events (whose houses and dancers were spoken of much earlier in the poem). But any possible connection is expressed only in the abrupt, irrelative juxtaposition of thought and occurrence: relation is hinted at by the device of irrelation.

What sort of world is this? The adjective *unreal* crops up frequently in *The Waste Land*. In *Ash Wednesday* we hear of "the unread vision in the higher dream" and "the word unheard." There is union here. The poet knows what he is doing. The authoritative power of the "dream" pulverizes the world, shifts the world into the unreal in order to beam-in mysteries that the world would never radiate as long as it remained real. The magical multiplicity of the language borders on the ineffable and manages to capture, in shattering words, the imperceptible music of dreams.

ST.-JOHN PERSE

Earlier, we spoke of Rimbaud's "sensory unreality." This term seems applicable to the poetry of St.-John Perse as well. The contents of his poems are barely tangible. Long lines, as in hymns or psalms, overwhelm the reader like cosmic floods; the technique and the enthusiasm recall Walt Whitman. St.-John Perse himself compares his verses to ocean waves. Evocations, sonorous and stately, sweep by in a concentrated sequence of new imagery that both stirs and bewilders the reader. None of the images ever calms down. A universe of soul and world surges and churns — an alien "universe of exile." Any reality it may contain is strange and unknown, coming to us from exotic lands, long forgotten civilizations, extraordinary myths. Reminiscences flare up of sacred writings of the Orient, Homer, Pindar, Greek tragedy. One idiosyncrasy of St.-John Perse's is the insertion of confirmable data into the fabrications of his fantasy; yet these data are so farfetched, and their statement so anomalous or so casual, that their reality is no longer perceptible, and they turn into a melody of a "song not meant for any shore." The reeling grasp at infinity contrasts sharply with precise information about sensory, corrosive details, mainly from the realm of animal smells. Yet even the details are enigmatic, encoded as they are in a specialized vocabulary of navigation, hunting, botany, medicine, for whose understanding even the French reader has to consult special dictionaries. One is better off if one yields to such vocables as he would to the sound of exotic instruments. Every totality of an object, a landscape, a situation, is deliberately lost between the details and an amorphous infinity. A passage in *Eloges* contains the following (summed up): a forehead under yellow hands, the memory of "arrows shot out by the sea of colors"; musical ships at the dock, mountains of logwood; "but what has become of the ships . . . ? Palms!"; then, "a sea, more credulous and haunted by invisible voyages, piled up like a sky above the orchards, swelled with golden fruit, with violet fishes, and birds"; fragrances wafting up to sumptuous heights, and, "because of the cinnamon tree in my father's garden, a confused world [reeling] on, resplendent in scales and armor."

A confused world. Its inhabitant is an adventurer in all ages and places, a prince penetrating the unexplored: Alexander. One of St.-John Perse's works is entitled *Anabase* [Alexander's campaign]. The conqueror must, however, destroy the entire past. A powerful passage in *Pluies* reads:

> Wash away the spot from the eye of the upright man . . . from the worthy man, the gifted . . . wash away the peoples' history from the tall tablets of memory: the great official annals and chronicles . . . wash away from the heart of man the finest words of man.

For the conqueror no longer lets himself be sullied "by the wine and the weeping of mankind." What and where is his goal? Not even St.-John Perse offers an answer. He speaks only about an escape into homelessness, "farther and farther away from the place of birth," and about the "never-written poem." All this is in every way Rimbaud's schema: destruction of the familiar for the sake of a violent escape into the unknown, the impotence of language when confronted with the unknown. Language can produce only exotic sounds from the innermost depths of words, which lie close to silence or madness.

And, as in Rimbaud, we find here a passionate creation of imagery which, though provided with sensory qualities, is no longer a part of any reality. A few examples will suffice: "the sea with medusa spasms"; "the black wool of typhoons"; "from the green sponge of a lonely tree, the sky [sucking] up its violent sap"; a man contemplating the morning sky, "[resting] his chin on the last fading star"; "pestilence of the spirit in the crackling of salt, in the milk of quicklime"; "mathematics, hanging from the icebergs of salt." Each part of an image is sensual, but the images themselves are unreal because of the union of incompatibilities; the product:

sensory unreality. It is odd that St.-John Perse so often adds "salt" to his imagery. Rimbaud did the same. Could it be a structural compulsion like Lautréamont's "saws," which we rediscovered in Eluard and Picasso (see above, p. 8)? The compulsiveness would be confirmed if this "salt" actually came from alchemical doctrines, which count it, along with sulphur and mercury, as a primal element of nature.

St.-John Perse has been translated into English by Eliot and into Italian by Ungaretti; the Spanish poet Guillén was his fervent admirer. In 1929, Hofmannsthal wrote several pages as a preface to *Anabase*, calling Mallarmé, Valéry, and St.-John Perse "creative individuals who plunge into language itself." Then comes an excellent observation: "This has always been the Latin approach to the unconscious: not in the semidreamy dissipation typical of the German spirit, but in a chaotic shaking up of objects, a smashing of orders," in a "dark and violent self-enchantment through the magic of words and rhythms."

DICTATORIAL IMAGINATION

"Creative individuals" is what Hofmannsthal calls Mallarmé, Valéry, and St.-John Perse. We are led back to a term that we used in connection with Rimbaud: dictatorial imagination, which in twentieth-century poetry, too, is the source of all transformation and/or destruction of the real world — and to such an extent that the products can be measured only heuristically rather than, in a definitive cognition, in terms of reality and the normal situation of mankind. Naturally, poetry has always blurred the distinction between "it is" and "it seems," subjugating its material to the power of the versifying mind. But in the modern age, the world issuing from creative imagination and sovereign language is an enemy of the real world. Baudelaire's comment that imagination begins with dissection and deformation and continues with a reconstruction by virtue of its own laws is verified not only in the poetic practice of the twentieth century but also in the statements made by the poets themselves — and by painters and sculptors as well. Conspicuous in these utterances is the prevalence of aggressive or negative phrasing.[33] García Lorca writes about Jiménez: "What a pure and great *wound* his imagination left in the infinite white!" Ortega y Gasset remarks: "The poetic soul attacks natural objects, *wounding or killing them.*" Diego calls poetry the creation of things we will *never see.* Proust writes: "The artist has the same effect as those high temperatures at which atomic compounds *disintegrate* and form a totally different compound." Benn speaks of the Western *Geist*, the spirit and mind — as well as the

33. [Italics in the following are Friedrich's. — *Trans.*]

art — of the Occident: *"disintegration* of life and nature, reintegration by human law." Picasso terms painting a *handiwork of the blind*, by which he means that art is free from any objective consideration. The power of the imagination, commencing in the late eighteenth century, has become almost definitive in the twentieth. And poetry, too, has become the language of a world created almost exclusively by the imagination and by leaping beyond or annihilating reality.

THE EFFECTS OF DICTATORIAL IMAGINATION

In contemporary verse, as in fiction, space disintegrates, losing its coherence and the normal order and orientation of its dimensions. Schiller once criticized a poem for shifting from the skirts of mountains to a valley meadow; on the basis of the structure of real space, he disapproved of the shift as a leap interrupting "the consistency of the framework." The reader may refer back to earlier quotations from T. S. Eliot and St.-John Perse to see how a modern poem, eschewing transition, reaches out to remote areas of space, poles apart from one another. Thus Trakl writes: "A white shirt of stars burns up the bearing shoulders." This fusion of stars and a human figure cancels space altogether. Such a fusion occurs even when a poet identifies the spatially separated objects: "The body of the mountain chain hesitates at my window" (Supervielle). In Apollinaire's *Zone*, all spatial areas are simultaneous: Prague, Marseilles, Coblenz, Amsterdam, form a single, simultaneous locale of one and the same outer and inner action. In most cases, locales are either nonexistent, or twisted beyond reality. In Valéry, the ocean sleeps *above* graves; in Alberti, the wind is *above* the star, and the sail *above* the wind. Eluard writes of "your eyes, in which both of us sleep." Likewise, we find a reversal of other objective orders: "Air exhales bitter leaves" (Quasimodo); "the dark, palpable moisture smells of bridge" (Guillén). This last example contains a stylistic device that we might call a "transposed adjective": *palpable*, although actually belonging to *bridge*, becomes a quality of the nonmaterial moisture. This practice — classified since antiquity as "hypallage," a rhetorical device to be used sparingly — had spread since Rimbaud and is ubiquitous today because of its great suitability for producing unreal crisscrosses and for strongly emphasizing the transposed epithet: "sorrowful branch and dry heart" (Jiménez), instead of "dry branch and sorrowful heart"; "Ursa Major, come down, hairy night" (Bachmann); parodistically, "a golden old man with a sad watch" (Prévert).

Time, too, acquires an abnormal function. First of all, it acts as a kind of fourth spatial dimension when things separated in time are drawn together in a single moment matched by a single image space; we saw examples of this in Eliot. The most frequent case, however, is the total cancellation of temporal hierarchy, of time itself. This cancellation is usually brought about by having a poem richochet between different tenses even though neither content nor statement may call for such shifts. The various tense forms are merely poetic perspectives of something static and beyond time, or are simply necessary as variants of tone and rhythm for the autonomous *ductus*. However, other devices are also possible. In Marie-Luise Kaschnitz's poem *Genazzano*, the opening five lines — nominal statements, without verbs — evoke a real action: a ride up to a tiny mountain town. Verbs join in, but in a virtually supratemporal past tense that encompasses the various tenses (including the future) in which the further — and now dreamlike — incidents could conceivably take place — if we had to "conceive" them. We see the following: the real action, occurring in empirical time, takes place without tenses; the unreal action is expressed by several verbs whose tenses are similarly unreal because, by stating things future as things past, the poem erases the distinctions between them.

García Lorca wrote an eight-line poem, *Cazador* [Hunter], which proceeds as an optical summing up: four doves fly up and return; "their shadows wounded," they lie upon the earth. The action is related in terse, spare diction. The causal concatenation is never stated; instead, it is replaced by the bland copula *y* ("and"), as well as the spatial shift (air-earth). For a moment, the language approaches the victim ("wounded"), but instantly draws away by transferring the adjective to the shadow. The cause 'of the shift in image and space is never mentioned: the hunter's shooting the doves. Furthermore, the poem begins and ends in the present tense, although each phase of the action belongs to a different stage of time — or *would* belong to a different stage if the poem were heedful of reality. Instead, the motion image of imagination depletes the action, stripping it of time and causal connection. We cite this poem as one of countless examples of the abolition of causality. Today, instead of expecting causality, "we must endure the adjacency of things," comments Gottfried Benn. However, the reverse is also possible. A line of Eliot's says, "Go, said the bird, for the leaves were full of children." This line posits a pseudocausal relation between unrelated things; it is only the imagination that makes the statement in the second part of the line a "reason" for the call of the bird. Paradox — possible, if rare, in older verse — has become a law in modern poetry. The paradox that relationships among objects or actions are destroyed by the absence of causal, final, adversative or other conjunctions, while, vice versa, objects or actions having nothing to do with one another are related by those very conjunctions: this is the spirit world of the imagination.

Another stylistic law, nearly a manner, is the coordination of the visual and the abstract: "the ashes of shame" (St.-John Perse), "change smiles at you" (Benn), "the rustle of withering tendencies" (Krolow), "sorrow and joy have their own foliage" (Supervielle) "forgetful snow" (Eliot).

And, finally, the imagination takes control of the visual and the aural by means of unreal colors, thereby raising objects out of the banal: "hyacinth silence" (Trakl), "hands conch-red-white" (Lasker-Schüler), "blue shudder" (García Lorca), "the earth is as blue as an orange" (Eluard). Green, however, predominates (as it did in baroque writing). Pablo Neruda's magazine, founded in 1935, was called *Caballo verde para la poesía* [Green horse for poetry]. And there are other examples: "a green silence from unraveled guitars" (Diego), "your hair, green from moist stars" (Jiménez), "green sun, green gold" (St.-John Perse), "time passes, green and heathen" (Krolow, in accordance with German usage, daringly employs *grün* half adjectivally, half adverbially); "green eyes of purple" (Trakl), "verdigris of stars" (Benn). This last metaphor, for all its abnormality, is still more intelligible than another one of Benn's: "hemstitch of stars." The first image, despite the mutual alienation of its parts, contains a possibility of rapprochement — albeit only in the outer zones of language. And last but not least we recall the dominance of green in García Lorca's *Romance sonámbulo* (see above, p. 154). In all these poems, "green" is no longer a color attribute but a substance issuing from unknown sources and spreading virtually like an epidemic. Syntactically and semantically, these are special cases of paradoxical adjectives: rather than adorn the noun or make it more precise, they alienate it: "golden sighs" (Lasker-Schüler), "a white absence" (Guillén), "crackling sun" (Aleixandre).

CROSSFADE TECHNIQUE AND METAPHORS

It was Rimbaud who first used the crossfade technique, and twentieth-century poetry has been following suit. *Die Tauben* [The doves], a late poem by Rilke, employs words other than those referring to the doves: *lamplight, smoke, love sacrifice, alms, container, priest*. These objects are neither similes nor metaphors. They fade a second realm, that of sacrificial ritual, into the realm of the doves. García Lorca writes: "Black horses move through the deep roads of the guitar." He composed a long poem of eleven individually titled sections and with the general title *The Forest of Clocks*. At first glance, the title image seems like a sustained metaphor (of the forest for the clocks, or vice versa); but we actually are dealing with a total integration of the clocks and the forest, with the metaphorical area (forest) gaining an objectivity equal to that of the clocks: "ticking leaves," "clusters of bells," "the whole confused forest is an enormous spider spinning a web of sound for hope." A past master in this technique is Diego. In his *Insomnio*, the insomniac speaks to the sleeping woman, whereby she and the sea fuse into an unreal unity which absorbs the speaker as maritime words are transferred to him: *island, reefs.* Another poem by Diego, *Sucesiva*, is a torrential interfusion of water and the human figure. At this point we can speak no longer of metaphors. The comparison possible in metaphor has given way to absolute equation.

But even when the metaphor in modern verse recalls one of its earlier functions, that of comparison, we may note a radical transformation: the things claimed (in metaphorical tone and structure) to be comparable are, in point of fact, totally incomparable. The metaphor has become the most useful stylistic device for the unbounded imagination of modern versecraft. Actually, the metaphor has always contributed to a poetic alteration of the world. As Ortega y Gasset put it in a series of similes: "The metaphor is the greatest power in man's possession. It verges on magic and is like an instrument of creation that God forgot inside his creatures, just as the absent-minded surgeon leaves an instrument inside the body of a patient." Yet this idea is contradicted by the point of view that the metaphor discloses an existing, but as yet unseen, similarity between two givens, and is therefore close to truth, functioning as a figurative label next to which an equally valid literal one exists. This opinion is applicable to the tamer cases of metaphorical speech; but the further one penetrates the land of poetry, the more useless this opinion becomes. It was least applicable to baroque writing and is equally incorrect with regard to modern poetry. Modern poetry does not arouse metaphorical similarity; instead, it uses the metaphor to clamp together things that strive to pull apart. The modern metaphor does not result from the need to reduce unknown entities to known entities. It executes a huge leap from the dissimilarity of its parts to a unity attainable only in linguistic experiment, and in such a way that the dissimilarity is obviously as extreme as possible and at the same time poetically abolished.[34] If a poem moves in a realm of imagery, it then creates a second domain in the midst of the first; the second is alien, and the poet is interested not so much in the perceptional values as in the violence of the collision between the two realms. Out of the metaphorical capacity to link near with far, modern poetry has developed the most amazing combinations in the metamorphosis of the far away into the totally unreachable; at the same time, modern poetry completely disregards all objective and logical considerations. Modern texts, more vehemently than classical literature, testify that metaphorical designations are not the "figurative"

---

34. ["Abolished" in the Hegelian sense of *aufheben.* — *Trans.*]

ones; quite the opposite — they are the irreplaceable and specific designations, specific for a poetry that primarily serves language rather than relate to the world. Such metaphors create an antiworld to the familiar world and the world of older (and happier) poetry. More often than not, the modern-day metaphor is no longer meant to be an image next to "reality," but to abolish the distinction between metaphorical and nonmetaphorical language.

Raymond Queneau has written a poem entitled *L'Explication des métaphores*, which claims that metaphors project their "negative images" into the Void; that they are a fermenting multiplicity, "created doubles of truth"; that they create a specific kind of reality, the kind that does not exist. Jiménez' metaphors have elicited the following comment: "They obscure the real in order to achieve a greater poetic clarity." Aleixandre remarked: "Only poetry knows that the wind is named *lips* at one time, and *sand* at another."

Several instances of poetic practice will serve as illustrations: "in the stormy plain the roots of sobbing decay" (Eluard); "the tongue is a red fish in the container of your voice" (Apollinaire); "the moon slowly mows the old trembling of the river" (García Lorca); "lightning sounds from the windows" (Ungaretti); "golden doves lie on your cheeks" (Lasker-Schüler); "the water of the air," "the flesh of bread" (Krolow); "the star gland" (Michaux). We easily recognize the feature common to all these examples the moment we observe their contents: absolute dissimilarity turns into identity.

We should, however, also observe which of the possible formal types of metaphor are used, and which of these, in turn, are preferred. We can thus gather evidence of modernity.

One category not conspicuous in form is the predicate metaphor of defining character. This type belongs to all periods of writing. "A black dove is the night" (Lasker-Schüler); "the guitar is a well full of wind and not water" (Diego). The same applies to attributive and verbal metaphors: "serpent-browed coasts" (Alberti; attributive); "icy winds weep in the dark" (Trakl; verbal). The unusual aspect of these metaphors is their material, which they use to alienate the everyday world mentally and sensually.

There is another category of metaphors that, beyond their abnormal contents, also change their formal conventionality — for example, metaphors of apposition. By omitting the article (a most powerful device in the Romance languages), they achieve a syntactical abbreviation: "church, stony woman" (Jouve); "face, sonorous shell" (Eluard); "October, island of precise profile" (Guillén). By abruptly placing these metaphors next to the objects, poetry approaches a total identification.

Another way in which modern metaphor approaches identification is through the technique of agglutination, which timidly began appearing during the first half of the last century: "gold-coin noon," "conjurer day," "boat imagination" (Krolow). In each case, the first noun is the metaphor of the second; basically we are dealing with predicate metaphors lacking the verb *to be*. It is precisely this foreshortening that makes the category specifically modern. Everyone knows the terse closing line of Apollinaire's *Zone*: "Soleil cou coupé [Sun head chopped off]." Here the agglutination abruptly juxtaposes the subject (sun) and its momentary phase (setting), but metaphorically, so that we may speak of an absolute metaphor whose basic meaning (sunset) is never stated.

The most frequent type of metaphor among the moderns is the so-called genitive metaphor (an imprecise term, since it is the object rather than the metaphor that appears in the genitive case). The pattern can be discerned in a simple example: "the round-dance of the stars." This is one of the oldest schemas of metaphor. Yet, because the function of the genitive has been weakened and has thus become a grammatical case-of-all-work, this type of metaphor permits feats of extraordinary boldness. Its usual task is to produce an alienation effect — a further polar tension in modern versecraft. However, we must distinguish between two subspecies. In the first, the genitive metaphor is simply one attribute or one condition or one situation, chosen from among several possibilities, in regard to an object, while the object itself remains primary. In such cases the metaphorical effect results from an exchange of domains or from semantic dissonance and the like — in other words, from the material. "Mute cries of mirrors" (Ungaretti): the glitter of the mirrors is simply one of a number of their possible modes and by no means totally identical with the mirrors. The conversion of glitter into the paradox of "mute cries" is thus an attributive metaphor signifying the transitory. "The scissors of the eyes cut up the melody" (Eluard): the reluctant glances at an unappreciated melody could just as easily be friendly or neutral. Thus this metaphor, too, is attributive and refers to something alterable.

The identifying genitive metaphor is different. Its daring is greater than that of the other subspecies. "The straw of the water" (Eluard): both parts are identified; we might also speak of a metaphor of the predicate genitive, insofar as the first noun, *straw,* is a predicate nominative of *water* (the water *is* straw). Of the authors we have cited, Eluard has used this kind of metaphor with the greatest frequency. A peculiar characteristic of his is that these metaphors consist of words which, if looked at individually, are as simple as can be and yet, by means of the identifying metaphor, enter into an unusual tension: "the sprigs of the wind," "the lakes of chance," "the mirrors of lips." Quotations from other poets are unnecessary, since their identifying genitive metaphors are of the same nature as Eluard's. We repeat only what is symptomatic of this phenomenon: the most worn and most multivalent of relational words, the genitive preposition and article, is most permissive of semantic disharmony and the magical union of mutually alien things.

We have to emphasize one more element, one that we have indicated above — the difference between metaphorical and nonmetaphorical diction seems to vanish: "the fruits of the wind," "the pebbles of din" (Eluard), "the ashes of the stars" (Montale). In these identifications, the metaphor is not so important as the combination of words. The metaphorical appearance can be misleading if one pays heed to it alone. We must be mindful of the identification of language levels — the metaphorical and the literal — beyond the identification of objectively dissimilar things. There is an excessive and constant shifting between the two strata in Eluard, Lasker-Schüler, and Aleixandre. We are dealing with a higher mathematics of poetry, as it were, an attempt to transcend the givens and the usual categories of language poetically.

With regard to metaphorical equations, the following may be added: while technological civilization connects material areas with one another, poetry, primarily in metaphor, connects things that can never be connected materially.

CONCLUSION

Now we can see how modern metaphor fits in with everything that we have thus far described. And so does its dissonance. With this concept, we return to the beginning of our book, where we quoted a statement of Stravinsky's. As early as 1914, the painters Marc and Kandinsky demanded a "law of color dissonance." Modern composers sometimes speak of "tense" or "hypersharp" chords, in reference to their intrinsic value rather than their function of constituting a transition to a resolving consonance. Modern poetry, in its dissonances, is obeying a law of its style. And this law, as we have frequently tried to point out, is, in turn, obeying the historical situation of the modern mind, which, because of the excessive imperiling of its freedom, has an excessive passion for freedom. Its art and artists can no more calm down in the objective, present-day historical reality than they can in genuine transcendence. Consequently, the poetic realm is an unreal world created by the modern *Geist*, a world existing only by virtue of the word, and whose totally intrinsic orders are in deliberately unresolved tension with things familiar and secure. Even when such verse is almost mute, it reveals the alien quality whose anguish can be magic and whose magic can be anguish. Modern poetry is a huge and lonely fairy tale previously untold. Its garden contains flowers, but also stones and chemical colors — fruit, but also dangerous drugs. Life in its nights and in its extreme temperatures is enormously strenuous. The acute ear will detect in this versecraft a harsh love that prefers to remain unconsumed and therefore to speak into chaos or even into the Void rather than to us. Reality, dismembered or torn to shreds by the power of imagination, becomes, in the poem, a landscape of ruins. Forced unrealities lie above it. Yet ruins and unrealities convey the mystery and the secret for whose sake the poets write.

What they compose, they state dissonantly: the indefinite by means of determinative words, the complicated by means of simple sentences, the causeless by means of causes (or vice versa), the unrelated by means of a relation (or vice versa), space or timelessness by means of indications of time, the abstract by means of magical verbal forces, haphazard contents by means of rigorous forms, the image of the invisible by means of sensory imagery. These are the modern dissonances of poetic language. Yet this language remains language, although very rarely one for comprehension. Language is used like a keyboard whose sounds and meanings are unpredictable. The poets are alone with language. Yet it is language alone that saves them.

All along, we have almost exclusively had to use negative concepts to describe modern poetry. But we were able to show that the various features of style, even the most abnormal ones, consistently proceed from one another or belong together. Thus, no matter how enigmatic or arbitrary modern poetry may become, it is always recognizable in its structure. The inner consistency in a striving away from reality and normality, as well as the despotism of even the boldest warpings of language, is a further hallmark indicating the quality of a poet and a poem. The old requirement that poetry have artistic evidence has not been abolished. Such evidence has merely shifted from the imagery and the ideas to the curves of language and tension beyond meaning. Even when they appear in obscure, multivalent material, their effect is compelling; and this effect makes a poem good. In the course of time, one learns how to discern such hallmarks and to sort out the truly competent from the avant-garde of the day, and the poets from the charlatans.

SELECTED BIBLIOGRAPHY

GENERAL CRITICISM

BOWRA, C. M. *The Heritage of Symbolism.* New York: St. Martin, 1943.
————. *The Creative Experiment.* New York: St. Martin, 1968.
BURNSHAW, STANLEY, ed. *The Poem Itself: 45 Modern Poets in a New Presentation.* New York: Schocken, 1967.
COHEN, JOHN M. *Poetry of This Age, 1908–1965.* Rev. ed. Chester Springs, Pa.: Dufour, 1966.
ELIOT, T. S. "From Poe to Valéry." In *To Criticize the Critic, and Other Writings.* New York: Farrar, Straus & Giroux, 1965.
MOSSOP, D. J. *Pure Poetry: Studies in French Poetic Theory and Practice, 1746–1945.* New York: Oxford University Press, 1971.
POE, EDGAR ALLAN. "A Philosophy of Composition." In *Poems and Essays.* New York: Dutton, n.d.
TINDALL, WILLIAM YORK. *The Literary Symbol.* Bloomington, Ind.: Indiana University Press, 1958.

FRENCH

GENERAL

CHIARI, JOSEPH. *Contemporary French Poetry.* Freeport, N.Y.: Books for Libraries, 1952.
GERSHMAN, HERBERT S. *Bibliography of the Surrealist Revolution in France.* Ann Arbor: University of Michigan Press, 1969.
GIBSON, ROBERT D. *Modern French Poets on Poetry.* New York: Cambridge University Press, 1961.
GRANT, ELLIOTT M. *French Poetry and Modern Industry.* 1927. Reprint. Millwood, N.Y.: Kraus, n.d.
HATZFELD, HELMUT. *Trends and Styles in Twentieth-Century French Literature.* 2d ed. Washington, D.C.: McGrath, n.d.

BAUDELAIRE

BAUDELAIRE, CHARLES. *Fleurs du Mal: Flowers of Evil.* Translated by FRANCIS DUKE. Charlottesville: University Press of Virginia, 1961.
————. *Selected Verse.* Translated by FRANCIS SCARFE. Baltimore, Md: Penguin, 1967.
————. *Twenty Prose Poems.* Translated by MICHAEL HAMBURGER. New York: Grossman, 1968.
MOSSOP, D. J. *Baudelaire's Tragic Hero: A Study of the Architecture of "Les Fleurs du Mal."* New York: Oxford University Press, 1961.

ELUARD

CARMODY, F. J. "Eluard's Rupture with Surrealism." PMLA, 1961.
ELUARD, PAUL. *Selected Writings.* Translated by LLOYD ALEXANDER. New York: New Directions, n.d.

MALLARMÉ

COHN, ROBERT G. *Toward the Poems of Mallarmé.* Berkeley and Los Angeles: University of California Press, 1965.
MALLARMÉ, STEPHANE. *Mallarmé.* Edited by ANTHONY HARTLEY. Baltimore, Md.: Penguin, 1965.
————. *Selected Poems.* Bilingual ed. Translated by C. F. MACINTYRE. Berkeley and Los Angeles: University of California Press, 1957.

RIMBAUD

RIMBAUD, ARTHUR. *Complete Works with Selected Letters.* Translated by WALLACE FOWLIE. Chicago: University of Chicago Press, 1966.
STARKIE, ENID. *Arthur Rimbaud.* Rev. ed. New York: New Directions, 1968.

ST.-JOHN PERSE

LITTLE, ROGER. *St.-John Perse: A Bibliography for Students of His Poetry.* London: Grant & Cutler, n.d.
PERSE, ST.-JOHN. *Collected Poems.* Princeton, N.J.: Princeton University Press, n.d.

VALÉRY

MacKay, Agnes E. *The Universal Self: An Introduction to the Work of Paul Valéry.* Toronto: University of Toronto Press, 1961.
Valéry, Paul. *Collected Works of Paul Valéry,* vol. 2. *Poems in the Rough.* Translated by Hilary Corke. Bollingen Series. Princeton, N.J.: Princeton University Press, 1970.
—————. *Collected Works of Paul Valéry,* vol. 7. *The Art of Poetry.* Edited by Jackson Matthews and translated by Denise Folliot. Bollingen Series. Princeton, N.J.: Princeton University Press, n.d.

OTHERS

Apollinaire, Guillaume. *Selected Writings of Apollinaire.* Rev. ed. Edited and translated by Roger Shattuck. New York: New Directions, 1971.
Callander, Margaret. *The Poetry of Pierre Jean Jouve.* New York: Barnes & Noble, 1965.

SPANISH

Guillén, Jorge. *Language and Poetry: Some Poets of Spain.* Charles Eliot Lecture Series, 1957–58. Cambridge, Mass.: Harvard University Press, 1961.
Ivask, Ivar, and Juan Marichal, eds. *Luminous Reality: The Poetry of Jorge Guillén.* Norman: University of Oklahoma Press, 1969.
Trend, John B. *Lorca and the Spanish Poetic Tradition.* 1956. Reprint. New York: Russell & Russell, 1971.

ENGLISH AND AMERICAN

GENERAL

Alvárez, Alfred. *The Shaping Spirit: Studies in Modern English and American Poets.* Folcroft, Pa.: Folcroft Press, 1961.
Brooks, Cleanth. *Modern Poetry and the Tradition.* Chapel Hill: University of North Carolina Press, 1970.

BULLOUGH, GEOFFREY. *The Trend of Modern Poetry*. London, 1934.

DE SOLA PINTO, VIVIAN. *Crisis in English Poetry, 1880–1940*. New York: Hutchinson University Library, 1951; 1967.

LUDWIG, R. M., ed. *Aspects of American Poetry: Essays Presented to H. Mumford Jones*. Columbus: Ohio State University Press, 1961.

PRESS JOHN. *The Chequer'd Shade: Reflections on Obscurity in Poetry*. New York: Oxford University Press, 1958.

ROBERTS, MICHAEL, ed. *The Faber Book of Modern Verse*. Rev. ed. London: Faber & Faber, 1965.

ROSENTHAL, MACHA L. *The Modern Poets: A Critical Introduction*. New York: Oxford University Press, 1960.

STRAUMANN, HEINRICH. *American Literature in the Twentieth Century*. New York: Harper & Row, 1968.

T. S. ELIOT

BRADBROOK, M. C. *T. S. Eliot*. British Writers and Their Work, edited by BONAMY DUBREE et al., vol. 5. Lincoln: University of Nebraska Press, 1965.

ELIOT, T. S. *Collected Poems, 1909–1962*. New York: Harcourt, Brace & World, 1963.

—————. *On Poetry and Poets*. New York: Farrar, Straus & Giroux, 1957.

—————. *Selected Essays*. Rev. ed. New York: Harcourt, Brace, 1950.

GALLUP, DONALD. *T. S. Eliot: A Bibliography*. Rev. ed. New York: Harcourt Brace Jovanovich, 1969.

KENNER, HUGH. *The Invisible Poet: T. S. Eliot*. 1959. Reprint. New York: Harcourt Brace Jovanovich, 1969.

MATTHIESSEN, F. O. *The Achievement of T. S. Eliot: An Essay on the Nature of Poetry*. 3rd ed. New York: Oxford University Press, 1959.

MAXWELL, DESMOND E. *The Poetry of T. S. Eliot*. 1952. Reprint. New York: Humanities Press, 1961.

SMIDT, KRISTIAN. *Poetry and Belief in the Work of T. S. Eliot*. Rev. ed. New York: Humanities Press, 1961.

WILLIAMSON, GEORGE. *A Reader's Guide to T. S. Eliot*. New York: Farrar, Straus & Giroux, 1953.

POUND

DEKKER, GEORGE. *The Cantos of E. Pound: A Critical Study*. New York: Barnes & Noble, 1963.

ELIOT, T. S. "E. Pound," *Poetry*, 1946.

POUND, EZRA. *Cantos of Ezra Pound*. New York: New Directions, 1970.

INDEX OF NAMES

175

Flaubert, Gustave, 25, 116–17, 135, 137, 156
Francis of Assisi, Saint, 131
Freud, Sigmund, 152

García Lorca, Federico, 3, 110, 111 n., 112, 113–14, 121, 126, 128, 133, 134, 136, 138–39, 142, 154–55, 157, 161, 163, 164–65, 166
Gautier, Théophile, 18, 37
Gengoux, J., 66 n.
George, Stefan, 70
Ghil, R., 86
Gide, André, 41
Goethe, J. W. von, 6, 7, 22, 107, 114, 136, 139, 157
Goll, Claire, 131
Goll, Yvan, 131
Gómez de la Serna, R., 108, 155–56
Góngora, Luis de, 5, 88–90, 111–12, 113–14, 126, 142
Gracq, Julien, 153
Grillparzer, F., 8
Guillén, Jorge, 3, 22, 24, 70, 86, 108, 110, 111 n., 112, 117, 119, 124, 125, 130, 132 n., 134–35, 141, 148–51, 156, 157, 161, 162, 164, 166

Haftman, Werner, 110, 127
Hebel, J. P., 114
Hegel, G. W. F., 93
Hemingway, Ernest, 137, 156
Hindemith, Paul, 130
Hofmannsthal, Hugo von, 6, 56 n., 161
Homer, 105, 159
Horace, 12
Hugo, Victor, 16, 17–18, 21, 26, 41, 44, 51, 83–84, 155

Iser, W., 124 n.

Jacob, Max, 60, 110, 137
Jiménez, Ramón, 110, 123, 132, 136, 145, 154, 161, 162, 164, 166
John of the Cross, Saint, 30
Jouve, Pierre Jean, 117, 129–30, 166
Jung, C. G., 131, 152

Kafka, Franz, 138
Kahn, Gustave, 60
Kandinsky, Wassily, 110, 168
Kant, Immanuel, 11, 102, 132
Kaschnitz, Marie-Luise, 123, 163
Kommerell, Max, 123
Krolow, Karl, 123, 127, 134, 138, 157, 164, 166, 167

La Fontaine, Jean de, 126
Lamartine, Alphonse de, 16
Langgässer, Elisabeth, 127
Lasker-Schüler, Else, 121, 164, 166, 168
Lautréamont (Isidore Ducasse), 8, 18, 151, 159, 161
Lessing, G. E., 11
Lévi, Eliphas, 101
Locke, John, 10
Lucretius, 148

Machado, Antonio, 10–11, 110
Maistre, Joseph de, 28
Mallarmé, Stéphane, 6, 14, 15, 17, 19, 20, 22, 24, 31, 33, 40, 41, 69–106, 107–16 passim, 120, 123, 128, 130, 140–51 passim, 157, 161
Manet, Edouard, 117
Marc, F., 35, 168
Marinetti, F. T., 134
Marino, G., 83
Ménard, Lewis, 66
Michaux, Henri, 145, 166
Michelet, V. E., 101
Montaigne, Michel de, 41
Montale, Eugenio, 4, 119, 131, 141, 157, 168
Morgenstern, Christian, 155
Musil, Robert de, 135, 137
Musset, Alfred de, 16

Napoleon I, 16
Neruda, Pablo, 206
Nervel, Gérard de, 16
Novalis (Baron Friedrich von Hardenberg), 8, 13–15, 17, 20, 24, 32–33, 35, 37, 54, 56 n., 65, 81, 90, 103, 107, 144

Index of Names

Ortega y Gasset, José, 110–11, 132, 161, 165
Ovid, 131

Palazzeschi, A., 3
Paracelsus, Philippus, 79
Petrarch, Francesco, 22
Picasso, Pablo, 8, 53, 57, 81, 96, 110, 161, 162
Pichette, H., 133
Picon, Gustave, 135, 143
Pindar, 159
Pinthus, K., 9
Poe, Edgar Allan, xi, 20, 24, 26, 31 n., 32–33, 34, 37, 48, 57, 65, 78, 81, 107, 112, 144, 157
Ponge, Francis, 130, 133, 135
Pound, Ezra, xi, 48, 124, 131, 140
Prévert, Jacques, 129, 162
Proust, Marcel, 62, 161

Quasimodo, Salvatore, 121, 141, 162
Queneau, R., 117, 166

Racine, Jean Baptiste, 9, 31
Régnier, Henri, 60
Renan, Ernest, 40
Reverdy, P., 115
Reyes, Alfonso, 111 n.
Richter, Jean Paul, 101
Rilke, Rainer Maria, 3, 126, 144, 146, 164
Rimbaud, Arthur, 6, 9, 15, 18, 19, 29, 31, 36, 37, 39–67, 70, 75, 76, 81, 85, 88–96 passim, 103, 104, 107–11 passim, 113, 116, 125, 130, 131, 137, 140, 143, 144, 145, 151–64 passim
Rivière, Jacques, 40, 67
Rousseau, Henri, 110
Rousseau, Jean Jacques, 9–11, 16, 27, 34, 42, 57, 95, 146

Sainte-Beuve, Charles Augustin, 102
St.-John Perse (Alexis Léger), 3, 4, 48, 114, 116, 117, 122, 125, 130, 131, 134, 136, 141, 142, 159–61, 162, 164

Salinas, Pedro, 115, 140–41
Sartre, Jean Paul, 135, 156, 157
Schelling, F. W. von, 85, 93
Schiller, Friedrich von, 7–8, 132, 162
Schlegel, Friedrich, 15, 17, 26, 37
Seneca, 10
Shakespeare, William, 49, 131
Spitzer, L., 143 n.
Staël, Madame de, 16
Stendhal (Marie Henri Beyle), 25
Sterne, Laurence, 10
Stevens, Wallace, xi
Stravinsky, Igor, 3, 24, 128–29, 168
Supervielle, Jules, 123, 125, 162, 164
Swedenborg, Emanuel, 30
Swinburne, A. C., 70

Taine, Hippolyte, 40
Tocqueville, Alexis de, 25
Trakl, Georg, 3, 107, 108, 136, 162, 164, 166
Tzara, Tristan, 152

Ungaretti, Guiseppe, 3, 70, 108, 114, 118, 119, 121–24, 126, 133, 137–38, 140, 142–43, 161, 166, 167

Valéry, Paul, 19, 24, 70, 78, 86, 91, 101, 102, 108, 109, 116, 117, 123, 126, 127, 128, 130, 133, 142, 145–48, 154, 157, 161, 162
Vergil, 9, 31
Verlaine, Paul, 9, 10, 18, 19, 48, 53, 56, 81, 112, 133
Vico, G. B., 12
Vigny, Alfred de, 16

Wagner, Richard, 131
Walter, J., 155 n.
Whitman, Walt, 159
Williams, William Carlos, xi

Yeats, William Butler, 3, 116, 140, 144

Zeltner-Neukomm, Gerda, 155 n.

INDEX OF SUBJECTS

Index of Subjects